TWO EARLY BYZANTINE BIBLE MANUSCRIPTS IN CHRISTIAN PALESTINIAN ARAMAIC

Cambridge Semitic Languages and Cultures

General Editor: Geoffrey Khan

This is the first Open Access book series in the field; it combines the high peer-review and editorial standards with the fair Open Access model offered by OBP. The series includes philological and linguistic studies of Semitic languages, editions of Semitic texts, and studies of Semitic cultures. Titles cover all periods, traditions and methodological approaches to the field. The editorial board comprises Geoffrey Khan, Aaron Hornkohl, Esther-Miriam Wagner, Anne Burberry, and Benjamin Kantor.

You can access the full series catalogue here: https://www.openbookpublishers.com/series/2632-6914

If you would like to join our community and interact with authors of the books, sign up to be contacted about events relating to the series and receive publication updates and news here: https://forms.gle/RWymsw3hdsUjZTXv5

Two Early Byzantine Bible Manuscripts in Christian Palestinian Aramaic

Codex Climaci Rescriptus II & XI

Kim Phillips

UNIVERSITY OF CAMBRIDGE
Faculty of Asian and Middle Eastern Studies

OpenBook Publishers

https://www.openbookpublishers.com

All external links were active at the time of publication unless otherwise stated and have been archived via the Internet Archive Wayback Machine at https://archive.org/web

Any digital material and resources associated with this volume will be available at https://doi.org/10.11647/OBP.0455#resources

Semitic Languages and Cultures 34

ISSN (print): 2632-6906
ISSN (digital): 2632-6914

ISBN Paperback: 978-1-80511-540-3
ISBN Hardback: 978-1-80511-541-0
ISBN Digital (PDF): 978-1-80511-542-7

DOI: 10.11647/OBP.0455

Cover image: Photo by Osama Shukir Muhammed Amin (2019). A Christian Palestinian Aramaic inscription, from the Kayanos Church. Inside the museum on Mount Nebo, Jordan. https://commons.wikimedia.org/wiki/File:Palestino-Aramaic_inscription,_from_the_Kayanos_Church._Inside_the_museum_on_Mount_Nebo,_Jordan.jpg.
Cover design: Jeevanjot Kaur Nagpal

The fonts used in this volume are Charis SIL, Estrangelo Edessa, SBL Greek, and SBL Hebrew.

CONTENTS

ACKNOWLEDGEMENTS

This volume has been a long time in the making. It was in 2015 that Dr Peter Williams of Tyndale House first gave me the opportunity to come and work on the Codex Climaci Rescriptus Project. I am grateful for his timely offer, and for the chance to have been involved for many years with Tyndale House, whose mission so closely echoes my own heart.

It was also in 2015 that I joined Cambridge University Library's Genizah Research Unit, and so began an informal, but thoroughgoing, apprenticeship in the various skills pertaining to the study of manuscripts. The head of the unit, Professor Benjamin Outhwaite, has been more than generous, over the interim years, with his time, knowledge, expertise and friendship.

Professor Roger Easton, of the Rochester Institute of Technology, has generously continued to lend his time and technical expertise long after the formal collaboration between Tyndale House and the team of multispectral imaging scientists came to an end. I am most grateful.

Late in 2023 I began working with Dr Nehemia Gordon at the Institute for Hebrew Bible Manuscript Research. I am immensely grateful for his willingness to allow me to finish this volume under the aegis of IHBMR.

It is a particular pleasure to thank Dr Anne Burberry for her patience and competence in guiding this volume through the final stages of publication, since she herself was one of the students involved in examining the codex as part of a Summer internship a decade ago (see §1.1.2. *infra*).

This has been a very difficult volume to produce. My long-suffering wife has borne with me patiently and steadfastly. In particular, at the time when it would perhaps have been more sensible simply to abandon the work, she accepted—even understood—my unwillingness to do so. *raḥoq mippəninim mikhrah.*

All CCR images used with kind permission of Museum of The Bible. Images from Sinai Palimpsests Project used with permission.

וַיִּקַּח שְׁמוּאֵל אֶבֶן אַחַת וַיָּשֶׂם בֵּין־הַמִּצְפָּה וּבֵין הַשֵּׁן וַיִּקְרָא אֶת־
שְׁמָהּ אֶבֶן הָעָזֶר וַיֹּאמַר עַד־הֵנָּה עֲזָרָנוּ יְהוָה׃

Ὥστε, ἀδελφοί μου ἀγαπητοί, ἑδραῖοι γίνεσθε, ἀμετακίνητοι, περισσεύοντες ἐν τῷ ἔργῳ τοῦ κυρίου πάντοτε, εἰδότες ὅτι ὁ κόπος ὑμῶν οὐκ ἔστιν κενὸς ἐν κυρίῳ.

ܫܒܚܝ ܢܦܫܝ ܠܡܪܝܐ
ܢܫܒܚ ܠܡܪܝܐ ܒܚܝܝ
ܘܢܫܒܚܝܢ ܠܐܠܗܝ ܟܕ ܐܢܐ ܩܐܡ...
ܡܪܝܐ ܫܪܐ ܐܣܝܪܐ
ܡܪܝܐ ܡܦܬܚ ܥܘܝܪܐ
ܡܪܝܐ ܙܩܦ ܟܦܝܦܐ

1. INTRODUCTION

1.1. Introduction to CCR, and to the CCR Project

1.1.1. Peregrinations of a Palimpsest

As the ninth century hastened into the tenth, while the Byzantine Macedonian Dynasty ruled from Constantinople, and the Muslim Abbasid Caliphate ruled from Iraq, a Christian scribe situated somewhere between the two sat at his writing desk, dry-ruling parchment. His task was to copy out a Syriac translation of John Climacus' popular manuals of spiritual discipline: *η κλίμαξ* '*The Ladder of Divine Ascent*' (CPG-7852) and *Εἰς τόν Ποιμένα* '*Liber ad Pastorem*' (CPG-7853).[1] He filled nearly 150 parchment folios in this endeavour, all of which were recycled from older, obsolete codices. These older codices contained biblical, liturgical and even astronomical texts, written either in Greek or in a dialect of Western Aramaic now referred to as Christian Palestinian Aramaic (CPA). The original Greek or Aramaic of these older codices had been more or less assiduously scraped off; the leaves were

[1] The scribe did not sign and date his work (or if he did, the colophon is now missing). Thus, the date of the Syriac superior writing in CCR is rather uncertain. Mingana (1939, 78) suggests "about A.D. 1100," whereas Lewis (1909, xi) reports the opinions of Margoliouth and Ellis, who date the hand to the beginning of the ninth century! Géhin (2017, 126–27) narrows this range to 9th–10th century. Williams et al. (2022, 507) report a private communication from a Syriac specialist noting that the script has several affinities with that of a dated Syriac manuscript from 885–86.

 https://doi.org/10.11647/OBP.0455.01

trimmed into uniformity and re-ruled in preparation for their new role.

It is possible that the 'somewhere in between' where our scribe was writing was none other than St Catherine's Monastery, Sinai, where John Climacus himself had served as Abbot a couple of centuries earlier.[2] At any rate, the codex certainly seems to have ended up there, as one quire of it was discovered at the monastery as recently as 1975.[3] Likely, it formed part of that ancient library for many centuries, until it was caught up in the great manuscript-hunting frenzy of the nineteenth century.[4] At some point, presumably in that century, the manuscript was dismembered, and parts thereof began to appear on the antiquities market.

---

[2] This opinion is rather widespread, but—in the absence of a colophon—impossible to prove. Géhin (2017, 20–21) notes that the great majority of Syriac parchment manuscripts from Sinai were not produced there, though he goes on to add that CCR probably was one of the few exceptions. He seems to base this opinion on the fact that the majority of the undertexts are written in CPA. However, the Cairo Genizah has revealed numerous Jewish manuscripts, almost certainly written in Palestine itself, with CPA undertexts. This strongly suggests that at least some CPA manuscripts were apparently scraped and washed for re-use *in the Land of Israel itself*. If this is the case, it is difficult to see why the Syriac of CCR could not have been produced in Palestine (or, indeed, further North) just as plausibly as at Sinai.

[3] Syriac New Finds 38. On the New Finds, see Desreumaux (2010). For some of the CPA fruits emerging from the New Finds, see, e.g., Müller-Kessler (2016; 2017; 2018; 2019a; 2019b; 2020; 2023b).

[4] For a brief outline of that frenzy, see Géhin (2017, 1–13).

In a series of three purchases between 1895 and 1906, the bulk of the manuscript was brought to Cambridge, England, and reassembled, thanks to the intrepid twin 'Sisters of Sinai', Agnes Lewis and Margaret Gibson.[5] The sisters perceived the immense value of the undertexts preserved in the codex, and it was Lewis herself who produced the *editio princeps* of all the CPA undertexts, and a small sample of the Greek undertexts (Lewis 1909). It was Lewis, too, who gave the manuscript the name by which it is now referred to: *Codex Climaci Rescriptus* (Lewis 1909).[6] The sisters eventually donated the manuscript to Westminster College (of which they were already benefactors), and it remained there until 2010.

In the mid-twentieth century, Ian Moir examined the Greek undertexts of the codex with the aid of infrared and ultraviolet lights and produced the first attempts at a full edition of those texts (Moir 1956; 1957). Then, towards the end of its century-long sojourn in Cambridge, all the Aramaic undertexts of CCR were re-edited by direct autopsy by Christa Müller-Kessler—also

---

[5] The sisters were not quite able to acquire the entire manuscript. Apart from the quire left at St Catherine's and only rediscovered in 1975, a single leaf was acquired by Alphonse Mingana during one of his three trips to the Middle East in the 1920s. It is now part of the University of Birmingham's Mingana Collection, with the classmark Mingana syr. 637. It was described by Mingana (1939, 78) and edited first by Duensing (1938) and shortly afterwards by Black (1939).

[6] Lewis (1909, xii) noted that, despite her best efforts, some leaves of the *Liber ad Pastorem* section of CCR had not yet been found at the time of the publishing of the *editio princeps*.

with the aid of an ultraviolet lamp (as she notes in passing: Müller-Kessler 2014, 4, n. 12). The resulting, vastly improved, transcriptions were included in the first three volumes of the monumental *Corpus of Christian Palestinian Aramaic* (Müller-Kessler and Sokoloff 1997; 1998a; 1988b).

In 2010, CCR was sold by Westminster College to the Green Collection. Subsequently, the Greens donated the manuscript to Museum of the Bible, in Washington, DC, where it resides today under classmark MS.000149. However, the codex's Cantabrigian link was not severed entirely: in 2012, Museum of the Bible invited Tyndale House, Cambridge, to take responsibility for the production of completely new editions of CCR's various Greek and Aramaic undertexts—this time aided by the latest advances in multispectral imaging (MSI).

1.1.2. Collaborative Codex Research

The study of the undertexts of CCR over the past decade at Tyndale House has been a collaborative exercise through and through. Most notably, the extensive collaboration between textual scholars and multispectral imaging computer scientists from 2017 onwards has resulted in a fruitful symbiosis for both sides, described in more detail below.[7]

In a different sort of collaboration: in Summer vacations between 2012 and 2017, students, mainly undergraduates, were

[7] Peter Williams, the overall project director, lists the various parties involved, and describes the nature of the collaboration, in Williams et al. (2022).

given the opportunity to contribute to the deciphering of the various undertexts of CCR. The students worked either on the Greek material or the Aramaic, depending on their previous linguistic experience. Again, the benefits were mutual. The students gained valuable experience in manuscript research, but also contributed, directly or indirectly, to the overall research outcomes. Williams et al. (2022) describe one such student-led contribution pertaining to the classical Greek material preserved in CCR. Among the students who worked on the CPA undertexts, one deserves particular mention. Between 2012 and 2015, Suzanna Millar[8] laboriously keyed in a first draft transcription of almost all the Aramaic undertexts, using digital photographs (but without any multispectral images), and Müller-Kessler's edition as a guide. When I examined her transcription as I started on CCR in 2015, the quality of her work was immediately obvious. With Millar's permission, her transcription was used as a starting point for the new CPA editions, saving many thousands of keystrokes. Moreover, among the student team working on CCR II, it was Millar who noted the differences in script between the Acts leaves and the Pauline epistles, and on that basis posited the presence of two distinct source manuscripts in CCR II (a hypothesis that is immediately confirmed by examination of the extant quire numbering—see *infra*).

---

[8] Now Dr Suzanna Millar, Chancellor's Fellow in Hebrew Bible/Old Testament, New College, University of Edinburgh.

1.1.3. Computer-Complemented Re-editing: A New Edition of CCR

In 2015, I was invited to prepare fresh transcriptions of the CPA portions of CCR for publication and so began the first of several complete re-examinations of the codex. At the same time, Dr Peter Malik took charge of the production of fresh editions of the Greek biblical undertexts. Our efforts received substantial fresh impetus in 2017 when the codex was photographed using multispectral imaging technology by a team from the Early Manuscripts Electronic Library (EMEL) and the Lazarus Project. These images were then computer processed in two stages: *deterministic* and (where necessary) *statistical* (Easton and Kelbe 2014, 38ff.). In essence, deterministic processing involves combining—for each individual page—a predetermined subset of the raw images in a predetermined manner, where such a combination has been shown to produce useful results in the past. The process can be automated, such that many pages can be processed relatively quickly with relatively little human input necessary. In the case of the CCR project, each page was 'batch-processed' using a programme designed by Keith Knox over the course of previous MSI palimpsest research—most notably, the Archimedes Palimpsest Project (Davies and Zawacki 2019, 180–81). For each page of CCR, four types of batch-processed images were generated:[9]

---

[9] As is perhaps inevitable with such multi-disciplinary scholarly collaboration, many so-called introductory articles to MSI abound with technical scientific jargon. Doubtless at the expense of nuance and accuracy, I have tried my best to keep the following descriptions jargon-free. For

Pseudocolour: this technique starts with monochrome images produced under ultraviolet light in which, typically, both the superior and inferior texts are visible. These are then combined with images in which only the superior text is visible. The result is an image in which the inferior text appears red, while the background appears greyish, and the superior text appears black.[10]

Figure 1: Snippet from CCR II f. 1r; unprocessed vs pseudocolour image

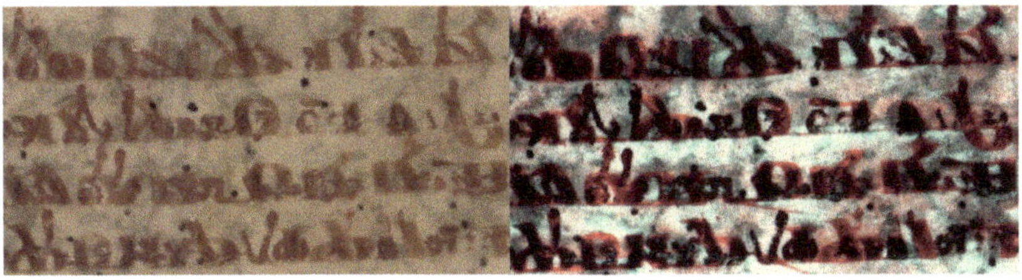

Sharpie: the *yin* to the pseudocolour *yang*. Whereas in the pseudocolour the separate images are combined additively, in the sharpie image they are 'subtracted' one from the other. The result is a greyscale image in which the undertext appears dark grey, while the superior text appears to have been erased.

---

a far fuller treatment of deterministic processing, yet still understandable by the non-specialist, see Knox (2023).

[10] The Archimedes Palimpsest Project has a helpful webpage introducing the pseudocolour processing method, including a video explanation from Knox himself: http://archimedespalimpsest.org/about/imaging/processing.php, accessed 4 July 2023.

Figure 2: Snippet from CCR II f. 1r; unprocessed vs sharpie image

Tx-ratio: these images were produced using transmissive illumination, relying on the corrosive effects of the iron-gall ink used to write the undertext. A thin sheet of acrylic placed beneath the leaf is used to shine infrared light *through* the object, towards the camera. Where the residual ink of the undertext has eaten away the parchment over the centuries, the parchment is thinner than the surrounding parchment, and thus allows more light through into the camera.

The usefulness of this particular method was highly dependent on the writing surface. The corrosive effects of the iron-gall ink were far more substantial on the flesh side of each folio, and in these cases the transmissive images were often remarkably useful.[11] Since iron-gall ink tends to adhere better to the hair side of parchment than the flesh side, erased text on the flesh side is often harder to recover using fluorescence-based techniques than that on the hair side. Thus, transmissive imaging goes a long way towards balancing this inequality.

The transmissive images have one particular benefit over all the other types of image: they can reveal text entirely covered by the superior text. The other processing methods can greatly

[11] By contrast, Tx-ratio images of the hair side of a folio would often only reveal a mirror-image of the text on the flesh side.

enhance the visibility of faded ink, but cannot render visible ink that has been covered over by the ink of the superior text. The transmissive images, on the other hand, inasmuch as they depend primarily on the degree of corrosion of the parchment, can still reveal the channels of corrosion, even when those channels have been subsequently written over.

Figure 3: Snippet from CCR II f. 1v; unprocessed vs Tx-ratio image

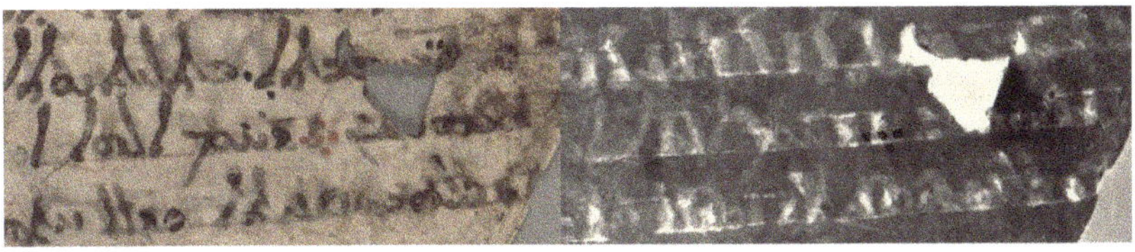

UVbyTx: these images are combinations of the images produced using ultraviolet light together with the images produced using transmissive illumination.

Figure 4: Snippet from CCR II f. 1v; unprocessed vs UVbyTx image

In many cases, these batch-processed images yielded such satisfactory results that further processing was not required. In a significant number of cases, however (particularly with the Greek material), the undertexts were not sufficiently clarified by the deterministic batch-processing.[12] In these cases, a second phase, or

[12] Statistical processing was regularly necessary (though not always successful) for re-editing the rubricated CPA texts, since the deterministic processing methods are calibrated to recover iron-gall ink.

mode, of processing was required: *statistical* processing. This umbrella term refers to an ever-expanding toolkit of different techniques (such as Principal Component Analysis, Independent Component Analysis, Minimum Noise Fraction).[13] What these techniques have in common is that neither the subset of raw images to be combined, nor their precise method of combination, are pre-determined. Rather, they are determined on a case-by-case basis, using statistical methods. Consequently, statistical processing is a slower process, requiring skilled human input at every stage. When successful, however, it can recover undertext that proved resistant to batch-processing.

Figure 5: Snippet from CCR II f. 18v; unprocessed vs statistically processed image (undertext appears purple)

1.1.4. Condensing a Century's Research: An Up-to-Date Description of CCR's Undertexts

The past century of CCR scholarship has substantially clarified our understanding both of the ninth–tenth-century Syriac codex, and—particularly—of the earlier codices whose parchment was harvested for palimpsesting. What follows, therefore, is an up-to-date description of the codex and its undertexts. Since less-complete descriptions abound in the scholarly literature, I have thought it worthwhile to preface the description with a brief

[13] For a recent overview of these processes, see Easton and Kelbe (2023).

overview of how, and on account of whom, our current understanding of the codex has developed.

When Lewis first published the undertexts of CCR, she found evidence of six different manuscripts (four CPA and two Greek) from which parchment was harvested for re-use. She labelled the CPA manuscripts Climacus I–IV, and the Greek manuscripts Climacus V–VI (Lewis 1909, xiii). Climacus I and II are early-period[14] CPA Bible manuscripts.[15] Climacus III was understood to be an early-period CPA Lectionary manuscript. Climacus IV is from an early-period collection of CPA homilies and apostolic myths.[16] This initial categorisation has been gradually refined over the past century.[17]

[14] Most CPA texts derive from either the Early Period (5th–8th centuries), when CPA was still a spoken dialect, or the Late Period (10th–13th centuries), when it seems to have been employed solely as a liturgical language. A few texts may derive from in between these periods (Morgenstern 2011).

[15] All the material from CCR I–III was re-edited by Müller-Kessler and appears in Müller-Kessler and Sokoloff (1997; 1998a; 1998b).

[16] The Dormition part of this manuscript was recently re-edited by Müller-Kessler (2019). The homily section is currently being re-edited and translated by the present author.

[17] Müller-Kessler (1999a, 81–82) explains that the identifications of distinct manuscripts can be made on the basis of letter size and shape, and number of lines per column (where cropping of the leaf in the palimpsesting process does not obscure this information), but also on orthographic and morphological grounds. However, given the possibility of multiple scribes contributing to a single manuscript (as with, for example, the Dormition manuscript from the Cairo Genizah: Müller-Kessler 2018, 78), I suggest that a more secure basis for such identifications is

With respect to the CPA undertexts: Bar-Asher (1977, 57, 142) noticed that folios 33 and 36 do not belong with the lectionary manuscript labelled CCR III by Lewis. He suggested naming the new manuscript CCR IIIb, but it appears in Müller-Kessler and Sokoloff (1997, 50–53) as CCR7, and is thus labelled here (though preserving Lewis' use of Roman numerals). CCR VII is a fragment from an early-period CPA Bible manuscript, containing portions of Leviticus.[18]

CCR III was divided yet again by Müller-Kessler and Sokoloff into two separate lectionary manuscripts: CCR3 and CCR8.[19]

Finally for the CPA undertext, we must consider Lewis' CCR II. Thanks to the recent multispectral images, sufficient quire numbering data are available to clearly demonstrate that CCR II must be divided into two distinct manuscripts. Hitherto understood to be a single manuscript containing Acts and the New Testament epistles, CCR II in fact consists of parts of an *Apostolos* manuscript (i.e., Acts + the Catholic Epistles), and parts of a

on the evidence of incompatible quire numbering (when such information is available).

[18] For a fresh re-editing and text-critical evaluation of CCR VII, see Phillips (forthcoming a).

[19] In Müller-Kessler and Sokoloff (1997, 148, 151–52), there is no mention of CCR8; folios 32 and 38 are still labelled as being part of CCR3. However, a year later, in Müller-Kessler and Sokoloff (1998a; 1998b), CCR8 has fully emerged. Recently, Müller-Kessler (2023a) has published some new fragments from the early CPA Jerusalem lectionary and situates these fragments among all the other early witnesses, including CCR3 and CCR8.

Pauline Epistles manuscript.[20] The full data are presented in the codicological descriptions of each manuscript. Far more of the Pauline Epistles manuscript has been preserved than the Apostolos manuscript (49 folios vs 12 folios). Thus, it is suggested that the Pauline Epistles manuscript remain as CCR II, and the Apostolos manuscript be renamed as CCR XI (the numerals IX and X having already been commandeered for the Greek material: see *infra*).[21]

---

[20] As noted above (§1.1.2.), Suzanna Millar was the first to recognise the clear differences in script within CCR II, and to posit the existence of two different source manuscripts on that basis.

[21] In the final stages of the preparation of this volume, Müller-Kessler (2023b) published her transliteration of Sin. syr. NF M38N, which consists of the 'missing' quire from CCR. These sheets of the tenth-century quire derive from the sixth-century manuscript CCR II. In the introduction she writes: "The siglum CCR2 has been used in the past for the part of CCR containing parts of the Acts of the Apostles and the Epistles, but it has become clear in the meantime that what was previously referred to as CCR2 now has to be divided into two different Bible manuscripts, CCR2A and CCR2B. The folios of CCR2A contain parts of Acts, and show a rather different scribal hand to the one containing parts of Corinthians—CCR2B" (Müller-Kessler 2023b, 148). In a private communication (2 January 2024), Müller-Kessler kindly confirmed to me that she first became aware of the need to distinguish between CCR2A and CCR2B during her examination of the 'missing' quire from CCR. Thus, this appears to be one of those reassuring situations where the same conclusion has been independently reached by two different scholars or groups of scholars (i.e., Müller-Kessler and Tyndale House). At any rate, it is gratifying that Müller-Kessler concurs with the basic division of *quondam*-CCR II into two distinct manuscripts. In addition to the differences in script and certain grammatical preferences between the two distinct

Pending further discoveries, therefore, the scribe responsible for the production of CCR appears to have used fragments from no fewer than seven CPA manuscripts.

The classification of the Greek undertext manuscripts has also been refined over the last century. Lewis (1909, xvi, xxvii–xxxi) identified CCR V (a harmony of the Gospels) and CCR VI (a fragment from a Greek Psalter). Moir (1956, ix) noted, and subsequently published (Moir 1957), a fragment of Greek Joshua, written in a different script-mode to the Greek Psalms, and hence unlikely to derive from the same codex. It is referred to below as CCR IX.

As part of the Tyndale House CCR project, Dr Peter Malik has begun to critically re-edit all the Greek biblical texts (Malik 2023a; 2023b).

Additionally, Moir's examination of the codex under ultraviolet light revealed that ff. 47–55 contained Greek text, which nonetheless eluded decipherment (Moir 1956, 15). Perhaps the most sensational outcome of the Tyndale House CCR project has

---

manuscripts, she points to the fact that the Acts portion of the manuscript occasionally carries headers (Müller-Kessler 2023b, 149, n. 17). The examination of the quire numbering below dovetails well with her findings.

In the same article, Müller-Kessler (2023b, 148) claims that one bifolium from Sin. syr. NF M64N also belongs with CCR II. Here, we must disagree. The evidence is given in an Appendix to this volume.

Finally, in an earlier publication from the same year (2023a, 208–9) Müller-Kessler claims in passing that CCR f. 23 (containing Tit. 2.7–3.3) cannot belong to CCR II. Again, we disagree with this assessment; the evidence will be presented below (§2.1.3.).

been the discovery of illustrated astronomical material of Aratus and Eratosthenes on these previously indecipherable pages (Williams et al. 2022). Williams et al. (2022, 506) label this text (and presumably, therefore, the manuscript whence it originated) CCR10.

Finally, then, we arrive at the following summary:

Codex Climaci Rescriptus consists of 146 leaves in 18 quires (16 quaternions and 2 quinions—quires VIII and XV). The majority of the first 17 quires reside in Museum of the Bible, Washington, DC (MS. 000149). The eighteenth quire remains at Sinai among the New Finds (Sin. syr. NF M38N).[22] An isolate leaf (f. 138) is held in the Mingana Collection, University of Birmingham (Mingana Syr. MS. 637).[23] Two folios from the beginning of the codex (those conjugate to the folios now numbered 5 and 6) are not extant.

Of those 146 folios, 109 contain CPA undertext. The remainder (all of which happen to belong to the Museum of the Bible portion of the manuscript) contain Greek undertext (though f. 55 may have no undertext).

The 146 folios derive from 11 earlier codices, seven of which contained CPA texts, and four of which contained Greek texts.

---

[22] Recently edited by Müller-Kessler (2023b).

[23] Edited first by Duensing (1938), then shortly later by Black (1939).

Table 1: The breakdown of CCR into its eleven component manuscripts

Source Manuscript	Folio Numbers from CCR (following sequence of undertext)	Content and Notes
CCR I (16 folios)	112; 80 (v, r); 73 (v, r); 105; 78; 75; 107 (v, r); 110 (v, r); 77 (v, r); 76 (v, r); 79 (v, r); 74 (v, r); 108 (v, r); 111; 106; 109 (v, r)	CPA Gospels manuscript; originally contained at least Matthew and Mark.
CCR II (41 CCR folios[24] + 8 NF folios)	127; 4; 1; 126; 45 (v, r); 40 (v, r); 16; 21; NF 38 f. 1; 11 (v, r); 10 (v, r); NF 38 f. 4; NF 38 f. 8 (v, r); NF 38 f. 5 (v, r); 19; 13 (v, r); NF 38 f. 7; 15; 22; NF 38 f. 6; 8 (v, r); 18; NF 38 f. 2; 20; 17; NF 38 f. 3; 3; 6; 2; 123; 130; 39; 125; 128; 46; 63 (v, r); 56 (v, r); 59 (v, r); 60 (v, r); 62 (v, r); 57 (v, r); 24; 29; 58 (v, r); 61 (v, r); 23; 30; 25 (v, r); 28 (v, r)	CPA Pauline epistles; Romans–Hebrews.
CCR III (18 folios)	114; 99 (v, r); 102 (v, r); 121; 97 (v, r); 117; 103; 101 (v, r); 100 (v, r); 98; 118; 104 (v, r); 122; 113; 116 (v, r); 115; 120; 119 (v, r)	CPA Lectionary.
CCR IV (6 folios)	9 (v, r); 12 (v, r) (Dormition) 14; 129; 124; 7 (Homily)	CPA Dormition; homily.
CCR V	67 (v, r); 84 (v, r); 85; 70; 87; 83 (v, r); 68 (v, r); 69; 86; 82 (v, r); 88 (v, r); 91; 94 (v, r); 81; 92 (v, r); 72 (v, r); 65; 93; 90 (v, r); 71 (v, r); 96 (v, r); 89; 66; 95[25]	Greek Gospel texts.

[24] Folio 6 lacks its conjugate; hence there is an odd number of folios in total.

[25] CCR V data according to Moir (1956, 97–98).

CCR VI	27; 26	Greek (biblical majuscule style) Psalms.
CCR VII (2 folios)	36; 33	CPA Leviticus.
CCR VIII (6 folios)	34; 35; 37 (v, r); 38; 31; 32	CPA Lectionary.
CCR IX	5 (v, r)	Greek (sloping ogival majuscule style) Joshua.
CCR X	51; 50; 48 (v, r); 53 (v, r); 64 (v, r); 52; 47 (v, r); 54 (v, r); 49	Greek (sloping ogival majuscule style) astronomical material from Aratus, Eratosthenes and Hipparchus.
CCR XI (12 CCR folios)	131; 43 (v, r); 42 (v, r); 138 (MSyr.637); 41 (v, r); 134; 132; 137; 135; 44 (v, r); 133; 136	CPA Apostolos (Acts and Catholic Epistles).

1.2. The Present Volume

This volume examines CCR II (Pauline Epistles) and CCR XI (Apostolos).[26] For each manuscript, a relatively detailed codicological introduction is offered (apparently for the first time). Thereafter, the re-edited text is presented, with notes clarifying where our text diverges from previous editions. At the end of the volume, a linguistic and textual commentary examines the points of textual and linguistic interest arising from the new edition.

[26] This study is part of a sequence of publications re-editing the four CPA biblical manuscripts: CCR I, CCR II, CCR VII, CCR XI.

Understanding something of the author's workflow in producing this edition may forestall some potential critiques. First, the various batch-processed images available for each page were stacked in layers using image manipulation software. These stacks contained five images per page: colour, pseudo, sharpie, Tx-ratio, UVbyTx (see *supra* §1.1.3.). For the more difficult pages, these stacks were then augmented with additional statistically processed images. In some cases, this resulted in stacks of 30–40 images for a single page. For the more legible pages, one image—typically the pseudocolour—served as the main reference point in the transcription process, complemented as and when necessary by the other layers—especially the Tx-ratio images.[27] Not infrequently, the Tx-ratio has rendered visible diacritical dots that are simply invisible otherwise. Anyone wishing to check these new transcriptions is therefore advised not to neglect the Tx-ratio images, even when the undertext seems legible without.

Re-editing the most illegible pages involved working letter-by-letter through each image in the stack. In the worst cases, one fraction of a letter might be visible in one image, while the rest of the letter might only be visible in another image 30 layers away.

The labour, though arduous, has not proved entirely fruitless. In terms of sheer recovery of text, the present edition fills more than twenty of the more substantial lacunae left in previous editions. Sometimes these lacunae consist of only a few words. In

---

[27] For the majority of the pages, the pseudocolour was the single most useful image—a result that conforms with other projects (Davies and Zawacki 2019, 181).

other cases, nearly entire columns of previously indecipherable material have been rendered legible thanks to the advanced imaging and image processing techniques (see, e.g., f. 18v; f. 21r; f. 23r; 30v; 123r). Additionally, the current edition contains several hundred improved readings compared to previous editions, more than 50 of which are of text-critical or linguistic significance.

This edition also pays renewed attention to *unit delimitation* within the manuscript, i.e., the various degrees of sense delimitation at the sub- and supra-sentential levels, and to how those boundaries are marked. Previously, this has been particularly difficult in CPA texts from the early period, in that nearly all the available evidence is in the form of palimpsests, where punctuation dots are all too readily obscured by the superior texts. Even at the supra-sentential level, though, previous editions of CPA have frequently neglected to represent the divisions found in the manuscripts themselves.

2. CCR II: PAULINE EPISTLES

2.1. CCR II Codicology

Sufficient sheets of CCR II survive to enable us to reconstruct the manuscript with confidence using the data available from the quire numbering and average number of verses per quire. CCR II began with Romans 1:1, and originally contained at least all the Pauline Epistles, in the order in which they are found today, in at least 25 quires.

2.1.1. Quire Structure

Summary: *The evidence afforded by the 49 extant leaves uniformly supports the reconstruction that the manuscript consisted of quaternions, each of which obeyed Gregory's Rule, with flesh side outermost. The quires were numbered using an alphanumeric numbering system found in several other CPA manuscripts. The numbering was arranged according to the mirror-signing technique typical of CPA manuscripts.*

The leaves of CCR from Museum of the Bible, together with those from the New Finds, preserve 49 folios from CCR II:[1] 24 bifolia, and one isolate folio.[2] These folios derive from 17 different quires, which themselves span a total range of 22 quires (quires 2–23) of the entire manuscript. In three cases (quires 9, 16 and 23), the outer sheet of the quire has been preserved (demonstrated by the presence of quire numbers on each folio), and in

[1] 41 in Museum of the Bible; eight in Sin. syr. NF M38N.

[2] The folio conjugate to f. 6 (apparently a cover leaf in the tenth-century codex) is not extant.

 https://doi.org/10.11647/OBP.0455.02

the case of quire 9, the entire quaternion quire is extant. This quire fully obeys Gregory's Rule, with flesh side outermost. In five other quires (nos 2, 6, 10, 11, 14), multiple sheets from the same quire have been preserved. When these sheets are contiguous, flesh–flesh, hair–hair layout is directly observable in all cases.[3] When the sheets are not contiguous, their orientation is consistent with Gregory's rule.[4] In all 17 quires for which at least one sheet is extant, the flesh–hair orientation of the sheets is consistent with a flesh-side-outermost quire structure (on the assumption that each quire is a quaternion).

The quires are mirror-signed, as is usual with CPA manuscripts.[5] In this system, quire number 'n' is signed with the number 'n - 1' on its opening side, and with the number 'n' on its final side. Thus, any opening containing the final side of one quire, and the first side of the next quire, will show the same number 'x' on both sides. In this case, the number 'x' indicates the total number of quires already read. In CCR II, the numbers are indicated using the alphanumeric numbering system that appears in several other CPA manuscripts (Desreumaux 2015, 134). Note the use of final *kaf* and final *nun* after their respective medial forms, and the use of *pe inversum* after *pe*:

---

[3] Quires 2, 9, 10 and 11.

[4] Quires 6 and 14.

[5] See Desreumaux (2015, 134) for a general discussion, and Desreumaux (2023, 135–36) for a helpful worked example, in the form of Sin. syr. NF M56N.

Table 2: Numbering system commonly found in CPA manuscripts

25	24	23	22	21	20	19	18	17	16	15	14	13	12	11	10	9	8	7	6	5	4	3	2	1
ܬ	ܫ	ܪ	ܩ	ܨ	ܦ	ܦ	ܥ	ܣ	ܢ	ܢ	ܡ	ܠ	ܟ	ܟ	ܝ	ܛ	ܚ	ܙ	ܘ	ܗ	ܕ	ܓ	ܒ	ܐ

Frustratingly, some of the quire numbers are only partially extant, due to the cropping of the leaves.

Table 3: Extant quire numbers in CCR II

Quire number	9	16	23
Number on opening side	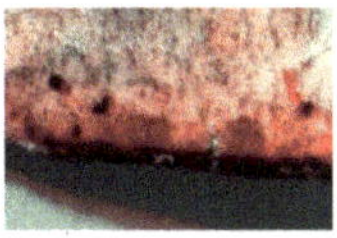 Upper traces of ܚ (F. 19r)	 ܢ (F. 59v)	 Upper traces of ܩ (F. 25v)
Number on closing side	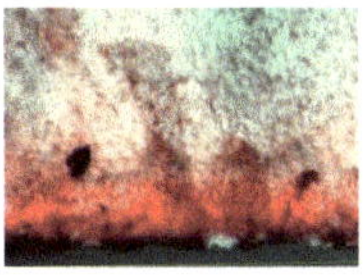 ܛ (F. 18v)	 ܢ (F. 60r)	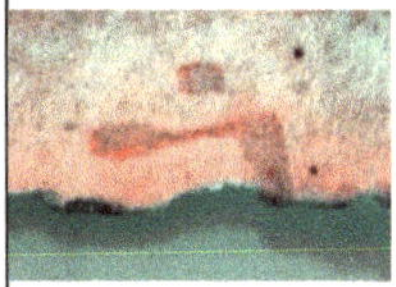 ܪ (F. 28r)

The three quires from which the outer bifolium has been preserved contain, on average, just over 100 verses each. A more accurate estimate of average quire content can be obtained by relying on the extant quire numbers. The range of text from the beginning of quire 9 to the end of quire 23 (1 Cor. 13:4–Heb. 7:27) comprises 1422 verses, which averages out as 94.8 verses/quire, or 11.85 verses/leaf.[6] This latter figure, in turn, affirms that quires 9, 16 and 23 (of each of which we have the outer

[6] Averaging the number of verses contained purely in the extant folios also gives an estimate of 11–12 verses per folio.

bifolium) are quaternions. This is confirmed in the case of quire 9, which is fully extant. This is unsurprising; Desreumaux (2015, 134) notes that "parchment manuscripts of the ancient period are regularly composed of quaternions (with an exceptional presence of some quinions)." Finally, using these data and a default assumption that each quire is a quaternion, the entire quire structure of almost all the manuscript can be reconstructed, as below.

Just three firm quire numbers are rather a thin foundation on which to build a 23-quire structure. Happily, though, the numbered quires are spread out widely across the full range. By using these numbered quires as anchor-points, and moving outwards therefrom, a reasonably solid quire sequence can be attained.[7] One part of the sequence remains problematic, and this is discussed below the following table.[8]

---

[7] In terms of process: I first established the position of each bifolium within the quire (using the average number of verses per folio alongside the total number of missing verses *between* each conjugate folio). With the added assumption that each quire is a quaternion, this was already sufficient to produce a full set of quires. Then, calculating the total number of missing verses between the outermost folios of consecutive quires served as a check to the proposed quire structure.

[8] Müller-Kessler (2023b), when publishing the 'missing' CCR quire from the New Finds (Sin. syr. NF M38N), containing parts of 1 and 2 Corinthians from CCR II, does not attempt to reconstruct the quire structure *in toto* for this part of the manuscript. She does, however, attempt to show how the leaves of Sin. syr. NF M38N (referred to simply as NF 38 in the table below) fit in sequence with the rest of CCR II 1-2 Corinthians. In a few places our respective analyses diverge, as will be indicated *ad loc.*

Table 4: The quire structure of CCR II

i. Quire No. *ii. Approx. quire range* *iii. Approx. No. Verses* iv. First extant verse v. Last extant verse vi. [No. missing verses between extant fols of adjacent quires]	Quire Structure
1 *Rom. 1:1–4:4* *96vv.* - -	
2 *Rom. 4:5–7:23* *88vv.* Rom. 4:17a Rom. 7:11a [23vv.; 2 fols]	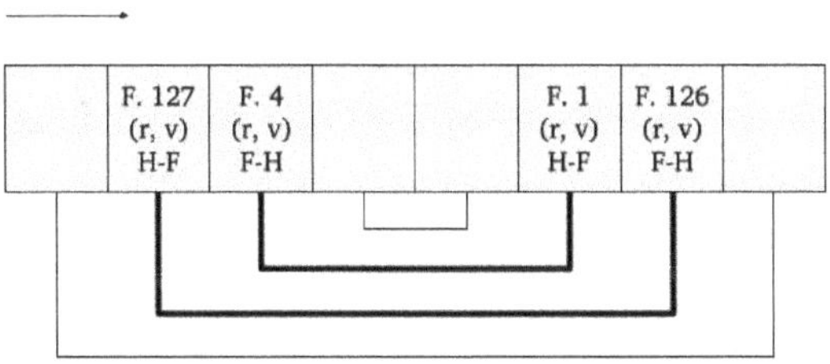
3 *Rom. 7:24–10:21* *95vv.* Rom. 8:9b Rom. 10:9b [117vv.; 10 fols]	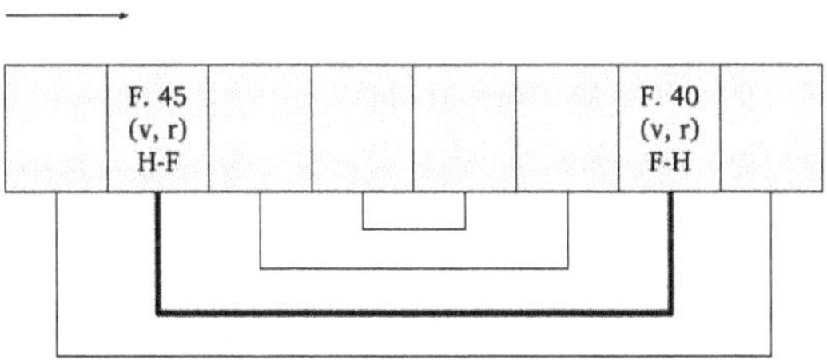
4 *Rom. 11:1–14:21* *92vv.* - -	

i. Quire No. *ii. Approx. quire range* *iii. Approx. No. Verses* iv. First extant verse v. Last extant verse vi. [No. missing verses between extant fols of adjacent quires]	Quire Structure
5 *Rom. 14:22–1 Cor. 1:28* *90vv.* Rom. 15:11b 1 Cor. 1:17 [23.5vv.; 2 fols][9]	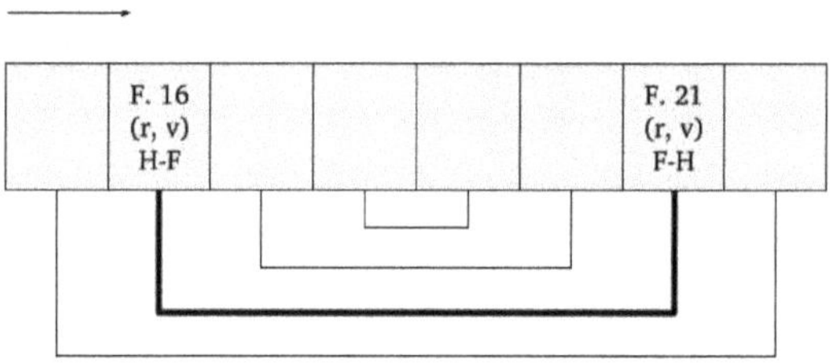
6 *1 Cor. 1:29–6:16* *92vv.* 1 Cor. 2:10c 1 Cor. 6:5a [113vv.; 10 fols][10]	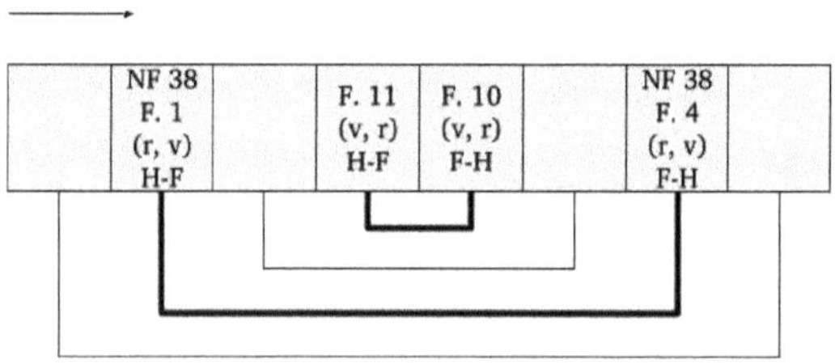
7 *1 Cor. 6:17–10:7* *91vv.* - -	

[9] Müller-Kessler (2023b, 151) posits just one missing folio between CCR II f. 21 and NF 38 f. 1. However, an average of 11.85 verses per folio requires precisely two missing folios for the intervening 23.5 verses.

[10] Müller-Kessler (2023b, 151) posits 8 missing folios between NF 38 f. 4 and NF 38 f. 8. The quire structure proposed here posits 10 missing folios, which coheres excellently with the count of an intervening 113 verses (at an average of 11.85 verses per folio).

i. Quire No. *ii. Approx. quire range* *iii. Approx. No. Verses* iv. First extant verse v. Last extant verse vi. [No. missing verses between extant fols of adjacent quires]	Quire Structure
8 *1 Cor. 10:8–13:3* *94vv.* 1 Cor. 10:18b 1 Cor. 12:24a[11] [10.5vv.; 1 fol.]	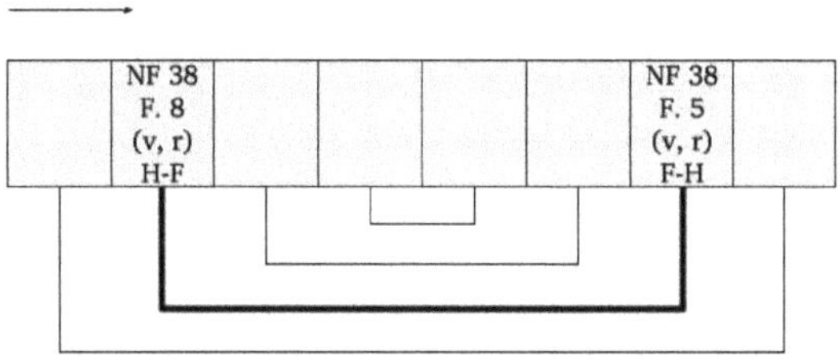
9 1 Cor. 13:4–15:49a 98.5vv. 1 Cor. 13:4 1 Cor. 15:49a [12vv.; 1 fol.]	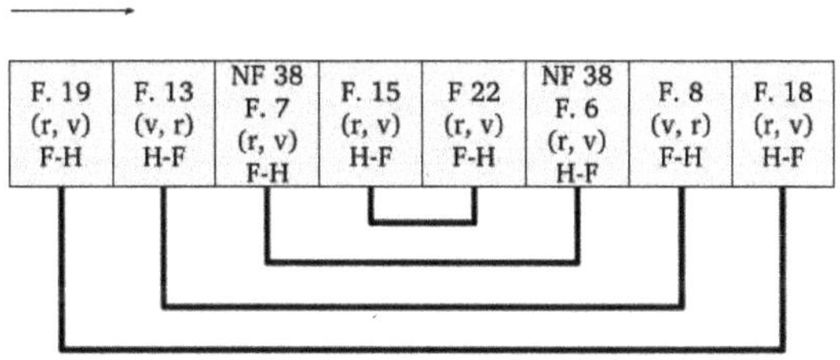

[11] Müller-Kessler (2023b, 151) posits two missing folios between NF 38 f. 8 and NF 38 f. 5. However, the total number of verses from the beginning of f. 8 (1 Cor. 10:18b) to the end of f. 5 (1 Cor. 12:24a) is 73. At 11.85 vv./fol, this implies 6 folios to contain this intervening material, and hence *four* missing folios between NF 38 f. 8 and NF 38 f. 5.

i. Quire No. *ii. Approx. quire range* *iii. Approx. No. Verses* iv. First extant verse v. Last extant verse vi. [No. missing verses between extant fols of adjacent quires]	Quire Structure
10 1 Cor. 15:49b–*2 Cor. 3:16* *90.5vv.* 1 Cor. 16:3b 2 Cor. 3:5a[12] [31vv.; 3 fols][13]	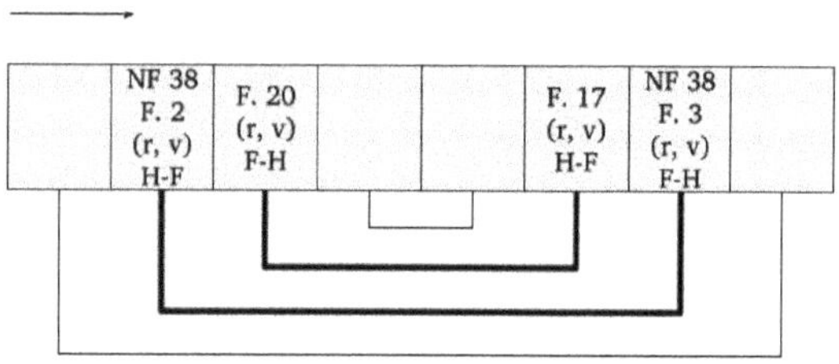
11 *2 Cor. 3:17–~ 2 Cor. 8* *~90vv.* 2 Cor. 4:18c 2 Cor. 7:8a [132.5vv.; 13 fols?]	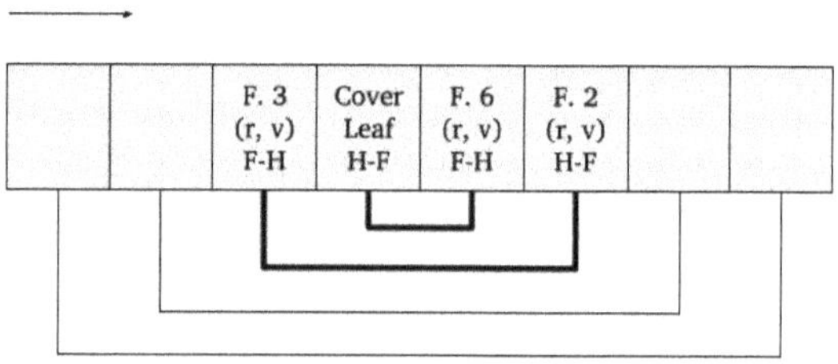

[12] Müller-Kessler (2023b, 151) omits to mention that an intervening bifolium must lie between the end of f. 20 (2 Cor. 1:3) and the beginning of f. 17 (2 Cor. 1:23).

[13] Müller-Kessler (2023b, 151) posits two missing folios between NF 38 f. 3 and CCR II f. 3. However, given the 11.85 vv./fol. average, the 31 intervening verses are far more likely to be contained in three folios each containing just over 10vv., than in two folios containing over 15vv. each.

i. Quire No. *ii. Approx. quire range* *iii. Approx. No. Verses* iv. First extant verse v. Last extant verse vi. [No. missing verses between extant fols of adjacent quires]	Quire Structure
12 *2 Cor. 8–~2 Cor. 12* *~80vv.(!)*[14] - -	
13 *~2 Cor. 12–Gal. 3:8* *~89vv.* Gal. 1:1 Gal. 1:23d [41vv.; 4 fols]	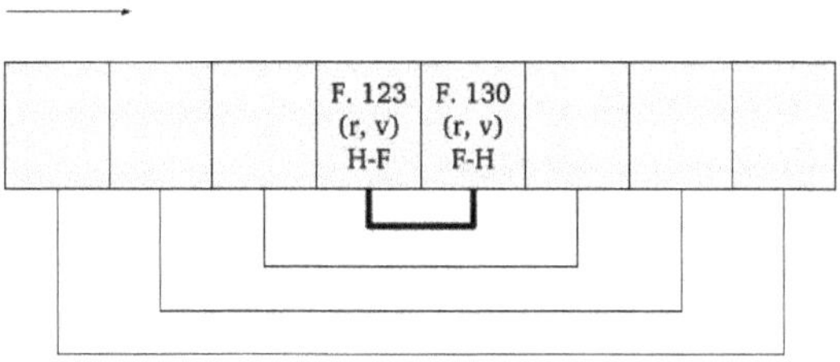
14 *Gal. 3:9–Eph. 1:6* *102vv.* Gal. 3:20 Gal. 6:12a [24vv.; 2 fols]	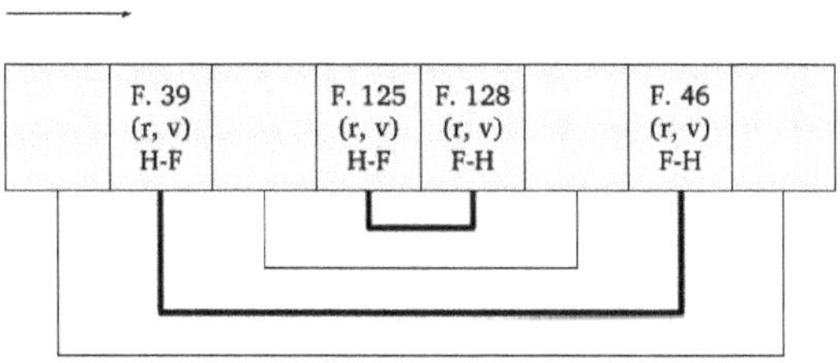
15 *Eph. 1:7*–Eph. 5:7 *99vv.* Eph. 1:18d Eph. 4:27 [12vv.; 1 fol.]	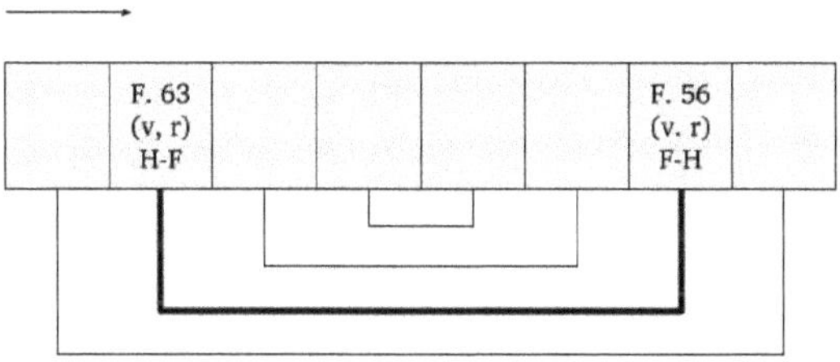

[14] See discussion *infra*.

i. Quire No. *ii. Approx. quire range* *iii. Approx. No. Verses* iv. First extant verse v. Last extant verse vi. [No. missing verses between extant fols of adjacent quires]	Quire Structure
16 Eph. 5:8–Phil. 2:26a 106vv. Eph. 5:8 Phil. 2:26a [131vv.; 11 fols]	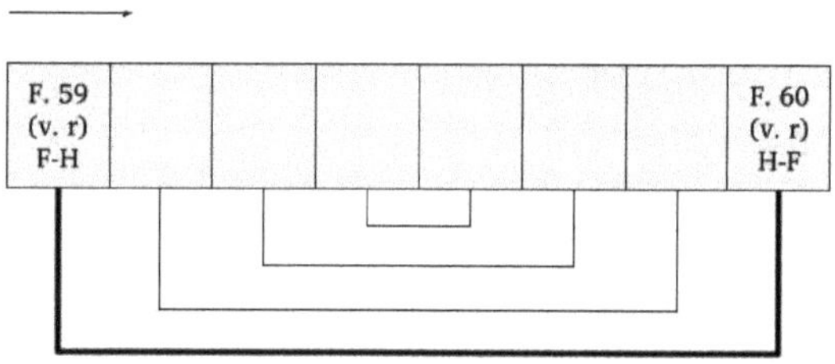
17 Phil. 2:26b–*Col. 2:18* *95vv.* - - 	
18 *Col. 2:19–1 Thes. 4:1* *92vv.* Col. 4:6b 1 Thes. 1:9a [67vv.; 6 fols]	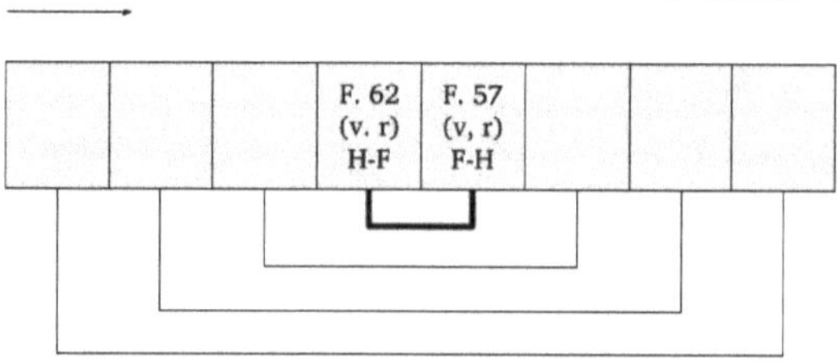
19 *1 Thes. 4:2–1 Tim. 1:3* *95vv.* 1 Thes. 5:15a 2 Thes. 2:2c [155vv.; 13 fols]	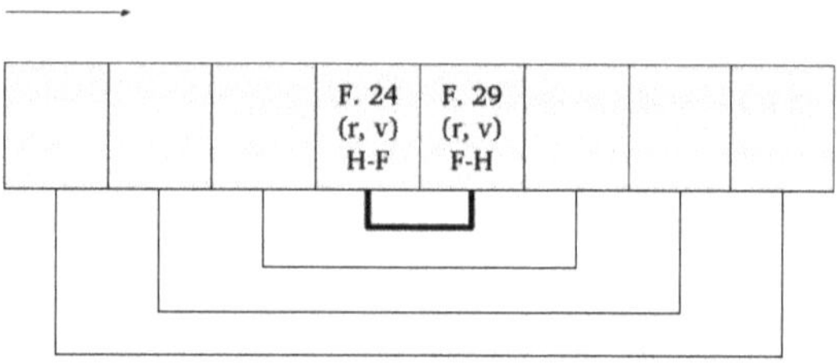

i. Quire No. *ii. Approx. quire range* *iii. Approx. No. Verses* iv. First extant verse v. Last extant verse vi. [No. missing verses between extant fols of adjacent quires]	Quire Structure
20 *1 Tim. 1:4–6:6* *95vv.* - -	
21 *1 Tim. 6:7–2 Tim. 4:20* *96vv.* 2 Tim. 1:9d 2 Tim. 3:14 [47vv.; 4 fols]	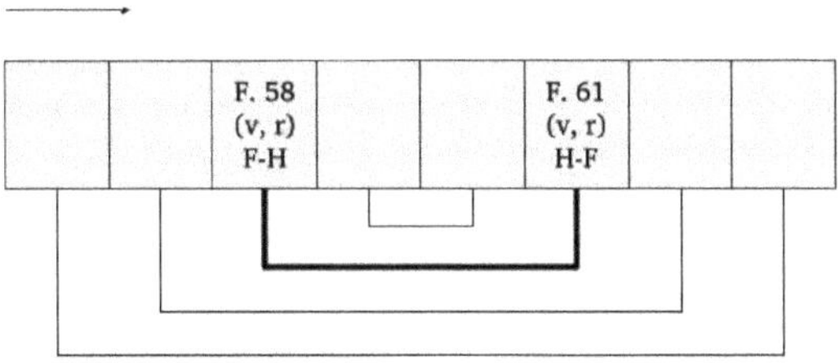
22 *2 Tim. 4:21*–Heb. 2:8 *95vv.* Tit. 2:7 Philem. 25 [22vv.; 2 fols]	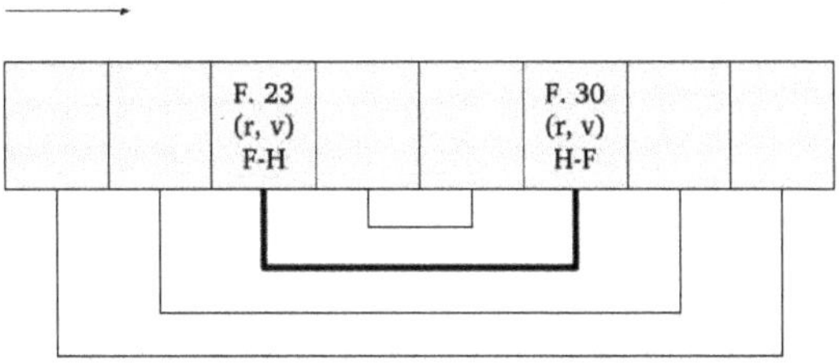
23 Heb. 2:9–7:27 106vv. Heb. 2:9 Heb. 7:27	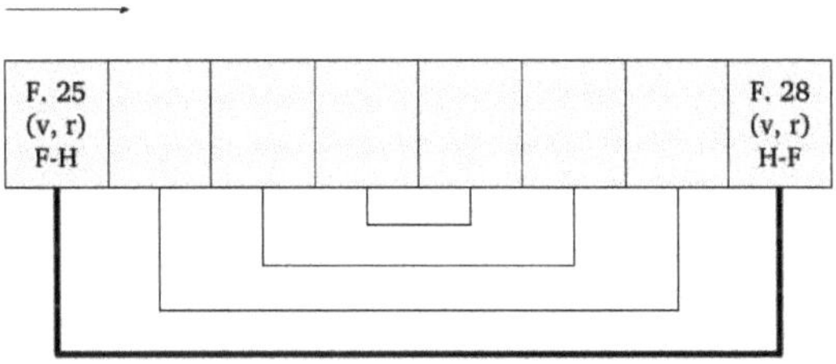

The remaining 175 verses of Hebrews would have required at least two further quires.

There is some uncertainty regarding the precise reconstruction of quires 11–13. Quires 9 and 16 serve as anchor-points, as the outermost bifolium of each is extant. Examination of the table above will confirm that the structures of quires 10, 14 and 15 are also secure. The heart of the difficulty is that only 132.5vv. lie between the last extant text of quire 11 (2 Cor. 7a; f. 2v; folio 6 out of 8 in quire) and the first extant text of quire 13 (Gal 1:1; f. 123r; folio 4 out of 8 in quire). If each of quires 11–13 is a quaternion, these 132.5vv. must be spread over 13 folios, averaging just over 10vv./fol. This is certainly not impossible, but it is rather low, given that the average over the codex as a whole is 11.85vv./fol. If one of these folios was a stub, this would raise the text density to just over 11vv./fol. This, though, is speculation; none of the extant material from CCR II gives any direct evidence of originally stunted sheets.

2.1.2. Dimensions, Ruling and Mise-en-Page

CCR II is arranged in portrait format. The average leaf measures approximately 230 × 183mm (after cropping), with a written area of approximately 180 × 137mm, and a lower margin height of approximately 32mm. As is usual for CPA manuscripts from the early period, the text is laid out in two columns per page. The average column measures approximately 180 × 60mm. Each column consists of 22 lines. Infrequently, one word is written at the bottom of a column on a twenty-third line, when doing so would complete a clear semantic unit. In these cases, the word on the twenty-third line is left-justified, rather than right-justified.[15] The average height of the *beth* is 3–4mm.

Both right and left margins of each column are strictly justified. Justification of the left-hand margin is achieved mainly by adjusting the space between letters, rather than dilation of the letters themselves. Rarely, simple line fillers are used, generally at the end of supra-sentential thematic units.[16]

Figure 6: Left: letter spacing for left justification in CCR II; right: line fillers at end of thematic unit in CCR II (f. 1r I.20)

Ruling is performed with a dry point, on the flesh side. It consists of four column-boundary vertical lines, extending over the full height of the sheet. Horizontal lines are drawn for each line of text, and apparently extend across the full width of the bifolium.

When describing the 'missing' CCR quire (originally from CCR II), Müller-Kessler claims that the folios are not ruled, either horizontally or vertically (Müller-Kessler 2023b, 149), and that

---

[15] This phenomenon is limited to the latter half of the manuscript. In Romans–2 Corinithians (42 sides), there are no cases of a twenty-third line. In Galatians–Hebrews (40 sides), there are seven occurrences.

[16] Fols 1r I.20; 57v I.10; 127v II.17.

there is no left-hand justification. Regarding the former, I submit that, in fact, the undertext of Sin. syr. NF M38N was ruled in the same way as the rest of CCR II, as the following snippets illustrate:

Figure 7: Left: snippet from Sin. syr. NF M38N f. 2r (pseudocolour); traces of the left-hand column boundary vertical line are visible, and several horizontal lines; right: snippet from Sin. syr. NF M38N f. 4v (raking light); two column boundary vertical lines are visible, as well as several horizontal lines.

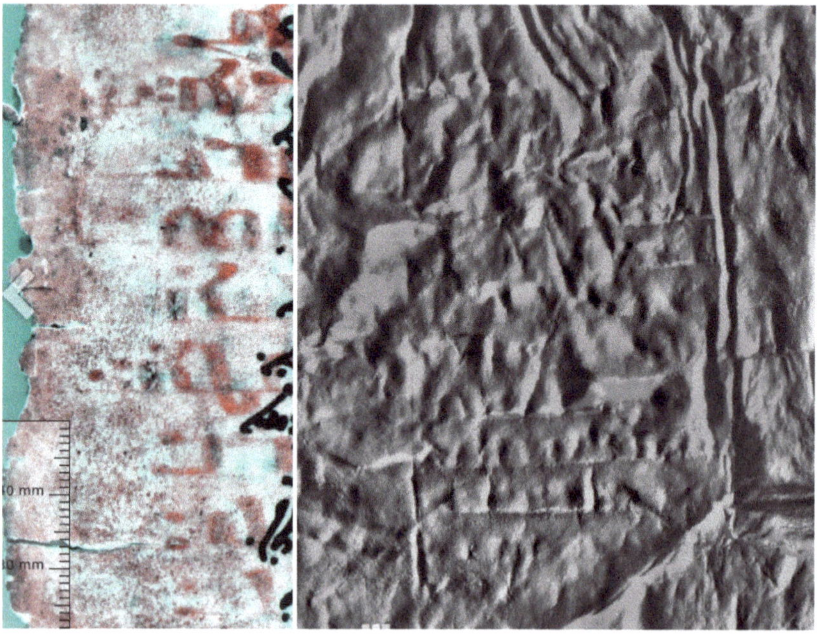

Regarding the left justification, I presume that Müller-Kessler and I are simply labelling the same phenomenon differently. As the left-hand image above illustrates, the scribe makes obvious efforts to adhere to the left vertical boundary line. Perhaps the most obvious locus is the end of line five, where the scribe elongates the base line between the penultimate letter and the final *alaf*, such that the left leg of the *alaf* nearly meets the column boundary line.

2.1.3. Paratextual Features

Overall, the manuscript is relatively unornate. Supra-sentential thematic units are indicated by ekthesis,[17] usually—though not always—with enlargement of the first letter. Usually, a simple four-dot rhombus is set over this initial letter, as can be seen in this snippet from f. 11v:[18]

Figure 8: Simple rhomboid ornament over enlarged letter with ekthesis

Larger textual units are demarcated using the ܪܝܫ ܡܩܠܝܘܢ rubric, usually with a blank line above and below the rubric. In general, the ink of the rubrics has not survived as well as the ink of the main text and has proved more resistant to MSI processing. In several cases, only blank lines are left where presumably rubric was originally to be found.

[17] I.e., the protrusion into the right-hand margin of the first letter of the first word of the new text unit.

[18] To be precise: this four-dot rhombus is almost always found from Romans 10 onwards (f. 40r), but only twice beforehand (and is absent in at least fifteen instances in Romans 1–9 where it would be expected to appear). Müller-Kessler (2023b, 149) notes comparable use of ekthesis, enlargement and the four-dot rhombus in CCR II's 'missing quire', Sin. syr. NF M38N.

In at least seven cases, the ekthesis following the ܪܫ ܦܩܠܝܘܢ rubric is adorned with a serifed cross in the right-hand margin.[19] The clearest example is found on f. 3r, introducing 2 Cor. 5:1.

Figure 9: Marginal decorative cross in CCR II (f. 3r)

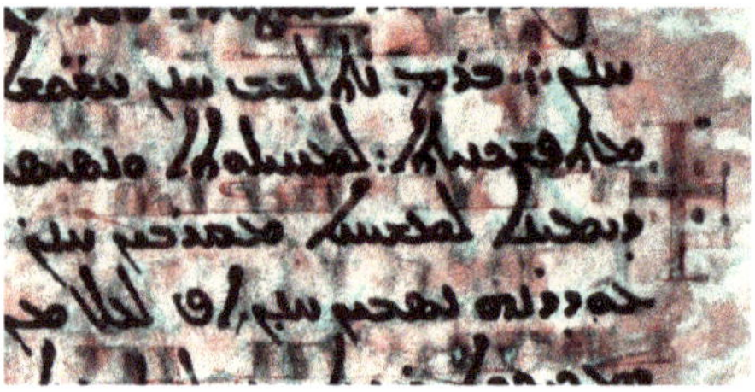

In the image above, the horizontal bar of the cross is in-line with the ܪܫ ܦܩܠܝܘܢ rubric (which is legible to an unusual degree in this instance). The rubric is separated from the main text by a blank line above and below. Ekthesis of the first word of the main text after the rubric (ܝܕܥܝܢ) means that the first letter of that word (*yod* in this case) is almost directly below the base of the cross. In one instance (f. 45r), the rubric appears at the bottom of column one, while the main text (with ekthesis) resumes at the top of column two. The ornate cross appears above the ekthesis, rather than beside the rubric, indicating that the decoration was seen to be adorning the biblical text itself.

The main body of these ornamental crosses was penned in the same ink as the rubric text. The basic cross shape was then surrounded by dots penned with the ink used for the main text:

---

[19] Fols 2r; 3r; 22r; 25r; 25v; 39r; 45r. In this latter case, the ܪܫ ܦܩܠܝܘܢ rubric appears on the last line of column one, whereas the cross appears above the first letter of the first word of column two. Moreover, in this instance, the cross is not surrounded by ornamental dots, but by small circles arranged in the same inner and outer pattern described below.

four inner dots surrounding the central vertex, and eight outer dots: two at each end of the vertical and horizontal bars of the cross. In the three other examples, the rubric ink has faded to such an extent that only the inner and outer dots remain visible. In the example below, from f. 2r, the main body of the cross has been reconstructed, such that the surrounding dots are more easily identified.

Figure 10: Reconstructed marginal decorative cross in CCR II (f. 2r)

In addition to the ܪܫ ܫܘܠܡܗ rubrics, CCR II also includes several rubrics pertaining to the lectionary.

Table 5: Lectionary rubrics in CCR II

4r I.11–13	Rom. 5:6ff.	ܫܘܠܡܗ ܠܚܪܘܒܬܐ ܕܫܘܒܬܐ ܡܕܢܚܬܐ
22r I.16–19	1 Cor. 15:1ff.	ܫܘܠܡܗ ܕܚܪܘܒܬܐ [...]
39r II.12–13	Gal. 3:24ff.	ܒܐܪܒܥܬܗ ܕܦܣܚܐ
23r II.9–11	Tit. 2:11ff.	ܫܘܠܡܗ ܕ[ܝܘܡܢܐ ܡܫܝܚܐ ܘܬܠܝܢܐ][20] ܕܬܗܘܦܢܝܐ
23v I.23	After Tit. 2:15	ܫܠܡ
25v II.1–3	Heb. 2:11ff.	ܫܘܠܡܗ ܕܚܪܘܒܬܐ [ܕܫܘܒܬܐ ܡܕܢܚܬܐ][21]

Müller-Kessler (2023a, 208–9) has recently claimed (*en passant*) that CCR f. 23 (Tit. 2:7–3:3) cannot originally have be-

[20] Reconstructed according to the reading in Lewis (1909, 176).

[21] Reconstructed according to the reading in Lewis (1909, 180, *sic*).

longed to CCR II, since it contains a lectionary rubric. This is untenable, for the following three reasons. First, the script of this folio, together with its codicological features, is identical to the rest of CCR II. Second, its position within CCR II's quire structure is seamless, which would be rather coincidental, to say the least, if the folio originated from a different manuscript.[22] Finally, the lectionary rubric on f. 23 is comparable with those on f. 4, f. 22 and f. 25. In particular, notice that in all three cases the ensuing reading is referred to as a ܡܦܠܩܘܢ, whereas in other (genuine lectionary) manuscripts, the term ܡܪܟܐܢ is used.[23] Thus, Lewis (1909, 176) was quite correct in assigning f. 23 to CCR II.

The most substantial paratextual additions in CCR II are the concluding rubric to each epistle. These notes (five of which are extant and at least partially legible) follow a set pattern:

- The letter to [recipient(s)] is complete
- It was written from [presumed location]
- And sent by [presumed letter carrier]

---

[22] See §2.1.1. The 47 missing verses between the end of f. 61 and the beginning of f. 23 (quires 21–22) perfectly match the four predicted folios between these leaves. The 22 missing verses between the end of f. 23 and the beginning of f. 30 (quire 22) perfectly match the two posited folios between these leaves. The 22 missing verses between the end of f. 30 and the beginning of f. 25 (which constitutes the outermost folio of quire 23, and carries a quire number) perfectly match the predicted two folios between these leaves. One could not ask for better alignment.

[23] Cf. the list of CPA rubrics in Müller-Kessler (2023a, 219–24).

Figure 11: Rubric concluding 2 Corinthians (f. 123r)

ܫܠܡܬ ܐ ܓܪܬܐ
ܬܢܝܢܬܐ
ܕܩܘܪ̈ܢܬ[...]
ܐܬܟܬܒܬ ܕܝ
ܡܢ ܦܝܠܝܦܘܣ
ܘܐܫܬܓܪܬ ܒܝܕ
ܛܛܘܣ ܘܠܘܩܣ:

~~~~~~~~~~~

ܐܓܪܬܐ ܕܠܘܬ
ܓܠܛܝܐ:

As can be seen in the image above: after the concluding comment and a simple line divider, the title of the next epistle appears, followed by the biblical text.

2.1.4. Punctuation

By far the most frequently used punctuation sign is a triangle of three dots (209 occurrences over 25 sides); a pair of vertically arranged dots is also frequently used (134 occurrences over 25 sides); the use of a single pausal dot is far less frequent (50 occurrences over 25 sides). Usually, the dots are arranged either in
~~~~~~~~~~~

line with the mid-height of the letters, or at the height of the top of the roofed letters.

The three-dot triangle is the default punctuation sign at the end of a sentence, and hence almost always appears at what we now consider to be verse divisions. However, it also frequently appears between two clauses in a compound sentence (e.g., 2 Tim. 1:12; f. 58v II.2), and between the constituents of a wide variety of complex sentences.

Two dots are used in a similarly broad manner, especially between the constituents making up compound and complex sentences. However, they are far less frequently used to mark significant semantic disjunction. For example, in the nine sides of 2 Corinthians (excluding the leaves from Sin. syr. NF M38N), two dots are used as end-of-verse punctuation in only three cases.

One dot tends to be used only to indicate minimal semantic or prosodic disjunction, as the following examples illustrate:

- After a vocative (1 Cor. 1:10; f. 21r)
- Between two closely related adverbial phrases (1 Cor. 1:10; f. 21r)
- Between a main clause and an adverbial accusative 'that'-clause (1 Cor. 1:14; f. 21v)
- Separating the end of a relative clause from the following main clause (1 Cor. 3:18; f. 11v)
- Separating a temporal clause from the following main clause (1 Cor. 13:10; f. 19r)
- Between the elements of a compound subject (1 Cor. 13:13; f. 19v)

However, the entire system of pausal dots appears to be applied in an causal, non-rigorous, manner. For example, in the list above, the post-vocative pause is marked with a single dot. However, at Gal. 5:11 (f. 128v) the same pause is marked with two dots, whereas at 2 Tim. 2:1 (f. 58r) there is no pausal dot whatsoever. Even more striking: at 2 Tim. 3:10–11 (f. 61r) two—and even three—dots regularly separate the elements of a compound object.

2.2. CCR II Text

Critical Symbols and Apparatus

[...]	Lacuna
[ܐܒܓ]	Reconstructed text
⸢ܐܒܓ⸣	Partially visible letter(s)
ܐܒܓ	Uncertain reading
ܐ ͨܒ ܓ	Supralinear secondary insertion
[a]ܐܒܓ	Word is commented on in the *sub loco* apparatus
[a]ܐܒܓ[a]	Text between the pair of superscript letters is commented on in the *sub loco* apparatus
*ܐܒܓ	Text is commented on in the Textual and Linguistic Commentary at the end of this volume

The critical apparatus is in two parts. The first part compares the present edition to previous editions, principally those of Müller-Kessler and Sokoloff (1997, 1998a, 1998b). For each page, this first apparatus begins with: MKS IIB, [page number(s)], indicating the page(s) of Müller-Kessler and Sokoloff (1998b) corresponding to the particular text at hand.

To avoid overcrowding, the following are *not* explicitly noted in the first apparatus: (1) differences in punctuation between the two editions; (2) disagreement as to the precise location of *seyame* over a particular word; (3) disagreement as to whether a letter is fully or only partially visible.

After this apparatus, and separated therefrom by double vertical lines ||, follows a brief textual apparatus. Substantial issues are reserved for the Textual and Linguistic Commentary at the end of this volume. Textual comments appearing *sub loco* in the second part of the apparatus are limited to minor issues such as the noting of a second hand, or an apparent error in the manuscript.

Romans 4:17–22 F. 127r

[17]ܗܝܟ ܕܟܬܝܒ:
ܕܐܒ ܠܣܓܝܢ
ܥܡܡܝܢ ܐܬܡܢܬ
ܝܬܟ: ܠܩܒܠ
ܕܗܝܡܢ
ܒܐܠܗܐ ܗܕܢ
ܕܡܚܝܐ
ܡܝܬܝܐ:
ܘܩܪܐ[a] ܠܗܠܝܢ
ܕܠܐ ܗܘܘ·
ܗܝܟ ܕܗܘܢ:
[18]ܗܕܢ ܕܗܝܡܢ
ܒܬܪ ܣܒܪ
ܥܠ ܣܒܪ: ܗܝܡܢ
ܕܝܗܐ ܐܒ
ܠܣܓܝܢ ܥܡܡܝܢ:
ܗܝܟ ܕܐܡܪ
ܕܗܟܢ ܝܗܐ
ܙܪܥܟ: [19]ܘܠܐ
ܕܝ ܐܬܟܐܫ
ܒܗܝܡܢܘܬܐ:
ܐܠܐ ܐܕܡܟ

ܒܦܘ ܓܪܗ
ܡܡܝܬ: ܕܗܘܐ
ܒܪ ܡܐܐ ܫܢܝܢ:
ܘܒܡܝܬܘܬܗ[b]
ܕܡܛܪܐ
ܕܣܪܐ:
[20]ܠܡܝܢ ܡܝܢ ܬܗ ܕܝ
ܕܐܠܗܐ ܠܐ
ܐܬܦܠܓ
ܒܚܣܝܪܘܬ
ܗܝܡܢܘ:
ܐܠܐ ܐܬܚܝܠ
ܒܗܝܡܢܘܬܐ:
ܘܝܗܒ ܬܫܒܘܚܐ
ܠܐܠܗܐ:
[21]ܘܐܫܬܘܕܥ
ܕܡܐ ܕܡܝܢ
ܠܗ ܝܟܠ ܗܘ
ܐܘܦ ܕܝܥܒܕ:
[22]ܠܟܝܠܠ ܒܕܢ
ܐܬܚܫܒܬ
ܠܗ ܠܟܝ ܕܘ:

MKS IIB, 55: **a** ܘܩܪܐ | **b** ܘܕܡܝܬܘܬܗ

Romans 4:23–5:4 F. 127v

[23] ܠܐ ܕܝ ܐܬܟܬܒܬ[a]
ܠܒܕܠܗ ܒܠܚܘܕ
ܕܐܬܚܫܒܬ[a]
ܠܗ: [24] ܐܠܐ ܐܘܦ
ܠܒܕܠܢ ⁖ ܠܗܠܝܢ
ܕܗܘ ܥܬܝܕ
ܕܢܚܫܒ: ܠܗܠܝܢ
ܕܡܗܝܡܢܝܢ ܥܠ
ܗܕܝ[b] ܕܐܩܝܡ
ܠܡܪܝ ܝܫܘܥ
ܡܫܝܚܐ ܡܢ
ܒܝܢ ܡܝ̈ܬܝܐ⁖
[25] ܗܕܝ ܕܐܬܡܣܪ
ܠܒܕܠ ܣܟ̈ܠܬܝ:
ܘܩܡ ܠܒܕܠ
ܙܕܘܩܢ⁖

ܪܫ ܩܠܝܘܢ

[5:1] ܐܢܝ ܙܕܩܢ ܐܘܝ
ܡܢ ܗܝܡܢܘ:
ܫܠܡ ܝܗܐ ܠܢ

ܠܘܬ ܐܠܗܐ
ܒܬܪܗ ܕܡܪܢ
ܝܫܘܥ ܡܫܝܚܐ⁖
[2] ܕܒܗ ܗܘܐ ܠܢ
ܐܘܦ ܠܢ ܒܝܘ
ܒܚܝܠܐ
ܒܗܝܡܢܘܬܐ
ܠܗܕܝ ܚܣܕܐ⁖
ܗܕܝ ܕܒܗ
ܐܢܢ ܩ̈ܝܡܝܢ
ܘܡܫܬ̈ܒܚܝܢ
ܥܠ ܣܒܪܐ
ܕܬܫܒܘܚܬܗ
ܕܐܠܗܐ⁖ [3] ܠܐ
ܐܘܝ ܐܠܐ ܐܘܦ
ܡܫܬ̈ܒܚܝܢ
ܒܠܚ̈ܘܨܝܐ[c] ⁖÷⁖
ܝܕܥ̈ܝܢ[d] ܕܠܚܘܨܝܐ
ܡܣܘܒܪܢܘ
ܗܘ ܡܥܒܕ:
[4] ܡܣܘܒܪܢܘܬܐ
ܕܝ ܒܕܘܩܝ:

MKS IIB, 56: **a** omit diacritical dot | **b** ܗܘ | **c** ܒܠܚܘܨܝ ܘܟܐ | **d** omit *seyame* || Scarcely visible pattern of dots in right margin, adjacent to ܪܫ ܩܠܝܘܢ; may be remains of an ornamental cross.

Romans 5:4–10 F. 4r

ܒܕܘܩܐ ܕܝ
ܣܒܪ: [5]ܣܒܪܐ
ܕܝ ܠܐ ܡܒܗܬ:
ܠܒܕܠ
ܕܚܒܬܗ
ܕܐܠܗܐ ܐܫܦܥܐ
ܒܠܒ̈ܒܝܢ:[a]
ܒܪܘܚܐ
ܕܩܘܕܫܐ ܗܘ̇ܢ
ܕܐܬܝܗܒ ܠܢ:
ܡܛܠܘܢ ܠܒܪܘܒܬܐ
ܕܚܘܒܬܐ
ܘܕܚܝܬܐ:
[6]ܐܢ ܓܪ ܡܫܝܚܐ
ܒܕ ܗܘܝܢ[a]
ܟܐ̈ܫܝܢ ܚܘܕ
ܒܡܫܪܘܦ ܚܠ
ܛܒ ܪ̈ܫܝܥܝܢ
ܡܝܬ: [7]ܒܡܫܐ̇[b]
ܓܪ ܚܠܛܒ[c] ܙܕܝܩ
ܐܢܫ ܡܡܐܬ:[d]

ܚܠ ܛܒ ܛܒܐ ܓܪ
ܛܒܐ ܡܚܝ ܦ
ܐܢܫ ܕܡܡܘܬ:
[8]ܡܚܘܐ ܕܝ ܐܠܗܐ
ܚܒܬܗ ܒܠܒ̈ܝܢ:
ܕܒܕ ܐܢܢ ܚܛ̈ܝܝܢ
ܡܫܝܚܐ ܚܠ
ܕܛܒܢ[e] ܡܝܬ:
[9]ܟܡ̈ܐ ܒܚܟܐ ܕܝ
ܒܕܘ ܢܬܙܕܩܐܝܬ[f]
ܕܐܢܝ ܛܕܡܝܢ
ܒܐܕܡܗ:
ܢܬܦܘܒ
ܒܬܪܚܗ ܡܢ
[g]ܘܪ ܓܙܐ:
[10]ܐܢ ܓܪ ܒܡܠܕ̈ܒܒܝܢ
ܗܘ̈ܝܢ ܡܢ
ܘܩܕܡ[g]
ܘܐܬܪ̈ܥ[ܝܢ] ⸢ܢ⸣[h]
ܠܐܠܗܐ
ܒܡܘܬܗ
ܕܒܪܗ:

MKS IIB, 57: **a** omit *seyame* | **b** ܒܡܫܐܢ | **c** ܚܠ ܛܒ | **d** omit diacritic | **e** ܕܛܒ̈ܢ | **f** ܒܕܘ [...]ܢܬܙܕܩܐܝܬ | **g–g** ܘܪ ܓܙܐ: ܐܢ / ܓܪ ⸢ܒܡܠܕ̈ܒܒܝܢ⸣ / [...] ܡܢ / [ܘܩܕܡ...] | **h** ܘܐܬܪ̈ܥ[ܝܢ]

Romans 5:10–15 F. 4v

ܣܓ̈ ܟܡܐ ܗܢ
ܕܝܬܝܪ ܒܕܘ
ܕܐܬܪ̈ܥܝܢ
ܢܬܦܪܩ ܒܚܝ̈ܘܝ܆
[11]ܠܐ ܕܝܢ ܒܠܚܘܕ:
ܐܠܐ ܐܘܦ [a]ܡܫܬ̈ܒܚܝܢ ܐܢܢ[a]
ܒܐܠܗܐ ܒܡܪܢ
ܕܡܪܢ ܝܫܘܥ
ܡܫܝܚܐ: ܕܝ
ܕܒܗ ܢܣܒܢ
ܫܘܒܐ: [12]ܠܒܓܠ
ܒܝ ܗܟܢ ܡܐ
ܕܒܬܪܗ ܕܒܕ[b]
ܒܪܢܫ ܥܠܬ
ܚܛܝܬܐ ܠܥܠܡܐ:
⌜ܘ⌝ܒܬܪܗ̇
ܕܚܛܝܬܐ
ܡܘܬܐ: ܘܗܟܢ
ܥܠ ⌜ܟܘܠ⌝ ܒܢܝ̈ܢܫܐ
[ܥ]ܒܪ ܡܘܬܐ:
ܒܡܐ ܕܟܘܠܐ
ܐܚ̈ܛܘ܆

[13]ܥܕ ܡܛܐ ܓܪ
ܢܡܘܣܐ
ܚܛܝܬܐ ܗܘܬ
ܒܥܠܡܐ: ܚܛܝܐ
ܕܝ ܠܐ ܗܘܬ
ܡܬܚܫܒܐ ܟܘܠ
ܐܡܬܝ ܕܠܐ
ܗܘܐ ܢܡܘܣܐ܆
[14]ܐܠܐ ܡܠܟ
ܡܘܬܐ ܡܢ
ܐܕܡ ܥܕ ܡܛܐ
ܡܘܫܐ ܐܘܦ
ܥܠ ܗܠܝܢ ܕܠܐ
ܐܚ̈ܛܘ܆
ܒܕܡܘܬܐ
ܕܥܒܪ ܦܘܩܕܗ
ܕܐܕܡ: ܗܝ
ܕܗܘ ܕܡܘܬܐ
ܕܗܝ ܕܥܬܝܕ:
[15]ܐܠܐ ܠܐ ܗܟܢܐ
ܕܐܚ̈ܛܝܘܬܐ·[c]
ܗܟܝ ܐܘܦ

a–a Interlinear insertion between lines 6 and 7, apparently in same hand as original text. | **b** MS *sic*; *expectaveris* ܕܚܕ | **c** MS *sic*; *expectaveris* ܕܚܛܝܘܬܐ. On guttural interchange in CPA, see Bar-Asher (1977, 367–420).

Romans 6:14–19 **F. 1r**

ܐܠܐ ܬܚܘܬ
ܛܝܒܘܬܐ:
[15]ܡܢܐ ܐܘܢ ܢܚܛܐ
ܕܠܝܬܝܢ ܬܚܘܬ
ܢܡܘܣܐ:
ܐܠܐ ܬܚܘܬ
ܛܝܒܘܬܐ. ܠܐ
ܗܘܐ ܟܢ:
[16]ܠܝܬ ܐܢܬܘܢ
ܝܕܥܝܢ ܕܠܡܢ
ܕܐܢܬܘܢ ܡܩܪܒܝܢ
ܓܪܡܝܟܘܢ ܥܒܕܝܢ
ܠܡܫܡܥܘܢ:
ܥܒܕܘܗܝ ܐܢܬܘܢ
ܕܗܘܢ ܕܐܢܬܘܢ
ܫܡܥܝܢ ܠܗ:
ܐܢ [a] ܠܚܛܝܬܐ
ܠܡܘܬܐ: ܘܐܢ
ܠܫܡܝܥܘܬܐ
ܠܝ ܕܩ : ÷ :
[17]ܛܝܒܘܬܐ ܕܝ
ܠܐܠܗܐ.

ܕܗܘܝܬܘܢ ܥܒܕܝܢ
ܠܚܛܝܬܐ:
ܐܫܬܡܥܬܘܢ
ܕܝ ܡܢ ܠܒܒܘܢ ܠܗܕܢ
ܕܐܬܡܣܪܬܘܢ
ܛܘܦܣ ܕܐܘܠܦܢ:
[18]ܐܬܚܪܪܬܘܢ
ܐܘܢ ܡܢ
ܚܛܝܬܐ:
ܘܐܫܬܥܒܕܬܘܢ
ܠܝ ܕܡܐ: [19]ܕܒܢܝܫ
ܐܢܐ ܐܡܪ:
ܠܒܕܠ
ܟܐܫܘܬܗ
ܕܒܣܪ⌜ܟ⌝ܘܢ :
ܕܗܝܟ ܡܢ
ܕܐܩܪܒܬܘܢ
ܐܒܪܝܟܘܢ ܥܒܕܝܢ
ܠܛܡܝܘܬܐ.
ܘܠܥܘܪ
ܢܡܘܣܐ ⌜ܗܟ⌝ܕܢ
ܥܒܕܘ ܐܩܪܒܘ

MKS IIB, 59: **a** omit diacritic

Romans 6:19–7:2 **F. 1v**

ܐܒܪ̈ܝܟܘܢ
ܥܒܕܝܢ ܠܗܝ ܕܩܫܛܐ
ܠܩܘܕܫ: 20 ܟܕ
ܓܝܪ ܗܘܝܬܘܢ
ܥܒܕܝܢ ܠܚܛܝܬܐ·
ܒܢܝ ܚܪ̈ܝܢ[a]
ܗܘܝܬܘܢ ܠܗܝ ܕܩܫܛܐ:
21 ܗܝܟ ܐܘܢ
ܦܐܪ̈ܝܢ ܗܘܐ
ܠܟܘܢ ܒܟܝܢ:[b]
ܗ̇ܠܝܢ[c] ܕܒܗܘܢ
[d]ܐܬܘܢ ܒܗܬܬܝܢ*[d]
ܒܗܘܢ:
ܫܘܝ ܘܣܘܦܗܘܢ
ܕ[ܡ]ܘܬ ܗܘ
ܡܘܬܐ: 22 ܒܪܡ ܗܝ
ܕܐܬܚܪܪܬܘܢ
ܡܢ ܚܛܝܬܐ:
ܐܬܥܒܕܬܘܢ
ܥܒܕ[ܝ]ܢ ܠܐܠܗܐ:
[e]ܗܐ ܐܒܥܘܢ[e]
ܦܐܪ̈ܝܟܘܢ[f] ܠܩܘܕܫ:

ܣܘܦܝ ܘܐܬܐ ܕܝ
ܠܚܝܝܢ ܕܠܥܠܡ:
23 ܦܪܘܣܗ[g] ܓܝܪ
ܕܚܛܝܬܐ
ܡܘܬܐ:
ܡܘܗܒܬܗ
ܕܝ ܕܐܠܗܐ
ܚܝܝܢ ܕܠܥܠܡ
ܒܡܪܢ ܝܫܘܥ
ܡܫܝܚܐ:
7:1 ܐܘ ܠܐ ܐܝܬܝܟܘܢ
ܝܕܥܝܢ ܐܚܝܐ:
ܠܕܝܕܥܝܢ ܓܝܪ
ܕܡܡܠܠܝܢ
ܢܡܘܣܐ
ܐܢܐ ܡܡܠܠ:
ܕܢܡܘܣܐ
ܫܠܝܛ ܥܠ ܒܪܢܫܐ
ܟܠ ܐܡܬܝ
ܕܗܘ ܚܝ:
2 ܐܬܬܐ ܓܒܪܐ
ܓܝܪ· ܟܠ ܢܩܒܬ

MKS IIB, 60: **a** omit *seyame* | **b** ܒܟܝܢ | **c** ܒܗܠܝܢ | **d** ܡܬܒܗܬܝܢ | **e** ܗܐ ܐܒܥܘܢ | **f** ܦܐܪܝܟܘܢ | **g** omit diacritic

Romans 7:2–6 F. 126r

ܕ ܒܥܠܗ̇ ܚܝ:
ܐܣܝܪܐ ܗܝ
ܠܢܡܘܣܗ ⁖
ܐܢ ܕܝ ܡܝܬ
ܒܥܠܗ̇ · ܒܛܠܬ
ܡܢ ܢܡܘܣܗ ⁖[a]
ܕ ܒܥܠܗ̇: [3]ܗܘܐ̇[b]
ܐܘܢ ܒܟܠ
ܐܢܬܬ ܕ ܒܥܠܗ̇
ܚܝ: ܠܓܒܪܐ ܗܝ
ܥܒܕܐ: ܐܢ
ܬܗܘܐ̇ ܠܓܒܪ
ܚܘܪܢ ⁖ ܐܢ ܕܝ
ܡܝܬ ܒܥܠܗ̇ ·
ܒܪܬ ܚܐ̈ܝܢ
ܗܝ ܗܘܝܐ ܡܢ
ܢܡܘܣܗ ܕܠܐ
ܬܗܘܐ̇ ܠܓܒܪܐ
ܐܢ ܬܬܒܥܒ
ܠܓܒܪ ܚܘܪܢ ⁖
[4]ܗܘܐ̇ ܐܘܢ
ܐܚ̈ܝ: ܐܘܦ

ܐܬܘܢ ܒܕܢ
ܡܝܬܘܢ
ܠܢܡܘܣܐ·
ܒܓܘܦ ܗܘ ܒܪܗ
ܕܡܫܝܚܐ:
ܕܬܬܚ̈ܒܪܘܢ
ܠܚܘܪܢ ܠܗܕܢ[c]
ܕܩܡ ܡܢ ܒܝܬ
ܡܝܬܝܐ: ܕܢܥܒܕ
ܦܐ̈ܪܝܢ ܠܐܠܗܐ ⁖
[5]ܟܕ ܓܪ ܗܘ̈ܝܢ
ܒܒܣܪܐ·
ܡܚܫ̈ܫܝܐ
ܕܚܛ̈ܝܬܐ
ܗܠܝܢ[d] ܕܒܬܪ
ܢܡܘܣܐ·
ܗܘܘ ܡܬܚ̈ܠܝܢ
ܒܐܒ̈ܪܝܢ:
ܠܡܥܒܕ ܕܢܥܒܕ
ܦܐ̈ܪܝܢ ܠܡܘܬܐ ⁖
[6]ܟܕܘ ܕܝ ܐܬܒܛܠܢ
ܡܢ ܢܡܘܣܐ:

MKS IIB, 61: **b** omit diacritic | **c** ܠܚܕܢ | **d** ܗܠܝܢ || **a** MS *sic*. Punctuation added in error?

Romans 7:6–11 F. 126v

ܕܡܦܠܚܝܢ ܒܚܕܬܐ
ܕܗܘܝܢ
ܡܬܬ̈ܝ ܚܕܝܢ
ܕܗܘܐ ܡܫ̈ܡܫܝܢ
ܒܚܕܘܬ ܕܪܘܚ:
ܘܠܐ ܒܥܬܝܩܘ
ܕܟܬܒ:
[7] ܡܢܐ ܐܘܟ ܐܡܪ
ܐܡܪ̈ܝܢ:
ܕܢܡܘܣܐ
ܚܛܝܐ ܗܘ·
ܠܐ ܝܗܘܐ ܒܢ: ܐܠܐ
ܚܛܝܬܐ ܠܐ
ܗܘܝܬ ܡܟܪ·
ܐܠܘ ܠܐ ܒܥܠܬ
ܢܡܘܣܐ:
ܬܐܘܝܕܬܐ ܕܝ
ܠܐ ܗܘܝܬ ܝܕܥ:
ܐܠܘ[a] ܠܐ ܢܡܘܣܐ
ܕܐܡܪ ܠܐ
ܬܬܐܘܝܕ: [8] ܥܠܐ
ܕܝ ܢܣܒܬ

ܚܛܝܬܐ
ܒܬܪܥܗ
ܕܦܘܩܕܐ:
ܘܥܒܕܬ ܒܝ
ܟܘܠ ܬܐܘܝܕܬܐ:
ܠܒܪ ܓܪ ܡܢ
ܢܡܘܣܐ
ܚܛܝܬܐ ܡܝܬܬܐ:
[9] ܐܢܐ ܕܝ ܗܘܝܬ
ܚܝ ܠܒܪ ܡܢ
ܢܡܘܣܐ ܒܙܒܢ:
ܟܕ ܕܝ ܐܬܬܐ
ܦܘܩܕܐ· ܚܛܝܬܐ
ܚܝܬ ܐܢܐ ܕܝ
ܡܝܬܬ:
[10] ܘܐܫܬܟܚ ܠܝ
ܦܘܩܕܐ ܗܕܝܟ
ܕܗܘܐ ܠܚܝ̈ܝܢ
ܠܡܘܬ:
[11] ܥܠܐ ܓܪ ܢܣܒܬ
ܚܛܝܬܐ
ܒܬܪܥܗ

a MS *sic*. Presumably the ekthesis and enlargement were added in error.

Romans 8:9–15 F. 45v

ܕܡܫܝܚܐ ܠܝܬ
ܒܗ: ܗܕܢ ܠܝܬ
ܗܘ ܕܝܠܗ:·
[10]ܐܢ ܕܝ ܡܫܝܚܐ
ܒܟܘܢ· ܦܓܪܐ
ܡܢ ܡܝܬ ܠܒܕܠ
ܚܛܝܬܐ: ܪܘܚܐ
ܕܝ ܚܝܐ ܠܒܕܠ
ܙܕܩܐ:· [11]ܐܢ ܕܝ
ܪܘܚܗ ܕܕܢ
ܕܐܩܝܡ ܝܫܘܥ
ܡܫܝܚܐ ܡܢ ܒܝܬ
ܡܝܬܝܐ ܒܥܡܪܐ
ܒܟܘܢ: ܗܕܢ
ܕܐܩܝܡ
ܝܫܘܥ ܡܫܝܚܐ
ܡܢ ܒܝܬ ܡܝܬܝܐ:
ܚܝܐ ܐܘܦ
ܦܘܓܪܝܟܘܢ
ܡܝܘܬܢܐ:
ܠܒܕܠ ܪܘܚܗ
ܕܥܡܪܐ ܒܟܘܢ:·

[12]ܗܫܐ ܐܘܢ ܐܚܝܐ
ܚܝܒܝܢ ܐܢܢ ܠܐ
ܠܒܣܪܐ· ܕܢܗܘܝ
ܒܣܪܐܝܬ
ܢܗܐ ܚܝܝܢ:· [13]ܐܢ
ܓܪ ܒܣܪܐܝܬ
ܐܬܘܢ ܚܝܝܢ:
ܥܬܝܕܝܢ ܐܬܘܢ
ܕܬܡܘܬܘܢ:·
ܐܢ ܕܝ ܒܪܘܚܐ
ܥܒܕܝܬܗ
ܕܒܣܪܐ ܐܬܘܢ
ܡܩܛܠܝܢ: ܚܝܝܢ
ܐܬܘܢ:· [14]ܟܘܠ
ܗܠܝܢ ܓܪ
ܕܒܪܘܚܗ
ܕܐܠܗܐ
ܡܬܕܒܪܝܢ:
ܗܠܝܢ ܒܢܘܗܝ
ܕܐܠܗܐ ܗܢܘܢ:·
[15]ܠܐ ܓܪ ܢܣܒܬܘܢ
ܪܘܚ ܕܥܒܕܘ

Romans 8:15–21 F. 45r

ܬܘܒ ܠܕܚܠܐ:
ܐܠܐ ܢܣܒܬܘܢ
ܪ̇ܘܚ ܕܒܪ̇ܘ:
ܗܕܐ ܕܒܗ̇[a]
ܐܢ ܚܢܢ ܩ̈ܥܝܢ
ܐܒܐ ܐܒܘܢ:·
[16]ܗܝ ܝܬܗ̇ ܪ̇ܘܚܐ
ܡܣܗܕܐ ܥܡ
ܪ̇ܘܚܢ: ܕܐܢܢ
ܒ̈ܢܘܝ ܕܐܠܗܐ:·
[17]ܐܢ ܕܝ ܒ̈ܢܝܢ
ܐܘܦ ܝ̈ܪܬܝܢ:·
ܝ̈ܪܬܘܝ ܡܢ
ܕܐܠܗܐ: ܒ̈ܢܝ
ܝ̇ܪܬܘܬܗ ܕܝ
ܕܡܫܝܚܐ: ܐܢ
ܐܘܦ ܚ̈ܫܝܢ
ܐܢ ܥܡܗ:
ܠܡܕܠ ܕܐܘܦ
ܥܡܗ ܢܫܬܒܚ:·
ܢ[ܫ ܡܦܠܝܢ][b]

✝

[18]ܡܬܚܫܒ ܐܢܐ
ܒ̇ܪ ܕܠܐ ܫܘ̈ܝܢ
ܚܫ̈ܫܘܝ
ܕܕܢ ܩܝܪܘܣܐ
ܕܒܕܘ: ܠܩܘܒܠ
ܬܫܒܚܬܐ
ܕܥܬܝܕܐ
ܕܬܬ ܓܠܝ ܒܢ:·
[19]ܣܒܘܝܗ̇
ܒܪ ܕܒܪܝܬܐ
ܠܓܠܝܢܗܘܢ
ܕܒ̈ܢܘܝ ܕܐܠܗܐ·
ܗܝ ܡܣܟܝܐ:·
[20]ܠܣܪܝܩܘܬܐ
ܒܪ ܒܪܝܬܐ
ܐܫܬܥܒܕܬ̇:·[a]
ܠܐ ܡܢ ܨܒܝܢܐ·
ܐܠܐ ܠܒܓܠ
ܗܕܢ ܕܫܥܒܕ
ܝܬܗ̇ ܥܠ ܣܒܪ:·
[21]ܠܒܓܠ ܕܐܘܦ
ܗܝ ܒܪܝܬܐ

MKS IIB, 64: **a** omit diacritic | **b** *nil*

Romans 9:30–10:3 F. 40v

[a][ ]
ܕ̈ܗܠܟܝܢ ܒܬܪ
ܨܕܩܐ ܡܛ̈ܘ
ܒܨܕܩܐ: ܨܕܩܐ
ܕܝ ܗܝ ܕܡܢ
ܗܝܡܢܘܬܐ:
[31]ܐܝܣܪܐܝܠ ܕܝ
ܕܗܠܟ ܒܬܪ
ܢܡܘܣܐ
ܕܨܕܩܐ:
ܠܢܡܘܣܐ
ܕܨܕܩܐ ܠܐ
ܡܛܐ: [32]ܠܒܕܝܠ
ܡܢ: ܠܒܕܝܠ
ܕܠܐ ܡܢ ܗܝܡܢܘ:
ܐܠܐ ܗܝܟ[b]
ܕܡܢ ܥܒ̈ܕܘܝ
ܕܢܡܘܣܐ:
ܐܬܬ̈ܩܠܘ ܓܪ
ܟܐܦܐ
ܕܬܘܩܠܬܐ·
[33]ܗܝܟ ܕܟܬܝܒ:

[ ]
ܕܗܐ ܐܢܐ
ܡܬܐܡ ܒܨܝܘܢ
ܟܐܦ ܕܬܘܩܠܬܐ·
ܘܟܐܦ ܕܡܟܫܘܠ:
ܘܟܠ[c] ܕܡܗܝܡܢ
ܒܗ[*c] ܠܐ ܢܒܗܬ:

ܪ[ܝ] ܡܩܠܘܢ

[10:1]ܐܚ̈ܝܐ ܨܒܝܘܢܗ
ܡܢ ܕܠܒܝ
ܘܒܥܘܬܝ ܠܘܬ
ܐܠܗܐ ܥܠ
ܕܛܒܗܘܢ ܠܚܝ̈ܝܢ:
[2]ܣܗܕ ܐܢܐ
ܓܪ ܥܠܝܗܘܢ[d]
ܕܩܢܬܗ[c]
ܕܐܠܗܐ ܒܗܘܢ:
ܐܠܐ ܠܐ ܒܡܕܥܘ:
[3]ܠܐ ܓܪ ܡܕ̈ܥܝܢ
ܨܕܩܗ ܕܐܠܗܐ:

MKS IIB, 65: **b** ܕܗܝܟ | **c** omit diacritic | **d** ܥܠܝܗ || **a** First ruled line of both columns is blank.

Romans 10:3–9 F. 40r

ܘܟ ܕܗܘܘܢ
ܕ ܟܐܢܗܘܢ ܒܥ̈ܝܢ
ܕܝܩܝ̈ܡܘܢ:
ܠܝ ܕܗܘ ܕܐܠܗܐ
ܠܐ ܐܫ̈ܬܥܒܕܘ:
[4]ܫܘܠܡܗ ܓܝܪ
ܕܢܡܘܣܐ
ܡܫܝܚܐ ܠܝ ܕܘ
ܠܟܘܠ ܡܢ
ܕܡܗܝܡܢ:
[5]ܡܘܫܐ ܓܝܪ ܟܬܒ
ܝ ܕܗܐ ܕܡܢ
ܢܡܘܣܐ:
ܕܒܪܢܫܐ ܕܥܒܕ
ܠܗ. ܚܝܐ ܒܗ:
[6]ܝ ܕܗܐ ܕܝ ܕܡܢ
ܗܝܡܢܘܬܐ. ܟܕܢ
ܗܘ ܐܡܪ:
ܠܐ ܬܐܡܪ
ܒܠܒܟ ܡܢ
ܣܠܩ ܠܫܡܝܐ:
ܡܢܐ ܕܗܘ

ܕܝܚܘܬ ܡܫܝܚܐ:
[7]ܐܘ ܡܢ ܢܚܘܬ
ܠܬܘܗܡܐ. ܡܢܐ
ܕܗܘ ܕܢܣܩ[a]
ܡܫܝܚܐ ܡܢ
ܒܝܢ ܡܝ̈ܬܐ:
[8]ܐ̈ܠܐ ܡܢܐ ܗܘ
ܐܡܪ ܟܬܒܐ:
ܩܪܝܒܐ ܗܝ ܠܟ
ܡܠܬܐ ܒܦܘܡܟ
ܘܒܠܒܟ: ܡܢܐ
ܕܗܝ ܡܠܬܐ
ܕܗܝܡܢܘܬܐ.
ܡܢܐ ܕܐܢܢ
ܡܟܪ̈ܙܝܢ: [9]ܕܐܢ
ܬܘܕܐ ܒܦܘܡܟ
ܕܡܪܐ ܗܘ
ܝܫܘܥ:
ܘܬܗܝܡܢ
ܒܠܒܟ ܕܐܠܗܐ
ܐܩܝܡ ܝܬܗ
ܡܢ ܒܝܢ ܡܝ̈ܬܐ:

MKS IIB, 66: **a** ܢܣܘܩ

Romans 15:11–16

F. 16r

ܝܬܗ ܟܘܠ
ܥܡܡܝܐ ·:· [12]ܘܬܘܒ
ܐܫܥܝܐܣ ܐܡܪ:
ܗܐ ܫܪܫܗ
ܕܐܝܫܝ: ܘܗܘܝ
ܕܩܐܡ ܪܫ
ܥܠ ܥܡܡܝܐ·
ܘܥܠܘܝ ܥܡܡܝܐ
ܡܣܒܪ̈ܝܢ ·:·
[13]ܐܠܗܐ ܕܝ
ܕܣܒܪܐ ܡܠܝܐ
ܝܬܟܘܢ ܟܘܠ
ܚܕܘܐ ܘܫܠܡ:
ܕܬܗܘܢ
ܡܬܬܝ̈ܪܝܢ
ܒܣܒܪܐ ܒܚܝܠܐ
ܕܪܘܚܐ
ܕܩܘܕܫܐ ·:·
[14]ܡܦܝܣܐ ܕܝ
ܐܚ̈ܝ ܐܘܦ
ܐܢܐ ܡܢܝ
ܥܠ ܕܝܠܟܘܢ:

ܕܐܘܦ ܐܬܘܢ
ܡܠ̈ܝܢ ܐܬܘܢ
ܛܒܘ ·:· ܘܡܫܡܠܝܢ
ܒܟܘܠ ܐܒܪܘ:
ܝܟܠܝܢ ܕܐܘܦ
ܠܚܕܕܝܢ
ܬܟܘܚܘܢ ·:·
[15]ܗܝܟ ܡܫܬܠܛ
ܕܝ ܟܬܒܝܬ[a]
ܠܟܘܢ ܐܚ̈ܝܐ
ܡܢ ܚܘܠܩ:
ܗܝܟ ܡܬܕܟܪ
ܠܟܘܢ ·:· ܠܒܓܠ
ܚܣܕܐ ܗܘ ܕܝ
ܕܐܬܝܗܒ ܠܝ
ܡܢ ܐܠܗܐ:
[16]ܠܒܓܠ ܕܝܗܐ
ܐܢܐ ܫܡܫܗ
ܕܝܫܘܥ
ܡܫܝܚܐ:
ܡܫܡܫ ܠܥܡܡ̈ܝܐ
ܒܣܒܪܗ
ܕܐܠܗܐ:[b]

MKS IIB, 67: **a** ܟܬܒܬ || **b** Written on an additional (i.e. 23rd) line, and left-justified.

Romans 15:16–21 **F. 16v**

ܠܒܕܝܠ
ܕܝܬܥܒܕ
ܩܘܪܒܢܗܘܢ
ܕܥܡܡܝܐ ܡܩܒܠ
ܘܡܩܕܫ
ܒܪܘܚܐ
ܕܩܘܕܫܐ:
[17] ܗܐ[a] ܠܝ ܐܘܢ
ܬܫܒܚܐ
ܒܝܫܘܥ
ܡܫܝܚܐ ܠܘܬ
ܐܠܗܐ܆ [18] ܠܝܬ
ܐܢܐ ܓܪ ܡܫܬܠܛ
ܕܝܡܠܠ ܟܠܘܡ
ܡܢ ܕܠܐ ܥܒܠ[b]
ܡܫܝܚܐ ܒܐܕܝ
ܠܡܫܡܥܘܬܗܘܢ
ܕܥܡܡܝܐ܆ ܒܡܠܐ
ܘܒܥܘܒܕ܆
[19] ܒܚܝܠܐ ܕܐܬܘܬܐ[c]
ܘܕ ܒܬܘܪܬܐ:
ܒܚܝܠܐ ܕܪܘܚܐ

ܕܩܘܕܫܐ:
ܠܡܠܘ ܕܐܢܐ
ܡܢ ܝܪܘܫܠܡ
ܘܚܘ ܟܠܗ̇[d] ܚܕ ܡܚܛ
ܐܠܝܪܝܩܘܢ[e]
ܐܡܠܝܐ̇[d] ܒܣܘܪܗ
ܕܐܠܗܐ܆ [20] ܒܕܝ[f]
ܕܝ ܐܢܐ ܡܠܝܐ̇[d]
ܒܣܝܠ
ܕܝܒܣܪ܆ ܠܐ
ܗܢ ܕܐܫܬܡܥ
ܡܫܝܚܐ: ܠܒܕܝܠ
ܕܠܐ ܥܠ ܐܘܫ
ܚܘܪܢ ܗܝܐ̇
ܐܢܐ ܒܢܐ̇܆
[21] ܐܠܐ ܗܝܟ
ܕܟܬܝܒ: ܢܚܙܘܢ
ܗܠܝܢ ܕܠܐ
ܐܬܢܝ[g] ܠܗܘܢ
ܥܠܘܝ: ܘܗܠܝܢ
ܕܠܐ ܫܡܥܘ
ܝܬܒܝܢܘܢ܆

MKS IIB, 68: **a** ܘܐܝܬ | **b** ܥܒܕ | **c** ܕܝܬܬܐ | **d** omit diacritic | **e** ܐܠܠܘܪܝܩܘܢ | **f** ܒܕ | **g** ܐܬ ܥܠ || **g** diacritic uncertain

1 Corinthians 1:6–12 — F. 21r

ܐܫܬܪܪܬ[a]
ܒܟܘܢ ⁘ [7] ܠܟܠܘ
ܕܠܐ ܬܗܘܘܢ
ܚܣܝܪܝܢ [b] ܐܘܦ
ܠܐ ܒܚܕܐ ܡܢ
ܡܘܗܒܬܐ: [c]
ܡܩܒܠܝܢ [d]
ܠܓܠܝܢܗ ܕܡܪܢ
ܝܫܘܥ
ܡܫܝܚܐ: [8] ܗܕܢ
ܕܐܘܦ ܝܫܪܪ
ܝܬܟܘܢ ܥܕ ܡܫܠܡܐ
ܠܥܝܢܘܝ ܦܨܝܢ
ܒܠܐ ܠܘܡܗ
ܕܡܪܢ ܝܫܘܥ
ܡܫܝܚܐ ⁘
[9] ܡܗܝܡܢ ܗܘ
ܐܠܗܐ
ܗܕܢ ܕܒܗ
ܐܬܩܪܝܬܘܢ
ܠܫܘܬܦܘܬܐ
ܕܒܪܗ ܝܫܘܥ

ܡܫܝܚܐ ܡܪܢ ⁘
[10] ܒܥܐ ܐܢܐ ܕܝ
ܡܢܟܘܢ ܐܚܝܐ·
[e]ܒܫܡܗ ܕܡܪܢ
ܝܫܘܥ
ܡܫܝܚܐ:
ܕܝܬܗ ܝܬܗ
ܬܗܘܘܢ ܐܡܪܝܢ
ܒܟܠܟܘܢ: ܘܠܐ
ܝܗܐ ܒܝܬܟܘܢ
ܒܪܝܢ ⁘ ܬܗܘܘܢ
ܕܝ ܡܫܬܠܠܝܢ
ܒܗ ܒܬܪܬܐ·[e]
ܘܒܗ ܒܡܕܥܐ:[f]
[11] ܐܬܕܒܪ ܠܝ
ܓܝܪ ܥܠ ܕܝܠܟܘܢ
ܐܚܝ ܡܢ ܕܒܝܬ
ܟܠܘܐܝܣ
ܕܦܠܓܝܢ ܐܝܬ
ܒܝܬܟܘܢ ⁘
[12] ܐܡܪ ܐܢܐ
ܕܝ ܗܕܐ:

MKS IIB, 69: **a** ܐܫܬܪܪܬ ܕܝ | **b** ܚܣܝܪܝܢ | **c** omit *seyame* | **d** ܡܩܒܠܝܢ | **e–e** *nil* | **f** ܕܡܕܥܐ || **c** MS *sic*; *expectaveris* ܡܘܗܒܬܐ

1 Corinthians 1:12–17 F. 21v

ܕܟܘܠ ܐܢܫ
ܡܢܟܘܢ ܐܡܪ:
ܐܢܐ ܡܢ
ܕܦܘܠܘܣ
ܐܢܐ: ܐܢܐ ܕܝ
ܕܐܦܘܠܘܢ: ܐܢܐ
ܕܝ ܕܟܐܦܐ:
ܐܢܐ ܕܝ
ܕܡܫܝܚܐ:
[13] ܕܡܐ ܡܦܠܓ
ܗܘ ܡܫܝܚܐ:
ܕܡܐ ܦܘܠܘܣ
ܐܨܛܠܒ ܥܠ
ܕܛܠܟܘܢ: ܐܐ̇
ܒܫܡܗ
ܕܦܘܠܘܣ
ܐܨܛܒܥܬܘܢ:
[14] ܡܘܕܐ̇ ܐܢܐ
ܠܐܠܗܝ. ܕܠܐ ܐܢܫ
ܡܢܟܘܢ ܠܐ
ܐܨܒܥܬ:
ܐܠܐ ܐܢ[a]

ܠܩܪܝܣܦܘܣ
ܘܠܓܐܝܘܣ: [15] ܕܠܐ
ܢܐܡܪ ܐܢܫ
ܕܒܫܡܝ ܕܝܠܝ
ܐܨܛܒܥܬܘܢ:
[16] ܐܨܒܥܬ ܕܝ
ܐܘܦ ܠܒܝܬܗ
ܕܐܣܛܦܢܘܣ:
ܒܪܡ ܠܝܬ ܐܢܐ
ܝܕܥ ܐܢ ܐܨܒܥܬ
ܠܐܢܫ ܐܚܪܢ:
[17] ܠܐ ܓܪ ܫܠܚ
ܡܫܝܚܐ ܕܝܗܐ̇
ܐܢܐ ܡܨܒܥ:
ܐܠܐ ܕܝܗܐ̇
ܐܢܐ ܡܣܒܪ:
ܠܐ ܒܚܟܡܬܐ
ܕܡܠܐ*[b] ܠܒܛܠ
ܕܠܐ ܢܬܪܘܩܢ
ܨܠܝܒܗ ܕܡܫܝܚܐ:

ܢܪ ܡܦ[ܠ]ܝܘܢ[c]

MKS IIB, 70: **a** ܐ̇ܢ | **b** ܕܡܠܝܐ | **c** *nil* || **b** There may be traces of a secondarily inserted *yod*.

1 Corinthians 3:17–23 **F. 11v**

ܢܘܣܗ ܓܪ
ܕܐܠܗܐ ܩܕܫ
ܐܝܬ ܗܘ· ܦܢ
ܕܐܬܘܢ ܗܘܢ·
[18] ܐܢܫ ܠܐ ܝܛܥܐ
ܒܪܗ·· ܦܢ
ܕܣܒܪ ܕܗܘ
ܚܟܝܡ ܒܥܠܡܗܘܢ
ܒܢܝ ܥܠܡܐ·
ܢܗܘܐ
ܫܛܝܐ ܠܒܪܠ
ܕܢܗܘܐ
ܚܟܝܡ:
[19] ܚܟܡܬܗ ܓܪ
ܕܗܢ ܥܠܡܐ
ܫܛܝܘ ܗܝ
ܠܘܬ ܐܠܗܐ:
ܟܬܝܒ ܓܪ ܕܝ
ܕܠܟܝ ܚܟܝܡܝܐ
ܒܚܬܠܬܘܬܗܘܢ·
[20] ܘܬܘܒ ܡܪܐ
ܝܕܥ ܚܫܒܬܗܘܢ[a]

ܕܚܟܝܡܝܐ
ܕܗܢܝܢ ܣܪܝܩܝܢ·
[21] ܗܘܐ ܐܘܦ ܐܢܫ
ܠܐ ܝܫܬܒܚ
ܒܒܢܝܢܫܐ·
ܟܘܠܐ ܓܪ
ܕܝܠܟܘܢ ܗܘ·
[22] ܐܢ ܦܘܠܘܣ:
ܘܐܢ ܐܦܘܠܘ:
ܘܐܢ ܟܐܦܐ:
ܘܐܢ ܥܠܡܐ:
ܘܐܢ ܚܝܝܐ:
ܘܐܢ ܡܘܬܐ:
ܘܐܢ ܗܠܝܢ ܕܩܝܡܝܢ
ܘܐܢ ܗܠܝܢ ܕܥܬܝܕ
ܟܘܠܐ ܕܝܠܟܘܢ:
[23] ܐܢܬܘܢ ܕܝ
ܕܡܫܝܚܐ:
ܡܫܝܚܐ ܕܝ
ܕܐܠܗܐ:
b

MKS IIB, 71: **a** omit *seyame* | **b** ⁘ ⁘ ⁘ ⁘

1 Corinthians 4:1–6 F. 11r

4:1 ܗܟܕܢ ܝܗܐ
ܒܪܢܫ ܡܚܫܒ
ܠܢ ܗܝܟ
ܫܡ̈ܫܝ
ܕܡܫܝܚܐ:
ܘܦܪ̈ܢܣܝܐ
ܕܪ̈ܙܘܗܝ
ܕܐܠܗܐ᠅ 2 ܟܐ
ܐܘܦ ܡܬܒܥܐ
ܒܦܪ̈ܢܣܝܐ
ܕܝܫܬܟܚ ܐܢܫ
ܡܗܝܡܢ᠅ 3 ܠܝ
ܕܝ ܠܙܥܘܪܘ
ܗܝ ܕܡܢܟܘܢ
ܐܬܕܝܢ: ܐܘ ܡܢ
ܒܪܢܫܘܬܐ:
ܐܠܐ ܐܘܦ ܠܐ
ܒܢܦܫܝ ܠܝܬ
ܐܢܐ ܕܐܝܢ᠄
4 ܠܝܬ ܐܢܐ ܒܪ
ܝܕܥ ܟܠܘܡ
ܒܢܦܫܝ.

ܐܠܐ ܒܗܕܐ
ܠܝܬ ܐܢܐ
ܡܢ ܕܐ: ܗܕܢ
ܕܝ ܕܕܐܝܢ
ܠܝ ܗܘ
ܡܪܐ᠅ 5 ܗܘܐ[a]
ܐܘܦ ܠܐ ܡܢ
ܩܘܕܡ ܥܕܢܗ
ܟܠܘܡ ܬܕܘܢ̈ܘܢ[b]
ܥܕܡܐ ܕܝܬܐ[a]
ܡܪܐ: ܗܕܢ
ܕܗܘ ܡܢܗܪ
ܠܛܡܫܘܪ̈ܝ
ܕܚܫܘܟܐ: ܘܡܓܠܐ
ܚܫܒ̈ܬܗܘܢ
ܕܠܒ̈ܒܝܐ: ܘܟܕܢ
ܡܬܟܒܕܐ
ܬܫܒܚܬܐ
ܠܟܠ ܐܢܫ
ܡܢ ܐܠܗܐ:
6 ܗܠܝܢ ܕܝ
ܐܚ̈ܝܐ ܕܡܚܝܬ

MKS IIB, 72: **a** omit diacritic | **b** omit *seyame*

1 Corinthians 4:6–10 F. 10v

ܒܓܝܢܟܘܢ
ܘܐܦܠܬܘܢ
ܡܢ ܠܒܪܠܒܘܢ:
ܠܒܪܠ ܕܡܢ
ܬܠܝܬܘܢ ܡܟܐ
ܕܠܐ ܡܟܬܒ
ܡܢ ܡܟܐ ܕܟܬܝܒ
ܬܗܘܘܢ ܡܬܢܦܚܝܢ:·
ܕܠܐ ܝܗܐ ܚܕ
ܥܠ ܕܚܠܒܗ
ܕܚܕ ܡܬܢܦܚ
ܥܠ ܚܒܪܗ:·
[7] ܡܢ[a] ܓܝܪ ܒܕܘ
ܠܟ: ܡܟܐ ܕܝ
ܒܕܝܟ ܡܟܐ
ܕܠܐ ܢܣܒܬ:
ܐܢ ܕܝ ܐܘܦ
ܢܣܒܬ: ܡܟܐ
ܐܬ ܡܫܬܒܚ
ܗܝܟ ܕܠܐ
ܢܣܒܬ: [8] ܟܒܪ
ܣܒܝܥܬܘܢ:[b]*

ܠܒܪ ܡܢ
ܡܠܟܬܘܢ:
ܘܠܘ ܡܠܟܬܘܢ·
ܕܐܘܦ ܐܢܢ
ܢܡܠܟ
ܥܡܟܘܢ:·
[9] ܣܒܪ ܐܢܐ
ܓܝܪ ܕܠܢ[c]
ܠܫܠܝܚܝܐ
ܒܚܪܝܬܐ
ܐܘܕܥ ܐܠܗܐ
ܗܝܟ ܕܡܝܬܝܢ
ܠܡܘܬܐ:·
ܕܡܣܟܘܢ
ܐܬܥܒܕܢ
ܠܥܠܡܐ
ܘܠܡܠܐܟܝܐ
ܘܠܒܢܝܢܫܐ:·
[10] ܐܢܢ ܫܛܝܢ
ܠܒܪܠ ܡܫܝܚܐ:
ܐܢܬܘܢ ܕܝ
ܚܟܝܡܝܢ

MKS IIB, 73: **a** omit diacritic | **b** omit *seyame* | **c** ܕܠܢ

1 Corinthians 4:10–15 F. 10r

ܒܡܫܝܚܐ:
ܐܢ ܒܐ̈ܫܝܢ
ܐܬܘܢ ܕܝ
ܚܝ̈ܠܝܢ: ܐܬܘܢ
ܡܫ̈ܒܚܝܢ. ܐܢ
ܕܝ ܡܒܙܠܝܢ:
[11] ܥܕ[a] ܡܫܥܬܐ
ܠܗܕܐ ܫܥܬܐ:
ܐܢ ܐܘܦ
ܟܦܢܝܢ ܘܨ̈ܗܝܢ
ܘܥܪ̈ܛܠܝܢ: ܘܐܢ
ܡܬܡ̈ܚܝܢ
ܘܡܬܛܪ̈ܦܝܢ:
[12] ܘܐܢ ܠܐ̈ܝܢ
ܒܥ̈ܡܠܝܢ ܒܐ̈ܕܝܢ:[b]
ܦ̈ܠܝܢ ܐܢ
ܘܐܢ ܡܒܪ̈ܟܝܢ:
ܡܬܪ̈ܕܦܝܢ ܘܐܢ
ܡܣܣܒܪ̈ܝܢ:
[13] ܡܬܓܕܦ ܒܠܥܝܢ
ܘܐܢ ܒܥ̈ܝܢ
ܡܢܗܘܢ:

ܗܟܢ ܦܣܠܘܬܗ
ܕܥܠܡܐ
ܐܬܥܒܕܢ:
ܥܠ ܟܘܠܐ ܐܢ
ܡܣܬܦܝܢ
ܥܕܡܐ ܠܥܕܘ:
[14] ܠܐ ܗܟܢ
ܡܟܬܒܬ ܠܟܘܢ
ܐܢܐ ܟܬܒ
ܗܠܝܢ: ܐܠܐ
ܗܟܢ ܠܒܢ̈ܝ
ܚܒܝ̈ܒܝ ܐܢܐ
ܡܟܘܢ: [15] ܐܢ
ܓܪ ܪ̈ܒܘܐܢ
ܕܡܠ̈ܦܝܢ
ܗܘܐ ܠܟܘܢ
ܒܡܫܝܚܐ:
ܐܠܐ ܠܐ ܣܓ̈ܝ[c]
ܐܒܗܢ:
ܒܝܫܘܥ ܓܪ
ܡܫܝܚܐ ܒܬܪܒ
ܒܣܘܪܬܐ. ܐܢܐ

MKS IIB, 74: **a** ܘܥܕ | **b** ܕܐ̈ܕܝܢ | **c** ܣ̈ܓܝ

1 Corinthians 13:4–11 F. 19r

[4]ܚܒܬܐ ܡܘܪܟܐ
ܪܘܚܐ
ܘܒܣܝܡܐ:· *
ܚܒܬܐ ܠܐ ܡܩܢܐ:
ܠܐ ܡܬܒܠܛܐ:·*[a]
ܠܐ ܡܬܢܦܚܐ:·
[5]ܠܐ ܡܬܦܠܠܐ:·
ܠܐ ܒܥܝܐ
ܕ ܒܪܡܗ̇:[b]
ܠܐ ܡܬܚܪܦܐ:·
ܠܐ ܡܬܚܫܒܐ
ܠܒܝܫܬܐ:·[c]
[6]ܠܐ ܚܕܝܐ ܥܠ
ܛܠܘܡܐ:
ܚܕܝܐ ܗܝ ܕܝ
ܥܠ ܩܘܫܛܐ:
[7]ܟܘܠܐ ܗܝ
ܡܣܝܒܪܐ:·
ܟܘܠܐ ܗܝ
ܡܗܝܡܢܐ:
ܟܘܠܐ ܗܝ
ܡܣܒܪܐ:

ܟܘܠܐ ܗܝ
ܡܣܝܒܪܐ:·*[d]
[8]ܚܒܬܐ ܠܐ[e]
ܢܦܠܐ ܠܥܠܡ:
[f]ܐܢ ܢܒܝܘ ܒܛܠܐ:
ܘܐܢ ܠܫܢܝܢ
ܫܬܩܢ· ܘܐܢ
ܐܕ̈ܘܐܢ* ܒܛܠܢ:
[9]ܡܢ ܚܘܠܡ ܓܪ
ܐܢܢ ܡܕ̈ܥܝܢ:[f]
ܘܡܢ ܚܘܠܡ
ܐܢܢ ܡܬܢ̈ܒܝܢ:
[10]ܟܕ ܕܝ ܬܐܬܐ̇[g]
ܫܠܡܘܬܐ·[h]
[i]ܒܝܢ ܡܐ ܕܡܢ
ܚܘܠܡ ܒܛܠ:[i]
[11]ܟܕ ܗܘܝܬ
ܛܠܝܐ· ܗܘܝܢ
ܛܠܝܐ ܗܘܝܬ
ܡܡܠܠ· ܗܘܝܢ
ܛܠܝܐ ܗܘܝܬ
ܡܬܚܫܒ:·*[j]

⌜ܝ⌝

MKS IIB, 75: **a** ܡܬܒܛܠܐ | **b** ܒܪܡܗ̇ | **c** ܥܠ ܒܝܫܬܐ | **d** ܡ[ܣܝ]ܒ[ܪ]ܐ | **e** ܚܒܬܐ [...]| **f–f** [...] / [...] ܘܡܢ ܚܘܠܡ / ܒܛܠܐ·: / [...] ܐܢ ܫܬܩ / [...] :ܒܛܠܢ / ܐܢ ܢܒܝܘܬܐ | **g** ܬܐܬܐ̇ | **h** ܫܠܡܘܬܐ | **i–i** *nil* | **j** ⌜ܡܬܪܥܐ⌝ || Quire number partially visible.

1 Corinthians 13:11–14:4 **F. 19v**

ܗܘܝ ܛܠܝܐ ܗܘܝܬ
ܡܬܚܫܒ: ܟܕ
ܕܝ ܐܬܥܒܕܬ
ܓܒܪ: ܒܛܠܬ
ܕܛܠܝܘܬܐ:[a]
[12]ܚܙ̈ܝܢ ܐܢ ܓܪ
ܟܕܘ ܗܘܝܢ
ܒܡܚܙܝ ܒܪܡܙ:
ܒܡ ܕܝ ܐܦܝܢ
ܠܩܒܠ ܐܦܝܢ:
ܟܕܘ ܐܢܐ ܡܟܪ
ܡܢ ܣܘܠܡ: ܒܡ
ܕܝ ܐܢܐ ܝܚܪ:
ܗܟܡܐ ܕܐܘܦ
ܐܬܝܚܪܬ:
[13]ܟ̈ܕܘ ܕܝ ܡܬܡܬܪܐ[b]
ܗܝ[c] ܗܝܡܢܘܬܐ.
ܘܣܒܪܐ.
ܘܚܒܬܐ. ܗܕܝܢ[d]
ܬܠܬܝܐ: ܪܒܐ
ܕܝ ܡܢ ܗܠܝܢ
ܗܝ ܚܒܬܐ:

[14:1]ܪ̈ܗܘܛܘ ܒܬܪ
ܚܒܬܐ: ܩܢܘ
ܕܝ ܒܪ̈ܘܚܢܝܬܐ:
ܡܠܘܢ ܕܝ
ܕܬܗܘܢ
ܡܬܢ̈ܒܝܢ: [2]ܗܕܝܢ
ܓܪ ܕܡܡܠܠ
ܒܠ̈ܫܢܝܢ: ܠܐ
ܠܒ̈ܢܝܢܫ ܗܘ
ܡܡܠܠ: ܐܠܐ
ܠܐܠܗܐ: ܐܢܫ
ܓܪ ܠܐ ܫܡܥ:
ܒܪܘܚܐ ܕܝ
ܗܘ ܡܡܠܠ
ܪ̈ܙܝܢ: [3]ܗܕܝܢ ܕܝ
ܕܡܬܢܒܐ
ܠܒ̈ܢܝܢܫ ܗܘ
ܡܡܠܠ ܒܢܝܢ
ܘܬܝܐܘܣܝܡ[e]*
ܘܦܝܓܘ ܠܒ:
[4]ܗܕܝܢ ܕܡܡܠܠ
ܒ̈ܠܫܢܝܢ ܓܪܡܗ

MKS IIB, 76: **a** ܒܛܠܘܬܐ | **b** [ܝ]ܡܬܬܪܐ | **c** omit | **d** ܗܠܝܢ | **e** ܘܬܝܐܘܣܝܡ

1 Corinthians 14:4–7 — F. 13v

ܗܘ ܡܒܢܐ܀
ܕܝ ܕܝ ܕܡܬܢܒܐ·
ܟܢܝܫܬܐ ܗܘ
ܡܒܢܐ܀ [5]ܒܝ ܒܥܐ
ܐܢܐ ܕܝ ܕܟܘܠܟܘܢ
ܡܡܠܠܝܢ
ܒܠܫܢܝܢ܀ ܡܠܘܢ
ܕܝ ܕܬܗܘܢ
ܡܬܢܒܝܢ܀ ܪܒ
ܗܘ ܕܝ ܗܕܝ
ܕܡܬܢܒܐ܀ ܐܢ
ܗܕܝ ܕܡܡܠܠ
ܒܠܫܢܝܢ܀ ܐܠܐ
ܐܝ ܗܘܐ ܡܦ
ܕܡܬܪ ܓܡ܀
ܠܒܪܠ
ܕܟܢܝܫܬܐ
ܬܣܒ ܒܢܝܢܐ܀
[6]ܟܥܢ ܕܝ ܐܚܝܐ
ܐܝ ܢܐܬܐ
ܠܘܬܟܘܢ
ܡܡܠܠ ܒܠܫܢܝܢ܀

ܡܐ ܐܢܐ
ܡܗܢܐ ܠܟܘܢ܀
ܐܠܐ ܐܝ ܡܡܠܠ
ܠܟܘܢ ܒܓܠܝܢܐ܀
ܐܢ ܒܐܡܪܘ܀
ܐܢ ܒܢܒܝܘ܀[a]
ܐܢ ܒܐܘܠܦܢ܀
[7]ܒܪܡ ܕܝ ܗܫܠܝܢ[b]
ܕܠܝܬ ܒܗܘܢ
ܢܦܫ ܘܠ
[c]ܗܘܝܢ ܝܗܒܝܢ܀[c]
ܐܝܟܢܐ ܐܒܘܒܐ܀
ܐܝܟܢܐ ܩܝܬܪܐ܀
ܐܢ ܐܦܪܫܘ
ܕܝ ܠܐ ܝܬܠ
ܠܩܠܝܬ ܙܡܪܐ܀
ܗܝܟ ܡܬܝܕܥ
ܡܐ ܕܡܙܕܡܪ
ܒܐܒܘܒܐ܀
ܐܢ ܡܐ
ܕܡܬܐܡܪ
ܒܩܝܬܪܐ܀

MKS IIB, 77: **a** ܒܢܒܘܐ | **b** ܗܠܝܢ | **c–c** ܝܗܒܘܢ ܗܕܝ܀

1 Corinthians 14:8–14 F. 13r

[a]8 ܡܟܝܪ ܐܢ ܟܠ[a]
ܕܠܐ ܢܚܪ
ܬܬܠ[b] ܩܪܢܐ.
ܡܢ[c] ܡܬܛܝܒ
ܠܩܪܒܐ: 9 ܗܟܕܝ
ܐܘܦ ܐܢܬܘܢ
ܐܢ ܒܠܫܢܐ
ܐܢ[d] ܠܐ ܡܠܐ
ܕܝܚܒܐ[e] ܬܬܠܘܢ.
ܗܝܟ ܡܬܝܕܥ
ܡܐ ܕܡܬܡܠܠ:
ܗܘܝܢ[f] ܐܢܬܘܢ ܓܪ
ܗܝܟ ܠܐܐܪܐ[g]
ܡܡܠܠܝܢ: 10 ܟܘܠ
ܒܝ ܗܝܟ
ܕܢܦܘܪ ܐܝܬ
ܛܘܦܣܝܢ
ܕܩܠܝܢ ܒܥܠܡܐ:
ܘܠܝܬ ܒܠܘܡ
ܕܠܝܬ ܠܗ ܩܠ
ܒܥܠܡܐ:[h] 11 ܐܢ
ܐܘܢ ܠܐ ܝܕܥܢܐ[i]

ܕܝܐ ܚܝܠܗ
ܕܩܠܐ: ܗܘܐ
ܐܢܐ ܠܒܝ
ܕܡܡܠܠ ܠܝ
ܒܪܒܪ: ܘܗܘ
ܕܡܡܠܠ ܠܝ
ܒܪܒܪ: 12 ܗܟܕܝ
ܐܘܦ ܐܢܬܘܢ
ܠܒܕܝܠ ܕܐܢܬܘܢ
ܡܛܝ ܕܪ̈ܘܚܢܝܐ.[j]
ܠܒܢܝܢܐ
ܕܟܢܝܫܬܐ
ܗܘܘ ܒܥܝܢ
ܕܬܗܘܢ
ܡܬܬܝ̈ܪܝܢ:
13 ܠܒܕܝܠ ܒܕܝ
ܗܕܝ ܕܡܡܠܠ
ܒܠܫܢ. ܝܗܐ
ܡܨܠܐ ܕܝܗܐ
ܡܬܪܓܡ:
14 ܐܢ ܓܪ ܗܘܐ[k]
ܐܢܐ ܡܨܠܐ ܒܠܫܢ:

MKS IIB, 78: **a–a** ܘܐܢ ܟܠ | **b** ܝܬܠ | **c** omit diacritic | **d** ܡܢ | **e** ܕܝܚܒܐ | **f** ܗܘܝܢ | **g** omit diacritic on *alaf* | **h** ܒܥܠܡܐ | **i** ܝܗܐ | **j** ܕܪܘܚܢܝܢ | **k** omit diacritic

1 Corinthians 14:24–30 **F. 15r**

ܘܡܬܕܝܢ ܡܢ
ܟܘܠܐ:
[25] ܘܛܡܘܪ̈ܝܐ
ܕܠܒܗ ܡܬ̈ܓܠܝܢ
ܢܦ̈ܩܝܢ ⁘ ܘܗܟܕܝܢ
ܗܘ ܢܦܠ ܥܠ
ܐܦ̈ܘܗܝ ܘܣܓܕ
ܠܐܠܗܐ:
ܡܘܕܐ ܕܐܠܗܐ
ܐܘܢܛܘܣ
ܒܟܘܢ ܗܘ⁘
[26] ܡܢܐ ܐܘܢ ܗܘ
ܐܚ̈ܝܢ: ܟܕ
ܐܬܘܢ ܡܬܟ̈ܢܫܝܢ:
ܟܘܠ ܐܢܫ ܡܢ
ܕܠܗ ܫܒܘܢ:
ܡܢ ܕܠܗ ܐܘܠܦܢ:
ܡܢ ܕܠܗ ܓܠܝܐ:
ܡܢ ܕܠܗ ܠܫܢ:
ܡܢ ܕܠܗ
ܬܪܓܡ: ܟܘܠܐ
ܠܒܢܝܢܐ ܝܗܐ

ܡܬܥܒܕ:
[27] ܐܢ ܒܠܫܢ[a] ܝܗܐ
ܐܢܫ ܡܡܠܠ:
ܬܪ̈ܝܢ ܐܘ ܟܕ
ܦܝܫ ܬܠܬܐ:
ܘܒܟܘܠ ܚܕ ܘܚܕ
ܠܚܘܪܗ:
ܘܚܕ ܝܗܐ
ܡܬܪܓܡ: [28] ܐܢ
ܕܝ ܠܐ ܗܘܐ
ܬܪܓܡܢ: ܝܗܐ
ܫܬܩ ܒܟܢܫܬܐ:
ܒܝܢܗ ܕܝ ܠܒܝܢ
ܓܪܡܗ· ܝܗܐ
ܡܡܠܠ: ܘܠܐܠܗܐ⁘
[29] ܢܒ̈ܝܝܢ ܕܝ ܬܪ̈ܝܢ
ܐܘ ܬܠܬܐ
ܝܗܘܢ ܡܡ̈ܠܠܝܢ:
ܘܫܪ̈ܟܐ
ܝܗܘܢ ܦܪ̈ܫܝܢ⁘[b]
[30] ܐܢ ܕܝ ܠܚܘܪܢ
ܕܗܘܐ ܝܬܒ

MKS IIB, 79: **a** ܠܫܢ | **b** omit *seyame*

1 Corinthians 14:30–37 F. 15v

ܬܘ ܓܝܪ܆ ܩܕܡܝܐ
ܗܘܐ ܫܬܘܩ܃
[31] ܝܟܠܝܢ ܐܢܬܘܢ
ܓܝܪ ܟܘܠ ܚܕ܆
ܘܚܕ ܡܬܢܒܝܢ
ܬܗܘܢ ܡܬܠܦܝܢ܆[a]
ܠܒܕܠ ܕܟܘܠܐ
ܝܗܘܢ ܝܠܦܝܢ܆
ܘܟܘܠܐ ܝܗܘܢ
ܡܬܒܝܐܝܢ܃
[32] ܘܪܘܚܝܐ
ܕܢܒܝܐ ܠܢܒܝܐ
ܡܫܬܥܒܕܝܢ܃
[33] ܠܝܬ ܓܝܪ ܐܠܗܐ
ܕܒܘܪܒܝܢ·
ܐܠܐ ܕܫܠܡ܃
ܗܝܟܕܐ ܕܒܟܘܠ
ܟܢܫܬܗܘܢ
ܕܩܕܝܫܝܐ· [34] ܢܫܝܐ
ܒܟܢܫܬܐ ܝܗܘܢ
ܫܬܩܝܢ܆ ܠܐ ܓܝܪ
ܫܠܝܛ ܠܗܘܢ ܕܡܡܠܠ܃

ܐܠܐ ܡܫܬܥܒܕܝܢ܃
ܗܝܟ ܕܐܘܦ
ܢܡܘܣܐ
ܐܡܪ܆ [35] ܐܢ
ܕܝ ܒܠܘܡ
ܗܢܝܢ ܒܥܝܢ
ܕܝܠܦܢ܆ ܒܒܝܬܐ
ܠܓܒܪܝܗܝܢ
ܢܗ̈ܢ ܢܫܐܠܢ܃
ܨܢܐ ܓܝܪ ܗܘ
ܠܐܢܬܬܐ ܬܡܠܠ
ܒܟܢܫܬܐ܃
[36] ܐܘ ܡܢܟܘܢ
ܢܦܩܬ ܡܠܬܗ
ܕܐܠܗܐ܆ ܐܘ
ܠܘܬܟܘܢ
ܒܠܚܘܕ ܡܛܬ܃
[37] ܐܢ ܐܢܬ ܐܢܫ
ܣܒܪ ܕܗܘ
ܢܒܝܐ· ܐܘ ܕܪܘܚ܆
ܡܢ ܗܘܐ
ܕܐܝܢܐ ܟܬܒ

MKS IIB, 80: **a** omit *seyame* || **a** *expectaveris* ܡܬܠܒܝܢ

1 Corinthians 14:37–15:3 F. 22r

ܠܟܘܢ܆ ܕܦܘܩܕܗ
ܗܘ ܕܡܪܢܐ܀
[38] ܐܢ ܕܝ ܐܝܬ
ܐܢܫ ܕܠܐ
ܡܚܪ· ܠܐ ܝܚܪ܀
[39] ܗܘܐ ܐܘܢ
ܐܚܝ ܡܢܘ
ܕܬܗܘܢ ܡܬܩܢܝܢ܆
ܘܕܬܡܠܠ
ܒܠܫܢܝܢ ܠܐ
ܬܗܘܢ ܟܠܝܢ܀
[40] ܟܘܠܐ ܕܝ
ܫܦܝܪܐܝܬ
ܘܒܐܬܩܘܢ ܢܗܝ
ܡܬܥܒܕ܀

✝ ܡܫܠܝܢ ܕܩܪܘܒܬܐ
[...]
[15:1] ܡܘܕܥ ܐܢܐ
ܠܟܘܢ ܕܝ ܐܚܝܐ
ܒܣܒܪܐ ܗܕܢ

ܕܣܒܪܬ ܠܟܘܢ܀
ܗܕܢ ܕܐܘܦ
ܩܒܠܬܘܢ܆ ܗܕܢ
ܕܒܗ ܐܬܘܢ
ܩܐܡܝܢ܆ [2] ܗܕܢ
ܕܒܬܪܒܗ
ܐܬܘܢ ܚܝܝܢ܀
ܡܢ ܠܒܪܠ
ܗܝܕܐ ܡܠܐ
ܒܣܒܪܬ
ܠܟܘܢ܀ ܐܢ
ܐܝܬ ܐܬܘܢ
ܡ̱ ܬܕܒܝܢ ܠܗ̇:[a]
ܐܢ ܕܝ ܡ ܠܒܠܐ
ܗܝܡܢܬܘܢ܀
[3] ܡܣܒܪܬ ܠܟܘܢ
ܓܪ ܒܩܕܡܝܬܐ
ܡܐ ܕܐܘܦ
ܩܒܠܬ:[b]
ܕܡܫܝܚܐ ܡܝܬ
ܥܠ ܕܚܛܗܝܢ
ܕܚܠܬܢ:

MKS IIB, 81: **a** omit diacritic | **b** ܩܒܠܬܗ

1 Corinthians 15:3–10 F. 22v

ܗܟܢ ܡܐ
ܕܒܟܬ̈ܒܝܐ:·
[4]ܘܕܐܬܩܒܪ:
ܘܕܩܡ ܠܝܘܡܐ
ܬܠܝܬܝܐ ܗܟܢ
ܕܒܟܬ̈ܒܝܐ:·
[5]ܘܕܐܬܚܙܝ
ܠܟܐܦܐ: ܐܦܠܐ
ܠܬܪ̈ܥܣܪܬܐ:·
[6]ܡܢ [a]ܒܬܪ ܟܢ·[a]
ܐܬܚܙܝ ܠܥܠ
ܡܢ ܚܡܫ
ܡܐܐ [b]ܐܢ̈ܫܝܢ
ܡܢ ܚܕܐ: ܡܐ
ܕܣܘ ܣܓܝܗܘܢ
ܩܝ̈ܡܝܢ ܥܕ
ܟܕܘ: ܐܢ̈ܫܝܢ
ܕܝ ܡܢܗܘܢ
ܕܡ̈ܟܘ:· [7]ܡܢ
[a]ܒܬܪ ܟܢ·[a]
ܐܬܚܙܝ
ܠܝܥܩܘܒ:·

ܐܦܠܐ ܠܟܘܠܗܘܢ
ܫܠܝ̈ܚܝܐ:· [8]ܒܬܪ
ܕܝ ܟܘܠܗܘܢ·
ܗܟܢ ܕܠܝܚܛܐ
ܐܬܚܙܝ
ܐܘܦ ܠܝ:·
[9]ܐܢܐ ܓܪ ܗܘ
ܙܥܘܪܗܘܢ
ܕܫܠܝ̈ܚܝܐ: ܗܕܢ
ܕܠܝܬܢܐ ܫܘܐ̇
ܕܢܬܩܪܐ̇
ܫܠܝܚ: ܠܒܕܝܠ
ܕܪܕܦܬ
ܟܢܫܬܗ
ܕܐܠܗܐ:·
[10]ܒܚܣܕܗ ܕܝ
ܕܐܠܗܐ· ܐܢܐ
ܡܐ ܕܐܢܐ:·
ܘܚܣܕܗ ܕܢ[c]
ܕܗܘܐ ܠܘܬܝ:
ܠܐ ܐܬܒܛܠ
ܪܝܩ:·

MKS IIB, 82: **a–a** ܒܬܪܟܢ | **b** ܡܐܐ̇ | **c** ܕܝ

1 Corinthians 15:24–31 **F. 8v**

ܟܕ ܡܣܘܪ
ܠܗ ܡܠܟܘܬܗ
ܕܐܠܗܐ ܘܐܒܐ:·
ܟܕ ܡܒܛܠ
ܟܠ ܪܫܘ[a] ܘܟܠ
ܫܘܠܛܢ ܘܚܝܠ:·
[25]ܗܐ ܠܗ ܓܪ
ܕܝܡܠܘܟ ܥܕܡܐ
ܕܝܫܘܝ ܟܠ
ܒܥܠܕܒ̈ܒܘܗܝ
ܬܚܘܬ ܪ̈ܓܠܘܗܝ:·
[26]ܒܥܠܕܒܒܐ ܚܪܝܐ
ܒܛܠ: ܡܢ ܕܗܘ
ܡܘܬܐ:· [27]ܟܘܠܐ[b]
ܓܪ ܫܥܒܕ
ܬܚܘܬ ܪ̈ܓܠܘܗܝ:·
ܟ̇ܕ ܕܝ ܝܐܡܪ
ܟܘܠܐ ܡܫܥܒܕ:
ܒܕܝܠܐ ܕܠܒܪ
ܡܢ ܗܘ ܕܫܥܒܕ
ܠܗ ܟܘܠܐ:· [28]ܟܕ
ܕܝ ܡܫܬܥܒܕ

ܠܗ ܟܘܠܐ:
ܒܟܢ ܗܘ ܒܪܐ
ܡܫܬܥܒܕ ܠܕܝ[c]
ܕܫܥܒܕ ܠܗ
ܟܘܠܐ܆ ܠܒܕܝܠ
ܕܝܗܘܐ ܐܠܗܐ
ܟܘܠܐ ܒܟܘܠ
ܐܚܪ:·[d] [29]ܐܝ ܕܝ
ܡܢܐ ܒܝ܆ ܡܢܐ
ܥܒ̈ܕܘܢ ܗܠܝܢ
ܕܡܬܛ̈ܒܠܝܢ
ܚܠܦܝ[e] ܡܝ̈ܬܝܐ:
ܐܝ ܗܘܠܗܘܢ
ܡܬܩ̈ܝܡܝܢ ܠܐ
ܡ̈ܝܬܝܢ܆ ܠܡܢܐ
ܗܘܝ ܡܬܛ̈ܒܠܝܢ
ܥܠ ܕܛܒܠܗܘܢ:·
[30]ܠܡܢܐ[f] ܐܘܦ ܐܢܢ
ܒܡܣܬܢܝܢܢ
ܒܟܘܠ ܫܥܐ:·
[31]ܒܟܘܠ ܝܘܡ
ܐܢܐ ܡܝܬ:·

MKS IIB, 83: **a** ܪܝܫܘ | **b** ܟܘܠ | **c** ܕܝ | **d** ⸢ܐܚ̈ܝܢ⸣ | **e** ܥܠ ܚܠܦܝ | **f** ܘܠܡܢܐ

1 Corinthians 15:31–37 F. 8r

ܐܝܟ ܬܫܒܘܚܬܟܘܢ
ܐܚ̈ܝܢܐ· ܗܕܐ
ܕܠܝ ܒܡܪܢ
ܝܫܘܥ ܡܫܝܚܐ:
32 ܐܢ ܠܒܪܢܫ
ܒܪܫ ܚܛܝܬ
ܠܚܝܘܬܐ[a]
ܒܐܦܣܘܣ:
ܡܐ ܗܢܝܬ݀:
ܐܢ ܡܝ̈ܬܝܢ
ܠܐ ܡܬ̈ܩܝܡܝܢ·:
ܢܝܟܘܠ ܘܢܫܬܐ·
ܡܚܪ ܓܝܪ ܐܢܢ
ܡܝ̈ܬܝܢ:
33 ܠܐ ܬܛܥܘܢ·:
ܡܚܒ̈ܠܝܢ ܡ̈ܠܝܐ
ܒܥ̈ܕܬܐ ܠܛ̈ܒܬܐ
ܒܡ̈ܫܪܝܐ:
34 ܐܙܕܗܪܘ
ܒܟܝܢܘ ܘܠܐ
ܬܚܛܘܢ:
ܐ̇ܝܬ ܓܝܪ ܐ̈ܢܫܝܢ

ܕܠܝܬ ܒܗܘܢ
ܐܒܪܘܬܗ
ܕܐܠܗܐ:
ܠܒܗܬܬܟܘܢ
ܐܢܐ ܐܡܪ:
35 ܐܠܐ ܐܡܪ
ܐܢܫ ܗܟܢ
ܡܬ̈ܩܝܡܝܢ ܡܝ̈ܬܝܐ:
ܒܗܕܝܢ ܕܝ
ܦܘ ܓܪ ܗܘܝܢ
ܐܬܝܢ: 36 ܦܟܗܐ:
ܐܬ ܡܐ ܕܐܬ
ܙܪܥ[b] ܠܐ ܚܝܐ·
ܐܠܐ ܐܢ ܡܝܬܬ:
37 ܘ̇ܡܐ ܕܐܬ ܙܪܥ:
ܠܐ[c] ܦܘ ܓܪܐ ܗܕܝܢ
ܕܡܬܠܕ ܐܬ
ܙܪܥ: ܐܠܐ
ܦܪܛܐ ܒܪܛܠܐ:
ܐܢ ܕܫ̈ܛܝܢ·
ܘܐܢ ܕܚܪܝܢܬ
ܕܙ̈ܒܘܢܐ:

MKS IIB, 84: **a** ܠܚܝ̈ܘܬܐ | **c** omit || **b** MS *sic*; *expectaveris* ܙܪܥ

1 Corinthians 15:38–42 F. 18r

[38]ܐܠܗܐ ܕܝ
ܝܗܒ ܠܗ
[a]ܦܓܪ ܗܝܟ[a]
ܒܡܠܟܐ[b] ܕܝ ܨܒܐ܀
ܘ̇ܠܟܠ ܚܕ ܡܢ
ܙܪ̈ܥܘܢܐ
ܦܓܪܗ
ܕܓܪܡܗ܀ [39]ܠܐ
ܟܠ ܒܣܪܐ
ܝܬܗ ܝܬܗ
ܒܣܪܐ܀ ܐܠܐ
ܚܘܪܢ ܗܘ
ܕܒܢܝ̈ܢܫܐ:
ܚܘܪܢ ܕܝ ܗܘ
ܒܣܪܗܘܢ[c]
ܕܒܥܝܪܐ܀[d] ܚܘܪܢ
ܕܝ ܒܣܪܐ
ܕܦܪ̈ܚܬܐ:
ܚܘܪܢ ܕܝ
ܕܢܘ̈ܢܐ:
[40]ܘܦܓ̈ܪܝܢ
ܕܫܡ̈ܝܢ:

ܘܦܓ̈ܪܝܢ
ܕܐܪܥ: ܐܠܐ
ܚܘܪܝ ܗܝ
ܬܫܒܚܬܗܘܢ
ܕܗܠܝܢ ܕܡܢ
ܫܡܝܐ: ܚܘܪܝ
ܕܝ ܕܗܠܝܢ ܕܡܢ
ܐܪܥܐ: [41]ܚܘܪܝ
ܬܫܒܚܬܗ
ܕܫܡܫܐ:
ܘܚܘܪܝ
ܬܫܒܚܬܗ
ܕܙܗܪܐ:
ܘܚܘܪܝ
ܬܫܒܚܬܗܘܢ
ܕܟܘܟ̈ܒܝܐ:
ܟܘܟܒ ܓܪ
ܡܢ ܟܘܟܒ:
ܡܝܐܬܪ
ܒܬܫܒܚܬܐ:
[42]ܘ̱ܗܟܢ[e] ܐܘܦ
ܩܝܐܡܬܗܘܢ

MKS IIB, 85: **a–a** ܦܓܪܗ | **b** ܒܡܠ ܨܒܐ | **c** add *seyame* | **d** omit *seyame* | **e** ܗܟܢ

1 Corinthians 15:42–49 F. 18v

ܕܡܝ̈ܬܐ܀
ܡܙܕܪܥ ܗܘ
[a]ܒܬܪܘܦܐ:* ܘܩܐܡ[a]
[b]ܕܠܐ ܬܪܘܦ:
43 ܡܙܕܪܥ ܗܘ
ܒܨܠܠ: ܘܩܐܡ
ܒܬܫܒܘܚܬܐ܀
ܡܙܕܪܥ ܗܘ
ܒܟܐܒܐ: ܘܩܐܡ
ܒܚܝܠ܀ 44 ܡܙܕܪܥ
ܗܘ ܦܓܪ
ܕܢܦܫ: ܘܩܐܡ
ܗܘ ܕܝ ܦܓܪ
ܕܪܘܚ:
ܐܢ ܐܝܬ ܦܓܪ
ܕܢܦܫ: ܐܝܬ[b]
[c]ܐܦ ܦܓܪ
ܕܪܘܚ: 45 ܗܟܢܐ
ܐܦ ܟܬܝܒ:[c]
ܐܬܥܒܕ
ܒܪܢܫܐ ܩܕܡܝܐ
ܐܕܡ: ܠܢܦܫ ܚܝܐ:[d]

[e]ܐܕܡ ܒܬܪܝܐ*
ܠܪܘܚ ܡܚܝܢ:[e]*
[f]46 ܐܠܐ ܠܐ ܩܕܡ
ܕܪܘܚܐ. ܐܠܐ
ܕܢܦܫܐ: ܘܡܢ
ܒܬܪ ܟܢ
ܕܪܘܚܐ:
47 ܒܪܢܫܐ ܩܕܡܝܐ
ܡܢ ܐܪܥܐ
ܕܪܓܫ:
ܒܪܢܫܐ
ܬܢܝܢܐ. ܡܢ
ܫܡܝܐ: 48 ܗܝܟ
ܕ ܕܡܢ ܪܓܫܝܐ.
ܗܟܢ ܐܦ
ܗܠܝܢ ܕܡܢ
ܪܓܫܝܐ:*[f]
49 ܘܗܝܟ ܕܡܢ
ܕܠܫܡ̈ܝܐ[g]
ܢ ܘܪܬܗ
ܕܕ ܕܡܢ
ܪܓܫܝܐ:[h]

MKS IIB, 86: **a–a** ܒܚܒܠܐ ܘܩܐܡ | **b–b** *nil* | **c–c** ܟܬܝܒ [...] / ܗܟܢ [...] / ܦܓܪ [...] | **d** ܚܝ | **e–e** ܐܕܡ [...] / ܠܪܘܚ ܡܢ ܚܝܐ | **f–f** *nil* | **g** omit *seyame* | **h** ܪ[ܓܫ]ܝܐ || Side contains quire number.

1 Corinthians 16:16–24 F. 20r

ܡܫܬܥܒܕܝܢ
ܠܕ ܟܘܬ ܗܠܝܢ:
ܘܠܟܘܠ ܡܢ
ܕܠܐܐ[a] ܘܡܟܠ:
[17] ܚ̈ܕܐ ܐܢܐ ܕܝ ܥܠ
ܡܝܬܝܘܬܗ
ܕܐܣܛܦܢܐ
ܘܦܘܪܛܘܢܛܘܣ:
ܘܕܐܟܐܝܩܘܣ:
ܠܚܠܠ ܕܚܣܪܘܢܟܘܢ
ܗܠܝܢ ܡܠܝܘ:
[18] ܐܢܝܚܘ ܓܪ
ܝܬܗ̇ ܠܪܘܚܝ[b]
ܘܠܕܝܠܟܘܢ:[c]
ܗܘܘ ܡܒܪ̈ܝܢ
ܐܘܢ ܠܕ ܟܘܬ
ܗܠܝܢ: [19] ܫ̈ܐܠܝܢ
ܒܫܠܡܟܘܢ[d]
ܟܢ[ܫ̈]ܬܐ[e]
ܕܐܣܝܐ:
ܫ̈ܐܠܝܢ[f] ܒܫܠܡܟܘܢ
[g]ܗܘܢ ܒܡܪܢܐ:[g]

ܐܩܘܠܣ
ܘܦܪܝܣܩܐ:
ܥܡ ܟܢܫܬܐ
ܕܒܒܝܬܗܘܢ:
[20] ܫ̈ܐܠܝܢ ܒܫܠܡܟܘܢ
ܐܚ̈ܝܐ ܟܘܠܗܘܢ:
ܫܐܠܘ ܒܫܠܡܐ
ܕܦܠܓܟܘܢ ܕܦܠܓ:*[h]
ܒܫܠܡ ܩܕܝܫ:
[21] ܫܐܠ ܫܠܡܐ
ܒܐ̈ܝܕܝ ܕܝܠܝ
ܦܘܠܘܣ: [22] ܡܢ[i]
ܕܠܐ ܪܚܡ
ܠܡܪܐ ܝܗܐ
ܚܪܡ: ܡܪܢ
ܐܬܐ: [23] ܚܣܕܗ
ܕܡܪܢ ܝܣܘܣ
ܥܡܟܘܢ: [24] ܚܒܬܝ
ܕܝܠܝ ܥܡ
ܟܘܠܟܘܢ
ܒܝܣܘܣ
ܡܫܝܚܐ ܐܡܝܢ:

MKS IIB, 87: **a** omit diacritic | **b** ܪܘܚܝ | **c** ܘܕܝܠܟܘܢ | **d** ܒܫ[ܠܡܟܘܢ] | **e** ܟܢ[ܫܬܐ] | **f** omit *seyame* | **g** ܐ[...]ܐ ܡܪܢܐ | **h** ܕܦܠܓ | **i** omit diacritic

2 Corinthians 1:1–3 F. 20v

~~~~~~~~~~~~~~~~~~~~[a]

ܦܘܪܛܘܢܣ
ܘܐܣܛܦܢܘܣ
ܘܐܟܐܝܩܘܣ
~~~~~~~~~~~~~~~~~~~~

ܐܓ[ܪܬܐ] ܕܠܘܬ
ܩܘܪ[...]
ܬܢܝܢܬܐ[a]

[1:1] ܦܘܠܘܣ ܫܠܝܚܗ
ܕܝܫܘܥ
ܡܫܝܚܐ
ܒܨܒܝܢܗ

ܘܛܝܡܬܐܘܣ
ܐܚܘܢ.
ܠܥܕܬܗ
ܕܐܠܗܐ· ܠܗܕܐ
ܕܝܗܝܒܐ
ܒܩܘܪܢܬܘܣ:
ܥܡ ܟܠܗܘܢ
ܘܩܕ̈ܝܫܐ ܕܐܝܬ
ܒܟܠܗ ܐܟܐܝܐ:
[2] ܫܠܡܐ ܥܡܟܘܢ.
ܘܛܝܒܘܬܐ ܡܢ
ܐܠܗܐ ܐܒܘܢ:
ܘܡܢ ܡܪܢ
ܝܫܘܥ ܡܫܝܚܐ:
[3] ܡܒܪܟ ܗܘ
ܐܠܗܐ ܘܐܒܘܗܝ
ܕܡܪܢ ܝܫܘܥ
ܡܫܝܚܐ:
ܐܒܘܗܝ
ܕܪ̈ܚܡܐ·
ܘܐܠܗܘܢ ܕܟܠ
ܬܘܢ̈ܚܡܐ:

MKS IIB, 94: **a–a** *nil*

2 Corinthians 1:23–2:4 F. 17r

[23] ܐܢܐ ܕܝ
ܣܗܕ ܐܢܐ
ܩܪܐ̇ ܠܐܠܗܐ
ܥܠ ܢܦܫܝ:
ܕܡܢ ܚܣܐ̇ܘ
ܥܠܝܟܘܢ ܠܐ ܐ̇ܬܝܬ[a]
ܠܩܘܪܢܬܘܣ:
[24] ܠܐ ܗܘܝ ܕܐܢܢ
ܡܪ̈ܘܡܢ ܥܠ
ܗܝܡܢܘܬܟܘܢ:
ܐܠܐ ܥܕ̈ܪ
ܚܠܘܬܗ̇ ܐܢܢ
ܕܚܕܘܬܟܘܢ:
ܒܗܝܡܢܘܬܐ
ܓܝܪ ܐܬܘܢ
ܩܝ̈ܡܝܢ: [2:1] ܗܕܐ
ܓܝܪ ܕܢܝܬ[b]*
ܒܓܪܡܝ: ܕܠܐ
ܬܘܒ ܒܥܝܩܐ
ܐܬܐ ܠܘܬܟܘܢ:
[2] ܐܢ ܓܝܪ ܐܢܐ
ܡܥܝܩ ܠܟܘܢ:

ܘܡܢ̇[c] ܗܘ ܕܝ
ܕܡܚܕܐ ܠܝ:
ܐܠܐ ܐܢ ܕܝ
ܕܡܬܥܝܩ ܡܢ
ܡܢܝ: [3] ܘܟܬܒܬ
ܐܬܗ̇ ܗܕܐ:
ܕܠܐ ܒܕ ܐܬܐ̇
ܗܘܐ̇ ܠܝ ܥܩܐ
ܡܢ ܗܠܝܢ ܕܗܘܐ
ܢܥܠ ܠܝ ܕܗܘܐ̇
ܐܢܐ ܚܕܐ̇:
ܕܐܢܐ ܪܚܝܢ
ܥܠ ܟܘܠܟܘܢ:
ܕܚܕܘܬܝ
ܕܟܠܝ ܕܟܘܠܟܘܢ[d]
ܗܝ: [4] ܡܢ ܠܥܝܩܘܢ
ܓܝܪ ܣܓܝ: ܘܡܢ
ܥܘܩܝ ܐ ܕܠܒ
ܟܬܒܬ ܠܟܘܢ
ܒܕ̈ܡܥܝܢ ܣܓܝ:
ܠܐ ܕܬܥܝܩܘܢ:[e]
ܐܠܐ[f] ܕܬܕܥ̈[ܘ]ܢ

MKS IIB, 95: **a** ܐ̇ܬܝܬ | **b** ܪܢܝܬ | **c** omit diacritic | **d** ܒܟܘܠܟܘܢ | **e** ܕܬܥܝ̈ܩܘܢ | **f** ܐ̇ܠܐ

2 Corinthians 2:4–11 F. 17v

ܚܒܬܐ ܗܕܐ
ܕܠܝ ܡܢ ܕܝܬܝܪ
ܠܘܬܟܘܢ ⁖ [5] ܐܢ
ܕܝ ܐܢ ܢܫ
ܐܥܩ: ܠܐ ܠܝ
ܐܢ ܢܫ: ܐܠܐ
ܡܢ ܚܘܠܩ·
ܕܠܐ ܢܒܪܐ̇[a]
ܥܠ ܟܘܠܟܘܢ ⁖ [6] ܣܦܩ
ܠܕ ܟܢܫܗ
ܕܗܕܝ ܗܕܐ
ܐܟܦܬܐ ܕܡܢ
ܣܘ ܟܢܫܐ ⁖ [7] ܗܘܐ̇
ܐܘܝ ܐܬܘܝ
ܡܠܘܝ ܫܒܩܘܢ
ܠܗ· ܘܢܝܚܘ
ܛܘܗ: ܕܠܐ
ܐܡܬܝ ܡܢ
ܣܘ ܟܢܫܐ ܕܝ ܩܬܐ
ܡܛܠܟ ܕ ܟܢܫܗ
ܕܗܕܝ ⁖ [8] ܠܒܕܝܠ
[ܒ]ܕܝ ܐܢܐ

ܒܥܐ ܡܢܟܘܢ
ܕܬܫܪ̈ܘܢ
ܥܠܘܝ ܚܒܬܐ:
[9] ܠܒܕܝܠ ܒܕܝ
ܟܪ ܐܘܦ
ܟܬܒܬ ܕܢܒܪ
ܒܕܘܩܢܟܘܢ:
ܐܢ ܐܢܬ
ܐܬܘܢ ܫܡ̈ܥܝܢ
ܟܟܘܠܐ ⁖ [10] ܠܡܢ
[b]ܕܝ ܕܐܬܘܢ[b]
ܫܒܩܝܢ ܐܘܦ
ܐܢܐ: ܡܢܟܪ
ܐܢܐ ܡܢܐ
ܕܫܒܩܬ· ܡܢ
ܠܒܕܝܠܟܘܢ
ܫܒܩܬ ܒܐܦ̈ܘܝ
ܕܡܫܝܚܐ:
[11] ܠܒܕܝܠ ܕܠܐ
ܢܬܥܫܩ[c] ܡܢ ܣܛܢܐ:
ܠܣܛܢ ܟܪ ܕܠܐ
ܡܕܥܝܢ ܡܚܫ̈ܒܬܗ:

MKS IIB, 96: **a** omit diacritic | **b–b** ܕܠܗ ܐܬܘܢ | **c** ܢܬܥܫܩ̈ܐ

2 Corinthians 4:18–5:6 **F. 3r**

ܡܬܚܙܝܐ
ܠܥܠܡ܀

✝ ܐܪܫ ܡܫܠܡ܀

5:1 ܝܕܥܝܢ ܐܢܢ ܓܪ
ܕܐܢ ܒܝܬܐ
ܕܡܫܟܢܢ ܕܝܢ
ܐܪܥܐ ܡܫܬܪܐ܀[a]
ܐܝܬ ܠܢ ܒܢܝܢ
ܡܢ ܐܠܗܐ:
ܒܝ[b]* ܕܠܐ ܒܥܒܕ
ܒܐܝܕܝܢ ܕܠܥܠܡ
ܒܓܘ[c] ܫܡܝܐ܀
2 ܡܛܠ ܒܗܕܢ
ܐܢܢ ܡܬܬܢܚܝܢ:
ܕܒܡܥܪܬܢ[d] ܕܝܢ
ܫܡܝܐ ܐܢܢ
ܡܬܪܓܓܝܢ
ܕܢܠܒܫ: 3 ܘܐܢ
ܢܠܒܫ ܐܢܢ
ܕܠܐ ܢܫܬܟܚ

ܥܪܛܠܝܢ:
4 ܡܛܠ ܐܢܢ ܗܠܝܢ
ܕܒܡܫܟܢܐ
ܡܬܬܢܚܝܢ ܐܢܢ
ܘܝܩܝܪܐ[e] ܥܠܝܢ܀
ܥܠ ܕܠܝܬ ܐܢܢ
ܨܒܝܢ[f] ܕܢܫܠܚ:
ܐܠܐ ܕܢܠܒܫ:
ܠܒܪ ܕܢܬܒܠܥ
ܡܝܘܬܐ ܡܢ
ܚܝܐ: 5 ܗܘ ܕܝ[g]
ܕܥܒܕ ܠܢ
ܠܗ[e] ܠܗܕܐ·
ܐܠܗܐ: ܗܘ
ܕܝܗܒ ܠܢ
ܪܗܒܘܢܐ
ܕܪܘܚܐ:
6 ܪܚܝܩܝܢ ܐܢܢ
ܒܟܠ ܓܪ
ܘܝܕܥܝܢ ܕܟܡܐ
ܕܐܢܢ ܥܡܪܝܢ
ܒܦܓܪܐ

MKS IIB, 97: **a** ܡܫܬܪܐ | **b** ܒܝ | **c** ܕܒܓܘ | **d** ܒܡܥܪܬܢ | **e** omit diacritic | **f** ܨܒܝܢ | **g** omit

2 Corinthians 5:6–12 F. 3v

ܐܢܢ ܕܝܕܥܝܢ
ܡܢ ܡܪܢܐ܆
[7] ܒܗܝܡܢܘ ܓܝܪ
ܐܢܢ ܡܗܠܟܝܢ.
ܘܠܐ ܒܚܙܘ܆
[8] ܪ̈ܚܝܨܝܢ ܕܝ
ܘܨܒ̈ܝܢ ܡܠܘܢ
ܕܢܦܘܩ ܡܢ
ܦܘ ܓܪܐ ܘܢ̈ܬܝܠ
ܠܘܬ ܡܪܢܐ܆
[9] ܠܒܕܠ ܗܕܝ
ܐܢܢ ܢܛܝ ܦܝܢ
ܕܐܢ ܡܗ̈ܘܝܢ
ܒܦܘ ܓܪܐ. ܘܐܢ
ܢܦ̈ܩܝܢ. ܕܢܗܘܐ
ܫܦ̈ܪܝܢ ܠܗ:
[10] ܟܘܠܝܢ ܓܝܪ
ܠܢ ܕܢܩܘܡ
ܩܘܕܡ ܒܝܡܐ
ܕܡܫܝܚܐ܆
ܕܢܣܒ ܟܘܠ
ܐܢܫ ܡܐ ܕܥܒܕ

ܒܦܘ ܓܪܐ. ܐܢ
ܛܒ ܘܐܢ ܒܝܫ:
[11] ܡܕ̈ܚܠܝܢ ܐܘܢ
ܕܚܠܬܗ ܕܡܪܢܐ܆
ܠܒܢ̈ܝܢܫܐ ܡܢ
ܐܢܢ ܡܦ̈ܝܣܝܢ܆
ܠܐܠܗܐ ܕܝ
ܐܢܢ ܢܗ̈ܝܪܝܢ܆
ܡܣܒܪ[a] ܐܢܐ
ܕܝ ܕܐܘܦ
ܒܡܕ̈ܥܬܟܘܢ
ܐܢܢ ܢܗ̈ܝܪܝܢ܆
[12] ܠܐ ܬܘܒ ܓܪܡܢ
ܐܢܢ ܡܫ̈ܒܚܝܢ
ܠܟܘܢ܆ ܐܠܐ
ܚܠܐ ܐܢܢ
ܝܗ̈ܒܝܢ ܠܟܘܢ܆
ܕܬܫܒܚܐ
ܥܠ ܕܝܠܢ:
ܕܢܗܐ ܠܒܟܘܢ
ܠܘܬ ܗܠܝܢ
ܕܒܐܦ̈ܝܢ

a The *mim* is secondary, written in a smaller hand to the main text. The right-hand edge of the *semkath* aligns with the margin.

2 Corinthians 6:3–10 F. 6r

ܬܘܩܠܬܐ: ܕܠܐ
ܢܗܐ[a] ܡܘܡ
ܒܬܫܡܫܬܢ:
[4]ܐܠܐ ܒܟܘܠܐ
ܐܝܟ ܡܩܝܡܝܢ
ܚܙ̈ܝܢ[a] ܗܘܝܢ
ܡܫܡ̈ܫܘܗܝ[b]
ܕܐܠܗܐ:
ܒܡܣܝܒܪܢܘ
ܣܓܝ: ܒܐܘ̈ܠܨܢܝܢ:
ܒܩܛܝܢ: ܒܥ̈ܩܬܝܢ:*[c]
[5]ܒܡܚ̈ܘܬܐ:[d]
ܒܐܣ̈ܘܪܝܢ:
ܒܛܘܪ̈ܦܝܢ:
ܒܠܐ̈ܘܝܢ:
ܒܫܗ̈ܪܝܢ:
ܒܨ̈ܘܡܝܢ:
[6]ܒܕܟܝܘ:
ܒܐܪܟܘ:
ܒܐܘܪܟܘܬ[a] ܪܘܚ:
ܒܒܣܝܡܘ:
ܒܪܘܚ ܕܩܘܕܫ:

ܒܚܘܒܐ ܕܠܝܬ
ܒܗ̇ ܥܘܪ:
[7]ܒܡܠܐ ܩܘܫܛܐ:
ܒܚܝܠܗ ܕܐܠܗܐ:
ܒܙܝ̈ܢܐ ܕܝܢ ܕܙܟܐ·
ܕܝܡܝܢܐ
ܘܕܣܡܠܐ:
[8]ܒܬܫܒܚܐ
ܘܒܨܥܪ:
ܒܛܘܒ:
ܘܒܫܡܥܘ:
ܗ̇ܘܝܢ ܡܛܥ̈ܝܢ·
ܘܐܝܢ ܡܫܪ̈ܪܝܢ:[b]
[9]ܗܘܝܢ ܕܠܐ
ܝܕ̈ܥܝܢ· ܘܐܝܢ
ܝܕ̈ܥܝܢ: ܗܘܝܢ
ܡܝ̈ܬܝܢ·[e] ܘܐܝܢ
ܚܝܝܢ: ܗܘܝܢ
ܡܬܪ̈ܕܝܢ· ܘܠܐ
ܡܝ̈ܬܝܢ: [10]ܗܘܝܢ
[f]ܗܟܝ ܬܥܝܢ· ܗܘ̈ܝܢ[f]
ܕܝ ܚܕ̈ܝܢ:

MKS IIB, 99: **a** omit diacritic | **b** omit *seyame* | **c** ܒܣܩ̈ܝܢ | **e** ܡܝ̈ܬܝܢ | **f–f** ܗܟܝ ܥܡ ܗܘܝܢ || **d** The *beth* is a marginal correction: the right-hand side of the following *mim* aligns perfectly with the margin.

2 Corinthians 6:10–16 F. 6v

ܗܝܟ ܡܣܟܢܝܢ·
ܠܣܓܝ ܕܝ
ܡܥܬܪܝܢ:
ܗܝܟ ܕܠܝܬ
ܠܝܬ ܠܢ· ܘܟܘܠܐ
ܐܝܬ ܠܢ ܬܕܝܪ:
[11] ܦܡܢ ܦܬܝܚ
ܠܘܬܟܘܢ
ܩܘܪܢܬܝܐ:
ܠܒܢ ܡܦܬܐ:
[12] ܠܝܬ ܐܢܬܘܢ
ܡܥܩܢܝܢ ܒܢ:
ܡܥܩܢܝܢ
ܐܢܬܘܢ ܕܝ
ܒܪܚܡܝܟܘܢ:
[13] ܚܠܦܗ ܕܝ ܚܠܦܗ
ܒܗܘܢܐ ܕܐ ܒܪܐ·
ܗܝܟ ܠܒܢܝܢ
ܐܢܐ ܐܡܪ:
ܐܬܦܬܚܘ ܐܘܦ
ܐܢܬܘܢ: [14] ܠܐ
ܬܬܥܒܕܘܢ ܥܡ

ܢܟܪܘܢ ܕܗܠܝܢ
ܕܠܐ ܡܗܝܡܢܝܢ·
ܡ̈ܢܐ ܓܪ ܫܘܬܦܘ
ܠܙܕܝܩܐ ܥܡ
ܥܘܠܐ· ܐܘ
ܡܢܐ ܫܘܬܦܘ
ܠܢܗܘܪܐ
ܠܘܬ ܩܒܠܐ:
[15] ܡܢܐ ܕܝ ܐܫܘܝܘ
ܠܡܫܝܚܐ ܠܘܬ
ܒܠܝܥܪ: ܐܘ
ܡܢܐ ܚܘܠܩ
ܠܡܗܝܡܢܐ
ܥܡ ܗܘ ܕܠܐ
ܡܗܝܡܢ:
[16] ܡ̈ܢܐ ܕܝ ܐܬܘܣܝܘ
ܠܢܘܣܗ
ܕܐܠܗܐ ܥܡ
ܕܝ ܠܦܬܟܪܐ· ܐܝܬ
ܓܪ ܢܘܣܗ
ܐܝܬ ܕܐܠܗܐ
ܚܝܐ:

2 Corinthians 6:16–7:3 F. 2r

ܗܟܢ ܕܐܡܪ̇
ܐܠܗܐ: ܕܐܢܐ
ܡܥܡܪ ܒܗܘܢ
ܘܡܗܠܟ܀ ܘܗܘܝ
ܐܢܐ ܠܗܘܢ
ܐܠܗ: ܘܗܢܘܢ
ܝܗܘܢ ܠܝ ܥܡܠ:
17 ܠܒܪܝܠ ܒܪܝ
ܦܘܩܘ ܡܢ
ܒܝܢܬܗܘܢ
ܘܐܬܦܪ̈ܫܘ
ܐܡܪ ܡܪܝܐ:
ܘܠܡܣܐܒ ܠܐ
ܬܩܪ̈ܒܘܢ܀
ܘܐܢܐ ܡܩܒܠ
ܝܬܟܘܢ܀ 18 ܘܐܢܐ
ܗܘܐ ܠܟܘܢ
ܠܐܒ: ܘܐܬܘܢ
ܗܘܝܢ ܠܝ
ܠܒܢܝܢ ܘܠܒ̈ܢܢ
ܐܡܪ ܡܪܝܐ
ܕܫܠܝܛ ܒܟܠܐ܀

✝ [a]ܪܫ ܦܘܠܘܣ[a]·
7:1 ܗܠܝܢ ܐܘܢ
ܡܢ ܕ̈ܝܢ ܬܐ ܐܝܬ
ܠܢ ܚܒܝܒ̈ܝܐ:
ܢܕܟܐ ܓܪ̈ܡܢ
ܡܢ ܟܘܠ
ܛܘܐܒܐ
ܕܒܣܪ
ܘܪܘܚ:·
ܘܢܫܠܡ
ܩܕܝܫܘܬܐ
ܒܪܘܚܗ
ܕܐܠܗܐ:
2 ܣܒ̈ܪܘܢ[b] ܠܢ:·
ܠܐܢܫ ܠܐ
ܐܠܘܠܢ[c]: ܠܐܢܫ
ܠܐ ܐܬܪ̈ܦܢ:
ܠܐܢܫ ܠܐ ܚܣ̈ܪܢ:·
3 ܠܡܚܝܒܘ ܠܝܬ
ܐܢܐ ܐܡܪ:·
ܩܕܡܬ ܓܪ

MKS IIB, 101: **a–a** *nil* | **b** omit *seyame* | **c** ܐܠܘܠܢ

2 Corinthians 7:3–8 F. 2v

ܐܡܪܬ ܕܐܬܘܢ
ܒܠܒ̈ܒܢ
ܕܬܡܘ̈ܬܘܢ
ܥܡܢ ܘܬܚܝ̈ܘܢ ܀[a]
[4] ܣܓܝ ܠܝ
ܦܪܗܣܝܐ[b]
ܠܘܬܟܘܢ ܃ ܣܓܝ
ܠܝ[c] ܬܫܒܘܚܐ
ܥܠ ܕܝܠܟܘܢ ܀
ܡܠܝ̇ܐ[d] ܐܢܐ
ܒܬܢܘ̈ܚܡܐ ܀[a]
ܘܡܝܬܪ ܐܢܐ
ܒܚܕܘܬܐ ܥܠ
ܟܘܠ ܠܚܨܝ̈ܘܢ ܀
[5] ܦ̈ܓܪ ܟܕ[e] ܐܬܝ̈ܢ
ܠܡܩܕܘܢܝܐ ܀[f]
ܐܘܦ ܠܐ ܢܚܐ
ܢܝܚܐ[g] ܠܐ
ܗܘܐ ܠܒܣܪܢ ܀
ܐܠܐ ܒܟܘܠܐ
ܡܬܠܚܨܝܢ ܀[*h] ܡܢ
ܠܒܪ ܝ ܣܚ̈ܬܐ ܀[a]

ܘܡܢ ܠܓܘ
ܕܚܠ̈ܬܐ ܀ [6] ܐܠܐ
ܗܘ ܕܡܒܝܣ
ܠܡܟܝ̈ܟܐ ܒܝܣ
ܒܝ ܐܠܗܐ
ܒܡܐܬܝܘܬܗ
ܕܛܛܘܣ ܀
[7] ܠܐ ܕܝ ܒܠܚܘܕ
ܒܡܐܬܝܘܬܗ ܀
ܐܠܐ ܐܘܦ
ܒܬܢܘ̈ܚܡܐ
ܕܐܬܒܝܣ
ܒܟܘܢ ܀[i]
ܕܗܘܐ ܡܬܢܝ̇ܐ[d]
ܠܝ ܬܫܘܥܕܬܐ[j]
ܕܠܟܘܢ ܀
ܘܒܟܝܟܘܢ
ܘܛܢܬܟܘܢ
ܕܒܠ[k] ܕܝܠܝ ܃
ܕܗܘܝ[l] ܡܠܝ*
ܚܕܝ̇ܐ ܀ [8] ܕܐܘܦ
ܐܢ ܐܝ ܥܝܬ

MKS IIB, 60: **a** omit *seyame* | **b** ܦܪܗܣ̈ܝܐ | **c** ܕܝ | **d** omit diacritic | **e** omit | **f** ܠܡܩܕܘܢܝܐ | **g** ܢܝܚ | **h** ܐܬܐܠܨܝܢ | **i** ܒܠ ܛܠܒܘܢ | **j** ܬܫܘܥܕܬܐ | **k** ܒܠ | **l** ܕܗܘܐ

Galatians 1:1–5 **F. 123r**

[a]ܫܠܡܬ ܐܓܪܬܐ
ܬܢܝܢܬܐ
ܕܩܘܪ̈ܢܬ[ܝ]
ܐܬܟܬܒܬ ܕ̈ܝ
ܡܢ ܦܝܠܝܦܘܣ
ܘܐܫܬܕܪܬ ܒܝܕ ܥܡ
ܛܝܛܘܣ ܘܠܘܩܣ:
~~~~~~~~~~~
ܐܓܪܬܐ ܕܠܘܬ
ܓܠܛܝ̈ܐ:[a]
1:1 ܦܘܠܘܣ ܫܠܝܚܐ:
ܠܐ ܡܢ ܒܢܝ̈ܫ:
ܘܠܐ ܒܝܕ ܒܪ
ܐܢܫ:
ܐܠܐ ܒܝܕܗ
ܕܝܫܘܥ
ܡܫܝܚܐ:
ܘܐܠܗܐ ܐܒܐ:
ܕܝ ܕܐܩܝܡ ܝܬܗ
ܡܢ ܒܝܬ ܡܝܬܝܐ:

2 ܘܟܘܠ ܐܚ̈ܝܐ
ܕܥܡܝ:
ܠܥܕ̈ܬܐ
ܕܓܠܛܝܐ:
3 ܛܝܒܘܬܐ ܠܟܘܢ
ܘܫܠܡܐ ܡܢ
ܐܠܗܐ ܐܒܐ:
ܘܡܢ ܡܪܢ
ܝܫܘܥ ܡܫܝܚܐ:
4 ܗܘ ܕܝܗܒ
ܓܪܡܗ ܥܠ
ܕܚܛܗ̈ܝܢ
ܕܦܨܬܢ:
ܠܒܪ
ܕܫܩ̈ܠܬܢ ܡܢ
ܕܝ ܥܠܡܐ ܒܝܫܐ
ܕܐܝܬ: ܗܝܟ
ܨܒܝܢܗ
ܕܐܠܗܐ[b]
ܘܐܒܘܢ:
5 ܗܘ ܕܠܗ
ܬܫܒܚܬܐ

MKS IIB, 107: **a–a** *nil* | **b** ܕܐܠܗܐ
~~~~~~~~~~~

Galatians 1:5–10 F. 123v

ܠܥܠܡܝܗܘܢ
ܕܥܠܡ̈ܝܐ ܐܡܝܢ:
[6] ܬܡܗ ܐܢܐ ܕܟܕܢ
ܒܥܘܪܒ
ܐܬܘܢ ܓ̈ܪܫܝܢ
ܒܡܕܒܟܘܢ
ܡܢ ܕܝ ܕܩܪܐ
ܝܬܟܘܢ
ܒܛܝܒܘܬܗ
ܕܡܫܝܚܐ:
ܠܚܘܪܢ ܒܣܘܪ·
[7] ܡܐ ܕܠܝܬ ܚܘܪܢ:
ܐܠܐ ܐܢ̈ܫܝܢ ܗܘܝܢ[a]
ܕܡܕ̈ܒܕܒܝܢ
ܝܬܟܘܢ· ܘܒܥ̈ܝܢ
ܕܝܦܟܘܢ
ܒܣܘܪܗ
ܕܡܫܝܚܐ:
[8] ܐܠܐ ܐܘܦ ܐܢ·
ܐܢ̇ ܡܠܐܟ ܡܢ
ܫܡ̈ܝܐ[b] ܡܣܒܪ
ܝܬܟܘܢ ܠܒܪ ܡܢ

ܡܐ ܕܒܣܪ̈ܢ
ܝܬܟܘܢ ܚܪܡ
ܝ̇ܗܐ⁖ [9] ܗܝܟ
ܕܐܡܪ̈ܢ ܡܢ
ܩܘܕܡ· ܘܬܘܒ
ܟܕܘ ܐܢܐ
ܐܡܪ: ܡ̇ܢ[c]
ܕܡܒܣܪ̇
ܝܬܟܘܢ
ܠܒܪ ܡܢ ܡܐ
ܕܩܒܠܬܘܢ
ܝ̇ܗܐ ܚܪܡ:
[10] ܟ̈ܕܘ ܟܪ ܠܒ̈ܢܝܢܫ
ܐܢܐ ܡܦܝܣ·
ܐܘ̇ ܠܐܠܗܐ:
ܐܘ̇ ܕܡܒܥܐ[d]
ܠܒ̈ܢܝܢܫ ܐܢܐ
[e]ܒܥܐ̇ ܕܝܫܦܪ⁖[e]
ܐ̈ܠܘ[c] ܕܝ ܟܕ ܟܕܢ
ܠܒ̈ܢܝܢܫ ܗܘܝܬ
ܫܦܪ: ܐܠ̇ܘ[c] ܕܝ
ܡܢ: ܟܕܘܗ

MKS IIB, 108: **a** ܗܘܘܢ | **b** omit *seyame* | **c** omit diacritic | **d** ܒܥܐ | **e–e** *nil*

Galatians 1:10–16

F. 130r

ܕܡܫܝܚܐ
ܠܐ ܗܘܝܬ܀
[11] ܡܘܕܥ ܐܢܐ ܠܟܘܢ
ܕܝ ܐܚܝܐ
ܒܣܘܪܐ ܗܕܢ
ܕܐܬܒܣܪ
ܡܢܝ: ܕܠܝܬ
ܗܘ ܕܒܪܢܫ:
[12] ܐܘܦ ܠܐ ܓܪ
ܐܢܐ ܡܢ ܒܪܢܫ
ܠܐ ܩܒܠܬ ܠܗ·
ܘܠܐ ܠܦܝܬ:
ܐܠܐ ܒܓܠܝܢܗ
ܕܝܫܘܥ
ܕܡܫܝܚܐ:·[a]
[13] ܫܡܥܬܘܢ ܓܪ
ܗܦܟܬܝ
ܗܠܝܢ ܕܗܘܘ
ܡܢ ܩܕܡ
ܒܝܗܘܕܝܘܬܐ:
ܕܒܠ ܕܠܝܬܪܐ*[b]
ܗܘܝܬ ܪܕܦ

ܠܟܢܫܬܗ
ܕܐܠܗܐ:
ܘܗܘܝܬ ܡܚܪܒ
ܠܗ:· [14] ܘܗܘܝܬ
ܡܬܝܬܪ[c]
ܒܝܗܘܕܝܘܬܐ·
ܝܬܝܪ ܡܢ ܣܓܝ
ܒܢܝ ܫܢܝ*[d]
ܒܫܪܒܬܝ:·[e]
ܘܡܛܢܬܪ[f]
ܗܘܝܬ ܡܛܠܬܐ
ܒܡܫܠܡܢܘܬܗܘܢ[g]
ܕܐܒܗܬܝ:· [15] ܟܕ
ܕܝ ܨܒܐ ܐܠܗܐ
ܕ ܕܐܦܪܫ ܠܝ
ܡܢ ܒܛܢܗ
ܕܐܡܝ:
ܘܩܪܐ ܠܝ
ܒܛܝܒܘܬܗ
[16] ܕܢܓܠܐ ܒܪ ܒܪܗ·
ܕܒܝ
ܠܗ ܒܥܡܡܐ:

MKS IIB, 109: **a** ܡܫܝܚܐ | **b** ܡܛܪܕ | **c** ܡܬܝܬܪ | **d** ܫܢܝ | **e** ܫܪܒܬܝ | **f** ܠ ܡܛܪܬ | **g** omit *seyame* || **g** *seyame* uncertain

Galatians 1:16–23 **F. 130v**

ܫܘܐܪ ܠܐ ܐܘܕܥܬ
ܠܒܣܪ ܘܐܕܡ:
[17]ܘܠܐ ܣܠܩܬ
ܠܝܪܘܫܠܡ
ܠܘܬ ܫܠܝܚܝܐ
ܕܩܕ ܩܘܕܡܝ:
ܐܠܐ ܐܙܠܬ
ܠܥܪܒܝܐ:
ܘܬܘܒ ܗܦܟܬ
ܠܕܪܡܣܘܩ:
[18]ܘ̈ܬܘܒܢ ܡܢ
ܒܬܪ ܬܠܬ
ܫܢܝܢ ܣܠܩܬ
ܠܝܪܘܫܠܡ
ܕܐܚܡܐ ܠܟܐܦܐ:
ܘܩܘܝܬ ܠܘܬܗ
ܚܡܫܬܥܣܪ
ܝܘܡܝܢ: [19]ܠܚܘܪܢܝ
ܕܝ ܡܢ ܫܠܝܚܝܐ
ܠܐ ܚܡܝܬ ܐܠܐ
ܐܢ ܠܝܥܩܘܒ
ܐܚܘܝ ܕܡܪܢܐ:

[20]ܡܐ ܕܝ ܕܐܢܐ
ܟܬܒ ܠܟܘܢ
ܗܐ ܩܕܡ
ܐܠܗܐ ܕܠܝܬ
ܐܢܐ ܡܕܓܠ:
[21]ܘ̈ܬܘܒܢ ܐܬܝܬ
ܠܬܚܘܡܝܐ
ܕܣܘܪܝܐ
ܘܕܩܝܠܝܩܝܐ:
[22]ܘܗܘܝܬ ܕܝ
ܕܠܐ ܝܕܝܥ
ܒܐܦܝ ܠܟܢܫܬܐ
ܕܝܗܘܕܐ ܗܠܝܢ
ܕܒܡܫܝܚܐ:
[23]ܒܠܚܘܕ ܕܝ
ܗܘܘ ܫܡܥܝܢ
ܕܕ ܕܗܘܐ
ܪܕܦ ܠܢ
ܒܙܒܢ: ܟܕܘ
ܗܘ ܡܣܒܪ
ܗܝܡܢܘܬܐ
ܗܕܐ ܕܒܙܒܢ

Galatians 3:20–24 **F. 39r**

[20] ܬܠܬܝܐ ܕܝ
ܚܕ ܠܝܬ ܗܘ⁖
ܐܠܗܐ ܕܝ ܚܕ
ܐܝܬ ܗܘ⁖
[21] ܢܡܘܣܐ ܐܘܟ
ܩܐܡ ܠܩܘܒܠ
ܡܠ̈ܝ ܬܗ*[a]
ܕܐܠܗܐ⁚ ܠܐ
ܗܘܐ ܟܢ⁚ ܐܠܘ
ܓܝܪ ܐܬܝܗܒ
ܢܡܘܣ
ܕܝܟܠ ܕܝܚܝܐ⁚
ܐܘܦܠܘܣ
ܡܢ ܢܡܘܣܐ
ܗܘܐ ܝ ܙܕܩܐ⁖
[22] ܐܠܐ ܚܒܫ ܟܬܒܐ
ܟܘܠܐ ܬܚܘܬ
ܚܛܝܬܐ⁚ ܠܒܓܠ
ܕܡܢ ܡܝ̈ ܬܐ ܡܢ
ܗܝܡܢܘܬܗ
ܕܝܫܘܥ
ܡܫܝܚܐ

ܬܬܝܗܒ ܠܗܠܝܢ
ܕܡܗܝܡܢܝܢ⁖
[23] ܩܕܡ ܥܕ ܠܐ ܕܝ ܬܐܬܐ
ܗܝܡܢܘܬܐ⁚
ܬܚܘܬ
ܢܡܘܣܐ
ܗܘܝܢ ܢܛܝܪܝܢ.
ܡܬܚܒܫܝܢ
ܠܗܝܡܢܘܬܐ
ܕܥܬܝܕܐ
ܕܬܬ ܓܠܐ ܒ⁚
✝ ܒܐܚܪܝܬܗ
ܕܗܪܐ⁖
[24] ܗܘܐ ܐܘܟ
ܢܡܘܣܐ
ܦܕܓܘܓ
ܐܬܥܒܕ ܠ
ܠܘܬ ܝܫܘܥ
ܡܫܝܚܐ⁖
ܠܒܓܠ ܕܡܢ
ܗܝܡܢܘܬܐ
ܢܙܕܩ⁖

MKS IIB, 111: **a** ܡܠ̈ܝ ܬܗ

Galatians 3:25–4:2

F. 39v

[25] ܟܕܘ ܕܝ ܕܐܬܬ[a]
ܗܝܡܢܘܬܐ:
ܒܬܪ ܠܝܬܝܢ
ܬܚܘܬ ܦܕܓܘܓ:
[26] ܟܘܠܟܘܢ ܓܪ
ܒܢ̈ܘܝ ܕܐܠܗܐ
ܐܬܘܢ ܒܬܪܒܗ[b]
ܕܗܝܡܢܘܬܐ
ܕܝܫܘܥ
ܡܫܝܚܐ:
[27] ܟܘܠ ܗܠܝܢ ܓܪ
ܕܒܡܫܝܚܐ
ܐܝܢ ܐܬܥܡܕܬܘܢ·
ܡܫܝܚܐ
ܠܒܫܬܘܢ:
[28] ܠܝܬ ܝܗܘܕܝ
ܘܠܐ ܐܪܡܝ:
ܠܝܬ ܥܒܕ ܘܠܐ
ܒܪ ܚܐܪ: ܠܝܬ
ܕܟܪ ܘܢܩܒܐ:
ܟܘܠܟܘܢ ܓܪ
ܚܕ ܐܬܘܢ
ܒܝܫܘܥ
ܡܫܝܚܐ: [29] ܐܢ
ܕܝ ܐܬܘܢ
ܕܡܫܝܚܐ:
ܗܘܐ ܡܢ ܙܪܥܗ
ܕܐܒܪܗܡ
ܐܬܘܢ ܒܡܝ ܚܝ ܐ
ܝܪ̈ܬܝܢ:
ܒܘܥܕܐ
[c]ܬܠܝܬܝܐ ܕܬܘܦܘܣܝܐ:[c]
[4:1] ܐܡܪ ܐܢܐ ܕܝ
ܕܟܕ ܟܘܠ
ܐܡܬܝ
ܕܝܪܬܐ ܛܠܝܐ·
ܟܠܘܡ ܠܝܬ
ܗܘ ܡܫܬܪ
ܡܢ ܥܒܕ: ܘܗܘ
ܡܪܐ ܕܟܘܠܐ:
[2] ܐܠܐ ܬܚܘܬ
ܐܦܝܛܪܘܦܝܢ[d]
ܐܝܬ ܗܘ
ܘܦܪܢܣܝܢ:

MKS IIB, 112: **a** ܐܬܬ | **b** omit diacritic | **c–c** *nil* | **d** ܐܦܝܛܪܘܦܝܢ

Galatians 4:15–22 **F. 125r**

ܡܣܗܕ ܐܢܐ
ܓܪ ܠܟܘܢ
ܕܐܠܘ ܗܘܬ[a]
ܝܟܠܐ· ܥܝ̈ܢܝܟܘܢ
ܗܘܝܬܘܢ ܢܣ̈ܚܝܢ
ܘܝܗ̈ܒܝܢ ܠܝ:
[16] ܗܘܐ ܒܥܠܕܒܒܟܘܢ
ܐܬܥܒܕܝܬ
ܡܢ ܡܡܠܠ
ܠܟܘܢ ܩܘܫܛܐ:
[17] ܡܩ̈ܢܝܢ ܗܢܘܢ
ܠܟܘܢ ܠܐ ܛܒܐܘܬ:
ܐܠܐ ܕܝܣܓ̈ܪܘܢ
ܝܬܟܘܢ ܗܢܘܢ
ܒܥܝܢ: ܕܬܗܘܢ
ܡܩ̈ܢܝܢ ܒܗܘܢ··
[18] ܛܒ ܕܝ ܕܬܗܘܢ
ܡܩ̈ܢܝܢ ܒܛܒ̈ܬܐ
ܒܟܘܠ ܥܕܢ:
ܘܠܐ ܒܠܚܘܕ
ܟܕ ܐܢܐ ܗܘܐ
ܠܘܬܟܘܢ:

[19] ܒܢ̈ܝ ܗܠܝܢ
ܕܬܘܒ ܐܢܐ
ܡܚܒܠ ܒܟܘܢ
ܥܕܡܐ ܕܬܬܨܝܪ
ܡܫܝܚܐ ܒܓܘܟܘܢ··
[20] ܨܒܐ ܗܘܝܬ ܕܝ
ܕܐܬܐ ܟܕܘ
ܠܘܬܟܘܢ ܘܫܠܦ
ܩܠܝ: ܕܐܢܐ
ܡܬܕܘܐ ܒܟܘܢ:
[21] ܐܡܪܘ ܠܝ
ܗܠܝܢ ܕܒܥܝܢ
ܕܝܗܘܢ ܬܚܘܬ
ܢܡܘܣܐ:
ܠܝܬ ܐܬܘܢ
ܫܡ̈ܥܝܢ ܠܗ
ܠܢܡܘܣܐ:
[22] ܟܬܝܒ ܓܪ
ܕܐܒܪܗܡ
ܬܪ̈ܝܢ ܒܢܝܢ
ܗܘܐ ܠܗ:
ܚܕ ܡܢ ܐܡܬܐ·

MKS IIB, 113: **a** omit diacritic

Galatians 4:22–28 **F. 125v**

ܘܚܕ ܡܢ ܚܐܪܬܐ܀
[23] ܐܠܐ ܕܝ ܕܗܘܐ
ܡܢ ܐܡܗܬܐ܂
ܒܒܣܪܐ*[a]
ܗܘܐ ܝܠܕ:
ܗܕܝ ܕܝ ܕܗܘܐ
ܡܢ ܚܐܪܬܐ ܒܬܪܒ
ܦܝ ܣܝ ܬܐ܀ [24] ܗܠܝܢ
ܕܗܠܝܢ ܐܝܬ
ܗܬܝܢ ܡܬܪ̈ܬ ܩܝܡ܀
ܗܠܝܢ ܓܝܪ ܐܝܬ
ܗܬܝܢ ܬܪ̈ܬܝܢ
ܕܝܐܬ̈ܝܩܘ܀
ܚ̈ܕܐ ܡܢ ܛܘܪܐ
ܕܣܝܢܐ܂ ܠܥܒܕܘ
ܝܠܕܐ ܡܢ ܕܗܝ
ܗ ܓܝܪ܀ [25] ܗ ܓܝܪ ܕܝ
ܗܘ ܛܘܪܐ
ܕܣܝܢܐ
ܕܒܥܪܒܝܐ:
ܥܠܡ ܗܘ ܕܝ
ܠܗܕܐ ܕܒܕܘ܂

ܠܝܪܘܫܠܡ:
ܡܫܥܒܕܐ[b] ܗܝ
ܓܝܪ ܒܥܒܕܘܬܐ
ܥܡ ܒܢ̈ܝܗ܀
[26] ܝܪܘܫܠܡ ܕܝ
ܕܠܥܠ ܒܪܬ[c] ܚ̈ܪܝܢ
[d]ܗܝ: ܡܢ ܕܗܝ[d]
ܐܡܢ ܕܟܘܠܢ܀
[27] ܟ̈ܬܝܒ ܓܝܪ
ܒܫܥܝܐ
ܚܩܪܬܐ ܗܕܐ
ܕܠܐ ܝܠܕܐ:
ܐܪܥܡܝ
ܘܐܝ ܚܝ ܗܕܐ
ܕܠܐ ܡܚܒܠܐ܀
ܕܣܓܝ ܒܢ̈ܝܗ
ܕܡܕܒܪܬܐ܂
ܐܢ ܓܝܪ ܕܗܕܐ
ܕܠܗ ܓܒܪ:
[28] ܐ̈ܢܬܘܢ ܕܝ ܐܚ̈ܝܢܐ
ܟܐܝܣܚܩ ܒܢ̈ܝܢ
ܐܬܘܢ ܒܡܠܝ ܚܝ܀

MKS IIB, 114: **a** ܒܕ ܒܣܪܐ | **b** ܡܫܬܥܒܕܐ | **c** omit diacritic | **d–d** ܗܕܝ ܡܢ ܕܗܝ

Galatians 4:29–5:4 — F. 128r

29 ܐܠܐ ܗܝܟ ܡܐ
ܕܒܝܢ: ܗܕܢ
ܕܗܘܐ ܡܠܝܕ
ܒܒܣܪܐ
ܗܘܐ ܪܕܦ
ܠܢ ܕܗܘܐ
ܒܪܘܚܐ:
ܗܟܢ ܐܘܦ ܟܕܘ:
30 ܐܠܐ ܡܐ
ܐܡܪ ܟܬܒܐ:
ܐܦܩ ܠܐܡܬܐ
ܘܠܒܪܗ: ܠܐ
ܓܝܪ ܝܪܬ ܒܪܗ
ܕܐܡܬܐ.
ܥܡ ܒܪܗ
ܕܚܐܪܬܐ:
31 ܠܒܕܠ ܒܢ
ܐܚܝܢ· ܠܝܬ
ܐܢܢ ܒܢܝܗ
ܕܐܡܬܐ:
ܐܠܐ ܕܚܐܪܬܐ:
5:1 ܒܚܐܪܘܬܐ
ܚܪܪ ܠܬܢ
ܡܫܝܚܐ:
ܩܘܡܘ ܐܘܢ ܘܠܐ[a]
ܬܘܒ[b] ܒܢܝܪ
[c]ܕܥܒܕܘ ܠܐ[c]
ܬܬܐܣܪܘܢ:
2 ܗܐ ܐܢܐ
ܦܘܠܘܣ ܐܡܪ
ܠܟܘܢ: ܕܐܢ
ܬܓܙܪܘܢ:
ܡܫܝܚܐ ܟܠܘܡ
ܠܐ ܡܗܢܐ ܠܟܘܢ:
3 ܡܣܗܕ ܐܢܐ ܕܝ
ܬܘܒ ܠܟܘܠ
ܒܪܢܫ ܕܡܬܓܙܪ:[d]
ܕܚܝܒ[e]* ܗܘ
ܕܢܥܒܕ ܟܘܠ
ܢܡܘܣܐ:
4 ܐܬܒܛܠܬܘܢ ܡܢ
ܡܫܝܚܐ: ܐܝܠܝܢ[f]
ܕܡܢ ܢܡܘܣܐ
ܐܬܘܢ ܡܙܕܕܩܝܢ:

MKS IIB, 115: **a** ܠܐ | **b** ܬܘܒܢ | **c–c** ܥܒܕܘܬܐ | **d** ܕܡܬܓܙܪ | **e** ܕܚܝܒ | **f** ܗܠܝܢ

Galatians 5:4–12 F. 128v

ܢܦܠܬܘܢ ܡܢ
ܛܝܒܘܬܐ܀
[5]ܐܢܢ ܓܝܪ ܒܪܘܚܐ
ܡܢ ܗܝܡܢܘ
ܣܒܪ ܕܝ ܕܙܟܘ
ܐܢܢ ܡܣܟܝܢ܀
[6]ܒܝܫܘܥ[a] ܓܝܪ
ܡܫܝܚܐ܂ ܠܐ
ܓܙܘܪܬܐ ܢܚܠܐ
ܥܠܘܡ: ܘܠܐ
ܥܘܪܠܘܬܐ܂ ܐܠܐ
ܗܝܡܢܘܬܐ
ܕܡܬܥܒܕ ܚܝܠܐ
ܡܚܒܬܐ:
[7]ܪܗܛܬ ܗܘܝܬܘܢ
ܕܫܦܝܪ: ܡܢ[b] ܟܠܐ
ܠܟܘܢ ܕܠܐ
ܬܬܦܝܣܘܢ
ܠܩܘܫܬܐ:
[8]ܐܦܝܣܬܟܘܢ.
ܠܐ ܡܢ ܕܝ
ܕܩܪܐ ܠܟܘܢ܀

[9]ܕܝ ܢܚܡܝܪ ܚܡܝܪ܁
ܟܘܠܗ ܓܒܝܠܬܐ
ܡܚܡܥ:
[10]ܐܢܐ ܕܝ ܪܚܝܨ
ܥܠܝܟܘܢ ܒܡܪܐ
ܕܟܠܘܡ ܚܘܪܢ
ܠܐ ܬܬܚܫܒܘܢ:
ܕܝ ܕܝ ܕܡܕܘܕܒ
ܠܟܘܢ ܢܛܥܘܢ
ܕܝܟܘܢ ܟܘܠ
ܡܢ ܕܗܘܐ:
[11]ܐܢܐ ܕܝ ܐܚܝܐ:
ܐܢ ܓܙܘܪܬܐ
ܟܕ ܟܕܘ ܐܢܐ
ܡܟܪܙ: ܠܡܐ
ܟܘܕ ܐܢܐ
ܡܬܪܕܦ:
ܐܪܐ ܒܛܠ
ܡܟܫܘܠܗ
ܕܝ ܨܠܝܒܐ· [12]ܠܘܝ
ܐܘܦ ܢܦܣܩܘܢ
ܗܠܝܢ ܕܡܕܘܕܒܝܢ
ܠܟܘܢ܀

MKS IIB, 116: **b** omit diacritic || **a** MS *sic*; *expectaveris* ܒܝܫܘܥ

Galatians 5:24–6:4

F. 46r

[24]ܗܠܝܢ ܕܝ̈
ܕܗܢܘܢ ܕܡܪܢܐ
ܝܫܘܥ ܡܫܝܚܐ:
ܒܣܪܐ ܝ̱ ܨܠܒܘ
ܥܡ ܚܫ̈ܘܫܘܝ
ܘܬܐܘ̈ܬܢܬܗ:
[25]ܐ̤ܢ ܒܪܘܚܐ ܐܝܢ
ܚ̈ܝܝܢ. ܠܪܘܚܐ
ܢܗܐ ܐܘܦ
ܥܠܩ̈ܝܢ: [26]ܠܐ
ܢܬܚܒܕ
ܕܬܫܒܚܐ
ܙܢܢܐ: ܡܓܪ̈ܝܢ
ܩ̈ܠܝܢ ܠܩܠܝܢ:
ܘܡܩܢܝܢ ܩ̈ܠܝܢ
ܒܩܠܝܢ:
[6:1]ܐ̤ܚܝܢ· ܐܘܦ
ܐܢ ܢܬܕܒܩ
ܒܪܢܫ ܡܢܟܘܢ
ܒܐܥܪܟܘ ܕܟܠܘܡ:
ܐܢܬܘܢ ܗܠܝܢ
ܕܒܪܘܚܐ·

ܗܘܘ ܡܫ̈ܟܠܠܝܢ
ܠ̈ܓܒܝܫܗ ܕܕܢ
ܒܪܘܚ ܕܚܢܢܘ:
ܝ̱ ܦܐ ܠܓܪܡܟ
ܕܠܐ ܐܘܦ ܐܬ
ܬܬܢܣܐ:
[2]ܘܛܥ̈ܢܐ ܕܩܠܝܒܢ
ܒܩܠܝܢ ܗܘܘ
ܠܚܒ̈ܝܢ: ܘܟܕܢ[a]
ܐܬܘܢ ܡܫ̈ܠܡܝܢ
ܢܡܘܣܗ
ܕܡܫܝܚܐ: [3]ܐܢ
ܓܪ ܣܒܪ
ܐܢܫ ܕܗܘ[b]
ܟܠܘܡ: ܘܟܠܘܡ
ܠܝܬ ܗܘ:
ܢܫܒܬܗ ܗܘ̱
ܡܠܦܐ:[c] [4]ܥܒܕܗ̱
ܕ̈ܝ ܕ ܓܪܡܗ
ܢܗܐ ܒܩܠ
ܐܢܫ ܒܢܦ: ܘܒܟܢ
ܬܫܒܚܬܗ[d]

MKS IIB, 117: **a** ܘܗܟܕܢ | **b** ܒܗܘ | **c** omit diacritic | **d** ܬܫܒܚܬܐ

Galatians 6:4–12 F. 46v

ܬܗܐ ܒܓܪܡܗ
ܒܠܚܘܕ· ܘܠܐ
ܠܘܬ ܚܒܪܗ܇
[5]ܟܿܠ ܐܢܫ ܓܪ
ܛܥܝܢ ܡܘܒܠܗ
ܕܓܪܡܗ:
[6]ܝܗܐ ܕܝ
ܡܫܬܬܦ ܕܢ
ܕܫܡܥ ܡܠܬܐ·
ܠܕܢ ܕܡܫܡܥ
ܠܗ̇ ܒܟܘܠ ܛܒ̈ܝܢ܇
[7]ܠܐ ܬܛ̈ܥܘܢ:
ܐܠܗܐ ܠܐ
ܡܬܓܚܟ܇ ܡܐ
ܓܪ ܕܙܪܥ
ܓܒܪ: ܝܬܗ ܗܘ
ܚܨܕ:܇ [8]ܕܕܢ ܕܙܪܥ
ܒܒܣܪܗ܇ ܡܢ
ܒܣܪܗ ܗܘ
ܚܨܕ ܬܪܦܘ:
ܕܢ ܕܝ ܕܙܪܥ
ܒܪܘܚܐ:

ܡܢ ܪܘܚܐ
ܚܨܕ ܚܝܝܢ
ܕܠܥܠܡ: [9]ܡܢ
ܥܒ̈ܕܝܢ ܕܝ
ܛܒ̈ܬܐ· ܠܐ ܢܗܐ
ܡܬܒܥܝܢ:
ܒܩܪܘܣܗܝܢ
ܓܪ ܐܢ ܚܝ̈ܕܝܢ
ܕܠܐ ܡܬܪܫܠܝܢ܇
[10]ܗܿܘܐ ܐܘܢ ܒܕ
ܒܟܢ [a]ܩܪܘܣܐ
ܢܥܒܕ ܛܒ̈ܢ
ܠܘܬ ܟܘܠܐ܇
ܚܕ· ܒܟܢܐ ܕܝ
ܠܒ̈ܢܝ ܒܝܬܗ̇
ܕܗܝܡܢܘܬܐ:
[11]ܚܿܙܘ ܒܕ ܓܠܝܘ[b]
ܗܠܝܢ ܟܬ̈ܒܝܢ
ܟܬܒܬ ܠܟܘܢ
ܒܐܝܕܝ ܕܝܠܝ:
[12]ܟܘܠ ܗܠܝܢ ܕܒܥܝܢ
ܕܝܫܦܪܘܢ

MKS IIB, 118: **a** omit diacritic | **b** ܕܓܠܝܘ

Ephesians 1:18–2:2 **F. 63v**

ܕܬܫܒܘܚܬܗ̇
ܕܝܪܘܬܬܗ
ܒܩܕ̈ܝܫܝܐ܆ [19]ܘܡܐ
ܗܘ ܝܬܝܪܘܬܐ
ܕܪܒܘܬܐ ܕܚܝܠܗ
ܠܘܬܟܘܢ܂
ܠܘܬ ܗܠܝܢ
ܕܡܗ̈ܝܡܢܝܢ܆
ܗܝܟ ܡܥܒܠܘܬܐ
ܕܠܒܘܒܬܐ
ܕܚܝܠܗ:
[20]ܗܕܐ ܕܥܒܕ
ܒܡܫܝܚܐ܆
ܕܐܩܝܡܗ ܡܢ
ܒܝܢ ܡܝܬ̈ܝܐ:
ܘܐܘܬܒ ܝܬܗ
ܡܢ ܝܡܝܢܗ
ܒܓܘ ܫܘܡܝܐ:
[21]ܠܥܠ ܡܢ ܟܘܠ
ܪܫܘ ܘܫܘܠܛܢܘ
ܘܚܝܠ
ܘܡܪܘ:

ܘܠܥܠ ܡܢ
ܟܘܠ ܫܡ
ܕܡܫܬܡܗ̇: ܠܐ
ܒܠܚܘܕ ܒܗܕܝܢ
ܥܠܡܐ܆ ܐܠܐ[a]
ܐܘܦ ܒܗ̇ܘ
ܕܥܬܝܕ: [22]ܘܟܘܠܐ
ܫܥܒܕ ܬܚܘܬ
ܪ̈ܓܠܘܝ܆: ܘܝܬܗ
ܝܗܒ ܪܫ
ܥܠ ܟܘܠܗ̇[b]
ܠܥܕܬܐ܂ [23]ܕܗ̇ܝ
ܕܗܘ̱ ܦܘ ܓܪܗ:
ܡܘܠܝܐ ܗܕܝܢ
ܕܟܘܠܐ ܒܟܘܠܐ
ܡܬܡܠܝܐ:
[2:1]ܘ̇ܐܢܬܘܢ ܕܗܘܝܬܘܢ
ܡܝ̈ܬܝܢ
ܒܐܫܕܒ̈ܘܬܟܘܢ:[c]
[2]ܗܠܝܢ ܕܒܗܝܢ
ܗܠܟ̈ܬܘܢ ܒܗܝܢ·
ܗܝܟ ܬܘܩܢܗ

MKS IIB, 128: **a** ܐܠܐ | **b** omit diacritic || **c** MS *sic*; *expectaveris* ܒܐܫܪ̈ܒܘܬܟܘܢ. Cf. f. 63r II.6.

Ephesians 2:2–8 F. 63r

ܕܗܕܢ ܥܠܡܐ܀
ܘܗܝܟ ܐܪܟܘܢܐ
ܕܫܘܠܛܢܘܬܗ
ܕܐܐܪ ܕܪܘܚܐ:
ܗܕܝ ܕܝ[a] ܕܟܕܘ
ܡܥܡܠ ܒܒܢ̈ܝܐ
ܕܠܐ ܡܬܦܝ̈ܣܝܢ܀
[3]ܗܠܝܢ ܕܥܡܗܘܢ
ܐܘܦ ܐܢܢ ܟܠܢ
ܗܬܐ̈ܦܟܝܢ[b] ܒܗܢ:
ܒܬܪܓܝ̈ܓܬܗ[c]
ܕܒܣܪܢ:
ܕܗܘ̈ܝܢ ܥܒ̈ܕܝܢ
ܨܒܝܢܘ
ܕܒܣܪܐ
ܘܕܡ̈ܚܫܒܬܐ:[c]
ܘܗܘ̈ܝܢ[c] ܗܡ
ܦܣܘܣܘ[d] ܒܢ̈ܝܢ
ܕܪ ܟܘܠ ܗܝܟ
ܕܐܘܦ ܫܪܟܐ:
[4]ܐ̤ܠܗܐ ܕܝ ܕܗܘ
ܥܬܝܪ ܒܪ̈ܚܡܘܗܝ:

ܠܒܪ̇ܢܫ ܗܘ ܟܢܐ
ܕܚܒܬܗ ܗܕܐ
ܕܐܚܒ ܠܬܝ:
[5]ܘܟܡܐ ܕܗܘ̈ܝܢ
ܡܝ̈ܬܝܢ
ܒܐܫܬܒܘ̈ܬܝ:[e]
ܐܚܝ ܬܝ̈ ܥܡ
ܡܫܝܚܐ: ܒܛܝܒܘ
ܒܪ ܐܬܦܪ̈ܩܝܢ܀
[6]ܘܐܩܝܡܢ[f] ܥܡܗ:
ܘܐܘܬܒܢ[g] ܥܡܗ
ܒܫܡܝܐ
ܒܝܫܘܥ
ܡܫܝܚܐ: [7]ܕܢܘܕܥ
ܒܥܠܡ̈ܝܐ ܕܐ̈ܬܝܢ
ܬܪܘܬܐ
ܕܒܘܬܪܐ
ܕܛܝܒܘܬܗ
ܒܒܣܝܡܘ ܥܠܝܢ
ܒܝܫܘܥ
ܡܫܝܚܐ: [8]ܒܛܝܒܘ
ܒܪ ܐܬܦܪ̈ܩܝܢ

MKS IIB, 129: **a** omit | **c** omit *seyame* | **d** ܦܣܘܣܘ | **f** omit diacritic | **g** ܘܐܬܒܢ || **b** MS *sic* | **e** MS *sic*; *expectaveris* ܒܐܫܬܒܘܫܬܝ. Cf. f. 63v II.19.

Ephesians 4:14–19 **F. 56v**

ܒܪܡܘܬܗܘܢ
ܕܒܢ̈ܝܢܫܐ·
ܒܡܬܠܬܠܘ:
ܠܣܠܘܦܐ
ܕܛܥܘܬܐ:[a]
[15] ܢܗܐ ܕܝ ܡܩ̈ܫܛܝܢ:
ܒܚܒܐ ܢܥܒܕ
ܒܗ ܒܟܠܐ: ܡܢ̇[b]
ܕܗܘ ܪ̇ܝܫܐ
ܡܫܝܚܐ: [16] ܗܕܝܢ
ܕܡܢܗ ܟܘܠ
ܦܘ ܓܪܐ
ܡܬܠܚܡ
ܘܪ̇ܒܐ ܒܟܘܠ
ܓܨܐ ܕܡܬܦܩܕܐ
ܒܟܠܘ:
ܒܡܫܚܬܐ
ܕܟܘܠ ܚܕ ܘܚܕ.
ܡܢ ܐܒ̈ܪܝܐ.
ܥܒܝܕܗ ܕܦܘ ܓܪܐ
ܗܘ ܡܬܒܢܐ.
ܠܒܢܝܢܐ ܕܠܗ
ܒܚܒܐ:

[17] ܗ̇ܕܐ ܐܘܢ ܐܡܪ
ܐܢ̇ܐ ܘܡܣܗܕ.
ܒܡܪ̇ܐ: ܕܟܘܕ
ܠܐ ܬܗܘܢ
ܡܗ̈ܠܟܝܢ
ܗܝܟ ܕܡܢܢ̈ܐ
ܡܗ̈ܠܟܝܢ·
ܒܪܝܩܘܬܐ
ܕܬܪ̈ܥܝܬܗܘܢ:
[18] ܘܡܚ̈ܫܟܝܢ
ܒܡܚ̈ܫܒܬܗܘܢ:[c]
ܕܗܘܝܢ ܢܘܟܪ̈ܝܢ
ܡܢ ܚ̈ܝܝܐ
ܕܐܠܗܐ
ܠܒܓܠ ܒܥܝܘܬ
ܐܒܪܘܬܗܘܢ
ܕܒܠܒܗܘܢ:
ܠܒܓܠ
ܒܥܘܪܘܬܐ
ܕܠܒܗܘܢ: [19] ܗܠܝܢ
ܕܐܡܪ̈ܥܘ
ܘܡܣܪ̈ܘ

MKS IIB, 130: **a** ܒܛܥܘܬܐ | **b** omit diacritic | **c** omit *seyame*

Ephesians 4:19–27

F. 56r

ܒܪܡܗܘܢ
ܠܢܦܫܝ ܘܐܬܐ·
ܠܡܥܒܕܗ
ܕܟܠܗ
ܡܣܐܒܘܬܐ
ܒܥܝܢ ܗܘܢ:
[20] ܐܢܬܘܢ ܕܝ ܠܐ
ܟܢ ܝܠܦܬܘܢ
ܠܡܫܝܚܐ:
[21] ܐܢ ܕܝ ܫܡܥܬܘܢ
ܠܗ· ܘܒܗ
ܝܠܦܬܘܢ: ܗܝܟ
ܕܗܘ ܩܘܫܛܐ
ܒܝܫܘܥ:
[22] ܫܠܚܘܢ ܠܗܘܢ
ܠܗܦܘܟܝܗܘܢ
ܩܕܡܝ: ܠܒܪܢܫܐ
ܥܬܝܩܐ· ܗܘ ܕ
ܕܡܬܚܒܠ ܗܝܟ
ܬܐܘܝܬܐ
ܕܐܛܥܝܘܬܐ:
[23] ܐܬܚܕܬܘ ܕܝ
ܒܪܘܚܐ
ܕܬܪܥܝܬܟܘܢ:
[24] ܘܠܒܫܘܢ
ܒܪܢܫܐ ܚܕܬܐ
ܗܘ ܕܐܠܗܐ
ܐܬܒܪܝ
ܒܟܐܢܘ ܘܒܚܣܝܕܘ
ܕܩܘܫܛܐ:
[25] ܠܒܕܠ ܟܢ
ܫܒܘܩܘ ܕܫܩܪܐ
ܘܡܠܠܘ ܩܘܫܛܐ
ܟܠ ܐܢܫ ܥܡ
ܚܒܪܗ: ܕܐܢܢ
ܗܕܡܝܢ ܚܕ
ܕܚܕ:[a] [26] ܪܓܙܘ·
ܐܠܐ ܠܐ ܬܚܛܘܢ:
ܫܡܫܐ[b] ܠܐ
ܝܥܪܒ ܥܠ
ܥܠ ܪܘܓܙܟܘܢ:
[27] ܘܐܦ ܠܐ
ܬܬܠܘܢ ܐܬܪ
ܠܣܛܢܐ:

MKS IIB, 131: **a** ܥܠܝܟ || **b** The *yod* may be a secondary addition.

Ephesians 5:8–16 F. 59v

ܗܘܝܬܘܢ ܓܝܪ
ܒܪܝܢ ܩܒܠ:
ܒܪܘ ܕܝ ܢܗܘܪ
ܒܡܪܢܐ: ܗܟܝܢ[a]
ܟܒܢܝ ܕܢܗܘܪܐ
[b]ܗܠܟܘ: [9]ܦܐܪܘܝ[b]
ܓܝܪ ܕܢܗܘܪܐ
ܒܟܘܠ ܛܒܘ[c]
ܘܙܕܩܘ ܘܩܘܫܛ:
[10]ܒܕܩܝܢ[d] ܡܗ
ܕܫܦܪ ܠܡܪܢܐ:
[11]ܘܠܐ ܬܗܘܢ
ܡܫܬܘܬܦܝܢ
ܠܥܒܕܝܐ[e]
ܕܡܟܠܐ ܕܠܝܬ
ܒܗܘܢ ܦܐܪܝܢ:
ܡܠܘܢ ܕܝ ܐܘܦ
ܗܘܘ ܡܟܣܝܢ:
[12]ܡܗ ܓܝܪ ܕܡܬܥܒܕ
ܡܢܗܘܢ
ܒܛܘܡܪܝܢ:
ܣܢܐ ܗܘ
[f]ܐܘܦ ܠܡܐܡܪ:
[13]ܟܘܠ ܡܗ ܕܝ
ܕܡܬܟܣܝܢ ܡܢ
ܢܗܘܪܐ ܡܬܓܠܐ:[f]
ܟܘܠ ܡܗ ܓܝܪ
ܕܡܬܓܠܐ
[g]ܢܗܘܪ ܗܘ:[g]
[14]ܠܒܓܠ ܕܝܢ
ܗܘ ܐܡܪ:
ܩܘܡ ܐܬ
ܕܕܡܟ[h] ܘܩܘܡ
ܡܢ ܒܝܢ ܡܝܬܝܐ
ܘܡܢܗܪ
ܒܟ ܡܫܝܚܐ:
[15]ܚܙܘ ܐܘܝ ܗܟܝܢ
ܙܗܝܪܐܝܬ
ܬܗܘܢ ܡܗܠܟܝܢ:
ܠܐ ܗܟܝܢ ܕܠܐ
ܚܟܝܡܝܢ: ܐܠܐ
ܗܟܝܢ ܚܟܝܡܝܢ:
[16]ܙܒܢܝܢ ܡܙܒܢܘܐ[i]
ܕܝܘܡܝܐ ܒܝܫܝܢ
ܗܢܘܢ:

ܒ

MKS IIB, 132: **a** *nil* | **b–b** *nil* | **c** *nil* | **d** omit *seyame* | **e** ܒܥܒܕܝܐ | **f–f** ܐܘܦ [...] ܢܗܘܪܐ / [......] / [...] ܟܘܠ / ܬܗܘܢ | **g–g** *nil* | **h** ܒܕܡܟ | **i** ܡܙܒܢܘܐ || Side contains quire number.

Ephesians 5:17–24 **F. 59r**

[17]ܠܩܒܝܠ ܟܢ
ܠܐ ܬܬܥܒܕܘܢ
ܕܠܐ ܡܕ̈ܥܝܢ:
ܐܠܐ ܗܘܘ
ܡܬܕ̈ܥܝܢ ܡܐ
ܗܘ ܨܒܝܢܗ
ܕܡܪܐ: [18]ܘܠܐ
ܬܗܘܘܢ ܪ̈ܘܝܢ
ܒܚܡܪܐ ܗܕܢ
ܕܒܗ ܒܣܘܛܝܐ:.*[a]
ܐ̈ܠܐ ܡܠܝܢ ܗܘܘ
ܡܬܡ̈ܠܝܢ
ܒܪܘܚܐ ܕܩܘܕܫܐ:
[19]ܡܡ̈ܠܠܝܢ ܠܓܪܡܟܘܢ
ܒܡܙܡ̈ܘܪܝܢ ܘܬܫ̈ܒܚܢ·
ܘܙܡܝ̈ܪܢ
ܕܪܘܚ· ܒܠܒܒܟܘܢ
ܠܡܪܐ:
[20]ܡܫ̈ܬܘܕܝܢ
ܒܟܠ ܙܒܢ ܥܠ
ܟܠܐ ܒܫܡܗ
ܕܡܪܢ ܝܫܘܥ
ܡܫܝܚܐ:

ܠܐܒܐ ܘܐܠܗܐ:
[21]ܡܫ̈ܬܥܒܕܝܢ
ܦܠܓܟܘܢ ܠܦܠܓ
ܒܕܚܠܬܗ
ܕܡܫܝܚܐ:
[22]ܢ̈ܫܝܐ ܠܓܒ̈ܪܝܗܝܢ[b]
ܕܝܠܗܝܢ ܝܗܘܢ
ܡܫ̈ܬܥܒܕܢ ܗܝܟ
ܕܠܡܪܐ: [23]ܠܩܒܝܠ
ܕ ܓܒܪܐ ܗܘ
ܪ̈ܝܫܗ ܕܐܢܬܬܐ:
ܗܝܟ ܕܐܘܦ
ܡܫܝܚܐ ܗܘ
ܪ̈ܝܫܗ ܕܥܕܬܐ:
ܘܗܘ ܡܚܝܢܗ
ܕܓܘ ܓܒܪܐ: [24]ܐܠܐ
ܗܝܟ ܡܐ
ܕܥܕܬܐ
ܡܫܬܥܒܕܐ
ܠܡܫܝܚܐ· ܗܟܢ
ܐܘܦ ܢ̈ܫܝܐ
ܠܓܒ̈ܪܝܗܝܢ·

MKS IIB, 133: **a** ܪܣܘܛܝܐ | **b** omit *seyame*

Philippians 2:12–19 — F. 60v

ܘܒܐܪܬܬܘ
ܗܘܘ ܚܫܠܝܢ
ܚܝ̈ܝܟܘܢ܀ [13] ܐܠܗܐ
ܓܪ ܗܘ ܗܘܕܝܢ
ܕܡܥܒܥܠ ܒܢ
ܐܘܦ ܕܨܒܝ ܒܟܢ·
ܘܕܢܥܒܥܠ ܒܠ [a]
ܛܒ ܒܨܒܝܢܐ:
[14] ܒܟܠܐ ܗܘܘ
ܥܒܕܝܢ ܠܒܪ
ܡܢ ܪ̈ܛܢܝܢ ܘܣܦ̈ܩܝܢ܀
[15] ܠܒܕܝܠ
ܕܬܬܚ̈ܒܕܘܢ
ܦܨܝ̈ܢ ܒܠܐ
ܘܬܡܢܥܝܢ:
ܒܢ̈ܝ ܕܐܠܗܐ
ܦ̈ܨܝܢ ܡܨܥ ܒܝܢ
ܕܪ ܡܥܩܡ
ܘܡܗܦܟܝܢ܀ ܡܢ
ܕܒܗܘܢ ܬܗܘܢ
ܡܬܚ̈ܙܝܢ ܗܝܟ
ܢܗܘ̈ܪܝܢ ܒܥܠܡܐ:

[16] ܝ̈ܬܕܝܢ ܡܠܐ
ܕܚܝ̈ܝܢ:
ܠܫܒܘܚܐ ܠܝ
ܠܝܘܡܗ
ܕܡܫܝܚܐ܀
ܕܠܐ ܠܪܝܩܘ
ܪܗܛܬ· ܘܠܐ
ܠܪܝܩܘ ܠܐܝܬ:
[17] ܐܠܐ ܐܘܦ ܐܠܘܬ
ܐܢܐ ܡܬܢܣܟܠ
ܥܠ ܢܟܣܬܐ
ܘܬܫܡܫܬܐ
ܕܗܝܡܢܘܬܟܘܢ:
ܚܕܐ [b] ܐܢܐ
ܘܡܬܚܕܐ ܥܡ
ܟܘܠܟܘܢ܀ [18] ܗܕܐ [b]
ܕܝ ܐܘܦ ܐܢܬܘܢ
ܚܕܘ ܘܐܬܚܕܘ
ܥܡܝ: [19] ܡܣܒܪ
ܐܢܐ ܕܝ ܒܡܪܝܐ
ܝܫܘܥ
ܕܛܝܡܬܐܘܣ

MKS IIB, 139: **a** ܡܢ | **b** omit diacritic

Philippians 2:19–26 F. 60r

ܒܡܪܢ ܢܫܠܚ
ܠܟܘܢ܆ ܠܛܝܡܬܐ
ܕܐܘܦ ܐܢܐ
ܬܬܘܒ ܢܦܫܝ·
ܒܡܕܥ ܕܐܢܐ
ܡܢ ܡܕܡ ܕܥܠ
ܕܝܠܟܘܢ܀ [20] ܠܝܬ
ܠܝ ܓܒܪ ܐܚܪ
ܕܗܘ ܫܘܐ[a]
ܠܢܦܫܝ: ܗܕܝ
ܕܝܢ ܘܦ ܡܫܬܛܠܬ
ܥܠ ܕܝܠܟܘܢ܀
[21] ܟܘܠܐ ܓܝܪ
ܕܓܪܡܗܘܢ
ܒܥܝܢ ܘܠܐ
ܕܝܫܘܥ
ܡܫܝܚܐ܀
[22] ܒܢܘܣܝܘܢ ܕܝ
ܡܟܪܝܢ[b] ܐܢܬܘܢ.
ܕܗܝܟ ܒܪ ܠܐܒܘܗܝ
ܥܡܝ ܫܡܫ
ܒܣܒܪܬܐ܀

[23] ܠܗܕܢ ܐܘܢ
ܐܢܐ ܡܣܒܪ
ܕܢܫܠܚ ܠܘܬܟܘܢ܆
ܟܪ ܚܙܬܗ ܒܕ
ܡܣܒܪܐ ܡܢ
ܕܠܘܬܝ܀ [24] ܪܚܝܨ
ܐܢܐ ܕܝ ܒܡܪܐ
ܕܐܘܦ ܐܢܐ
ܒܡܪܢ ܢܬܐ܀
[25] ܐܘܟܬ ܕܝ
ܐܬܚܫܒܬ
ܠܐܦܦܪܘܕܝܛܘܣ
ܐܚܘܢ ܘܒܪ
ܥܡܠܬܝ: ܘܒܪ
ܦܠܚܘܬܝ:
ܠܟܘܢ ܕܝ ܫܠܝܚ
ܘܫܡܫ ܠܝ ܘܪܚ·
ܕܫܠܝܚܗ
ܠܘܬܟܘܢ܆ [26] ܡܛܠ
ܠܟܠ ܕܗܘܐ
ܡܬܚܡܕ ܕܚܙܐ
ܠܟܘܠܟܘܢ:

MKS IIB, 140: **a** omit diacritic | **b** omit *seyame* || Side contains quire number.

Colossians 4:6–11 F. 62v

ܗܝܟ ܢܦܠ ܠܟܘܢ
ܕܬܗܘܢ ܡܬ̈ܝܒܝܢ
ܠܟܘܠ ܐܢܫ
ܐܢܫ: [7] ܡܐ
ܕܠܘܬܝ ܟܘܠܐ
ܡܘܕܥ ܠܟܘܢ
ܛܘܟܝܩܘܣ
ܐܚܘܢ ܚܒܝܒܐ:
ܘܡܗܝܡܢܐ
ܫܡܫܐ ܘܚܒܪܢ
ܒܡܪܐ: [8] ܗܕܝܢ
ܕܫܠܚܬ ܠܘܬܟܘܢ
ܥܠܝܗ̇ ܥܠ ܗܕܐ:
ܠܡܕܥ ܕܬܕܥܘܢ
ܡܐ ܕܠܘܬܢ·
ܘܢܝܚ
ܠܒ̈ܒܝܟܘܢ: [9] ܥܡ
ܐܘܢܝܣܝܡܘܣ
ܡܗܝܡܢܐ
ܘܚܒܝܒܐ ܐܚܘܢ:
ܗܕܝܢ ܕܗܘ
ܡܢܟܘܢ:

ܟܘܠܐ ܗܢܝܢ
ܡܘܕܥܝܢ ܠܟܘܢ
ܡܐ ܕܗܟܐ:
[10] ܫܐܠ ܒܫܠܡܟܘܢ
ܐܪܝܣܛܪܟܘܣ
ܒܪ ܫܒܝܬܝ:
ܘܡܪܩܘܣ
ܒܪ ܕܕܗ
ܕܒܪܢܒܣ:
ܗܕܝܢ ܕܢܣܒܬܘܢ
ܥܠ ܕܦܩܕܗ
ܦܩܘܕܝܢ [a] ܐܢ
ܐܬܐ ܠܘܬܟܘܢ
ܩܒܠܘ ܝܬܗ:
[11] ܘܝܫܘܥ ܗܕܝܢ
ܕܡܬܐܡܪ
ܝܘܣܛܘܣ:
ܗܠܝܢ ܕܗܢܝܢ
ܡܢ ܓܙܘܪܬܐ:
ܗܠܝܢ ܒܠܚܘܕ
ܥܡܝ ܦܠܚܘܬܝ
ܗܢܝܢ ܠܡܠܟܘܬܗ

MKS IIB, 155: **a** ܦܩܘܕܝ

Colossians 4:11–17 F. 62r

ܕܐܠܗܐ: ܗܠܝܢ
ܕܐܬܥܒܕܘ
ܠܝ ܦܝܣܘ ܟܝ:
[12] ܫܐܠ ܒܫܠܡܟܘܢ
ܐܦܦܪܣ
ܗܘ ܕܡܢܟܘܢ.
ܥܒܕܗ ܕܝܫܘܥ
ܡܫܝܚܐ: ܒܟܘܠ
ܙܒ ܡܬܟܬܫ
ܥܠ ܕܝܠܟܘܢ
ܒܨܠܘ̈ܬܐ:
ܕܬܩܘܡܘܢ[a]
ܫܠ̈ܡܝܢ ܘܡ̈ܫܡܠܝܢ
ܒܟܘܠ ܨܒܝܢܗ
ܕܐܠܗܐ:
[13] ܣܗܕ ܐܢܐ ܓܪ
ܥܠܘܝ ܕܐܝܬ ܠܗ
ܡܥܘܫ ܣܓܝ
ܥܠ ܕܝܠܟܘܢ:
ܘܥܠ ܗܠܝܢ
ܕܒܠܕܝܩܝܐ
ܐܚ̈ܝܐ:[a]

ܘܕܗܠܝܢ
ܕܒܝܪܘܦܘܠܝܣ:·
[14] ܫܐܠ ܒܫܠܡܟܘܢ
ܠܘܩܣ ܐܣܝܐ
ܚܒܝܒܐ· ܘܕܝܡܣ:
[15] ܫܐܠ̈ܘ ܒܫܠܡܗܘܢ
ܕܐܚ̈ܝܐ[a] ܗܠܝܢ
ܕܒܠܕܝܩܝܐ
ܘܕܢܘܡܦܐ:
ܘܕܟܢܫܬܐ
ܕܒܒܝܬܗܘܢ:·
[16] ܘܟܕ ܬܬܩܪܐ[b]
ܐܓܪܬܐ ܠܘܬܟܘܢ.
ܥܒ̈ܕܘ ܕܐܦ
ܒܟܢܫܬܐ
ܕܠܕܝܩܝܐ
ܬܬܩܪܐ:·
ܘܗܕܐ ܕܡܢ
ܠܕܝܩܝܐ ܩܪ̈ܘ
ܐܦ ܐܢܬܘܢ:·
[17] ܘܐܡܪ̈ܘ[c]
ܕܒܝܪܘܦܘܠܝܣ:·

MKS IIB, 156: **a** omit *seyame* | **b** ܬܬܩܪܐ | **c** ܘܐܡܪܘ || **b** MS *sic*; *lapsus calami*; *expectaveris* ܬܬܩܪܐ

Colossians 4:17–18; 1 Thessalonians 1:1–3 F. 57v

ܚܙܝ ܬܫܡܫܬܐ
ܗܕܐ ܕܩܒܠܬ
ܒܡܪܐ· ܬܫܠܡܝܢ
ܝܬܗ̇:[a] [18] ܫܐܠ
ܫܠܡܐ ܕܐܝܕܝ[b]
ܕܝܠܝ ܦܘܠܘܣ:
ܗܘܘ ܡܬܕܟܪܝܢ
ܠܐܣܘܪܝ:
ܫܝܢܐ ܥܡܟܘܢ
ܐܡܝܢ ·:·:·

ܫܠܡܬ[a] ܐܓܪܬܐ
ܕܠܘܬ ܩܘܠܣܝܐ:[c]
ܐܬܟܬܒܬ ܕܝ ܡܢ
ܪܘܡܝ ܘܐܫܬ ܓܪܬ[a]
ܥܡ ܛܘܟܝܩܘܣ
ܘܐܘܢܝܣܝܡܘܣ

~~~~~~~~~~
ܕܬܣܠܘܢܝܩܝ[d]
ܡܫܠܡܬܐ:

[1:1] ܦܘܠܘܣ
ܘܣܝܠܘܐܢܘܣ
ܘܛܝܡܬܐܘܣ:[e]
ܠܥܕܬܐ
ܕܬܣܠܘܢܝܩܝ:[d]
ܒܐܠܗܐ ܐܒܘܢ·
ܘܒܡܪܢ ܝܫܘܥ
ܡܫܝܚܐ: ܚܣܕܐ
ܥܡܟܘܢ ܘܫܠܡܐ:
[2] ܡܫܬܘܕܝܢ ܐܢܢ
ܠܐܠܗܐ ܒܟܘܠ
ܙܒ ܥܠ ܕܟܠܟܘܢ:
ܥܒܕܝܢ ܕܟܪܘܢܟܘܢ
ܒܝ ܠܨܘܬܢ ܕܠܐ ܫܠܝܢ:
[3] ܡܬܕܟܪܝܢ
ܒܥܒܕܗ̇
ܕܗܝܡܢܘܬܟܘܢ:
ܘܠܐܘܬܐ
ܕܚܒܬܟܘܢ:
ܘܕܡܣܒܪܢܘܬܐ
ܕܣܒܪܐ ܕܡܪܢ
ܝܫܘܥ ܡܫܝܚܐ:

MKS IIB, 157: **a** omit diacritic | **b** ܒܐܝܕܝ | **c** omit *seyame* | MKS IIB, 163: **d** omit *seyame* | **e** ܘܛܝܡܬܐܘܣ
~~~~~~~~~~

1 Thessalonians 1:3–9 F. 57r

ܩܘܕܡ ܐܠܗܐ
ܐܒܘܢ: [4] ܐܚܝܢ
ܐܫܟܐ ܕܡܚܒܝܢ[a]
ܠܐܠܗܐ
ܒܚܝܪܘܬܟܘܢ:
[5] ܕܒܣܘܪܢ ܠܐ
ܐܬܚܒܪ ܠܘܬܟܘܢ
ܒܡܠܐ ܒܠܚܘܕ:
ܐܠܐ ܐܘܦ ܒܚܝܠ
ܘܒܪܘܚ ܕܩܘܕܫ·
ܘܒܫܘܠܡܐ،
ܣܓܝ: ܗܟܢ
ܕܐܬܘܢ ܝܕܥܝܢ
ܗܟܢ ܐܬܚܒܪܢ
ܠܘܬܟܘܢ
ܠܒܕܝܠܟܘܢ:
[6] ܕܐܘܦ ܐܬܘܢ
ܬܬܚܒܪܘܢ
ܕܝܠܝ ܘܠܡܪܢܐ:
ܕܩܒܠܬܘܢ
ܡܠܬܐ ܒܐܘܠܨܢ ܣ
ܣܓܝ:

ܒܚܕܘܐ ܕܪܘܚ
ܕܩܘܕܫ: [7] ܗܟܢ
ܕܬܬܚܒܪܘܢ
ܕܡܘ ܠܟܠ ܗܠܝܢ
ܕܡܗܝܡܢܝܢ
ܒܡܩܕܘܢܝܐ
ܘܒܐܟܐܝܐ: [8] ܡܢ
ܠܘܬܟܘܢ ܓܝܪ
ܐܫܬܡܥܬ
ܡܠܬܗ ܕܡܪܢܐ:
ܠܐ ܒܠܚܘܕ
ܒܡܩܕܘܢܝܐ
ܘܒܐܟܐܝܐ:
ܐܠܐ ܒܟܠ ܐܬܪ
ܗܝܡܢܘܬܟܘܢ
ܕܠܘܬ ܐܠܗܐ
ܢܦܩܬ: ܗܟܢ
ܕܠܐ ܢܗܐ
ܝ ܕܢܗܝܢ ܡܡܠܠܝܢ
ܠܗܘܢ ܒܠܘܡ:
[9] ܗܢܘܢ ܓܝܪ
ܡܬܢܝܢ ܥܠ

MKS IIB, 164: **a** ܡܚܒܝܢ

1 Thessalonians 5:15–26 F. 24r

ܛܒܬܐ ܗܘܘ
ܪܕܦܝܢ ܠܟܠܗܘܢ
ܠܘܬ ܟܠܢ:
ܘܠܘܬ ܟܘܠܐ:
[16]ܒܟܘܠ ܙܒ̈
ܗܘܘ ܚܕܝܢ:
[17]ܕܠܐ ܫܠܝܢ
ܗܘܘ ܡܨܠܝܢ:
[18]ܒܟܘܠܐ ܗܘܘ
ܡܫܒܚܝܢ:
ܗܕܐ ܓܝܪ ܗܘ
ܨܒܝܢܗ
ܕܐܠܗܐ
ܒܡܫܝܚܐ[a]
ܝܫܘܥ ܠܘܬܟܘܢ:
[19]ܪܘܚܐ ܠܐ ܬܛܦܘܢ
ܡܛܦܝܢ:
[20]ܢܒܝܘܬܐ[b] ܠܐ
ܬܗܘܘܢ ܦܣܠܝܢ:
[21]ܒܟܘܠܐ ܗܘܘ
ܒܕܩܝܢ· ܡܐ
ܕܛܒ ܗܘܘ ܐܚܕܝܢ:

[22]ܡܢ ܟܘܠ
ܕܡܘܬܐ ܒܝܫܐ
ܗܘܘ ܪܚܝܩܝܢ:
[23]ܗܘ ܕܝܢ ܐܠܗܐ
ܕܫܠܡܐ ܢܩܕܫ
ܝܬܟܘܢ ܫܘܠܡܢܝܬ:
ܘܫܠܡ ܝܬܗ
ܠܪܘܚܟܘܢ
ܘܠܢܦܫܟܘܢ
ܘܓܘ ܦܓܪܟܘܢ:
ܦܢܝ̈ܡ ܟܠܐ
ܒܡܬܝܬܘܬܗ
ܕܡܪܢ ܝܫܘܥ
ܡܫܝܚܐ ܢܛܪܝܢ:
[24]ܡܗܝܡܢ ܗܘ
ܗܘ ܕܩܪܐ[c]
ܝܬܟܘܢ· ܕܗܘ
ܐܘܦ ܝܥܒܕ:
[25]ܐܚܝܐ ܨܠܘ ܐܘܦ
ܥܠ ܕܝܠܢ: [26]ܫܐ̈ܠܘ
ܒܫܠܡܗܘܢ
ܕܟܘܠ ܐܚܝܐ·

MKS IIB, 165: **a** ܕܒܡܫܝܚܐ | **b** omit *seyame* | **c** omit diacritic

1 Thessalonians 5:26–28; 2 Thessalonians 1:1–3 F. 24v

ܒܫܠܡܐ[a] ܩܕܝܫ:
[27]ܡܘܡܐ[b] ܐܢܐ
ܠܟܘܢ ܒܡܪܢܐ·
ܕܬܬܩܪܐ[c]
ܐ ܓܪܬܐ ܠܟܘܠ
ܐܚܝܐ ܩܕܝܫܝܐ:
[28]ܛܝܒܘܬܗ ܕܡܪܢ
ܝܫܘܥ ܡܫܝܚܐ
ܥܡܟܘܢ:
~~~~~~~~~~~[d]
ܫܠܡܬ ܐ ܓܪܬܐ
ܕܬܣܠܘܢܝܩܝܐ
ܩܕܡܝܬܐ: ܐܬܟܬܒܬ
ܕܝ ܡܢ ܐܬܢܘܣ:
[d]~~~~~~~~~~~

[e]ܕܬܣܠܘܢܝܩܝܐ
ܬܢܝܢܝܬܐ:[e]
[1:1]ܦܘܠܘܣ
ܘܣܝܠܘܢܘܣ
ܘܛܝܡܬܐܘܣ:[f]

ܠܥܕܬܐ
ܕܬܣܠܘܢܝܩܝܐ[g]
ܒܐܠܗܐ ܐܒܘܢ
ܘܒܡܪܢ[h] ܝܫܘܥ
ܡܫܝܚܐ: [2]ܛܝܒܘܬܐ
ܥܡܟܘܢ· ܘܫܠܡܐ
ܡܢ ܐܠܗܐ ܐܒܐ
ܘܡܢ ܡܪܢ ܝܫܘܥ
ܡܫܝܚܐ: [3]ܚܝܒܝܢ
ܐܢܢ ܕܢܘܕܐ
ܡܫܬܘܕܝܢ
ܠܐܠܗܐ ܒܟܘܠ
ܙܒܢ ܥܠ ܕܠܒܟܘܢ
ܐܚܝܐ· ܗܝܟ
ܕܫܘܐ ܗܘ·
ܕܟܠ[i] ܕܡܬܪܒܐ
ܥܒܝܢܐ[j]
ܗܝܡܢܘܬܟܘܢ:
ܘܡܣܬܓܝܐ
ܚܒܬܐ ܕܟܘܠ
ܚܕ ܘܚܕ
ܡܢܟܘܢ:

MKS IIB, 166: **a** ܒܫܠܡ | **b** *nil* | **c** ܕܡܬܩܪܝܐ | **d–d** *nil* | MKS IIB, 172: **e–e** *nil* | **f** ܘܛܝܡܬܐܘܣ | **g** omit *seyame* | **h** ܘܡܪܢ | **i** ܟܠ | **j** ܥܒܝܢܐ
~~~~~~~~~~~

2 Thessalonians 1:3–9 F. 29r

ܦܠܓܒܘܢ ܠܘܬ
ܦܠܓ܃ [4]ܗܝܟ
[a]ܕܢܗܐ ܐܢܚ
ܡܫ̈ܬܒܚܝܢ ܒܟܘܢ
ܠܟܢ̈ܫܬܗ[a]
ܕܐܠܗܐ܃
ܥܠ ܕܛܒ
ܡܣܝܒܪܘܬܟܘܢ
ܘܗܝܡܢܘܬܟܘܢ
ܒܟܠܗܘܢ
ܪ̈ܕܘܦܝܟܘܢ܃
ܘܥܠܝܨܝ̈ܢ ܘܥܩܐ[b]
ܗܠܝܢ ܕܐܬܘܢ
ܡܣܝܒܪ̈ܝܢ܃
[5]ܠܐܘܕܥܘܬܐ
ܕܕܝܢܐ ܕܝ ܕܩܘܗ
ܕܐܠܗܐ܃
ܕܬܗܘܢ ܫܘ̈ܝܢ
ܒܡܠܟܘܬܗ
ܕܐܠܗܐ ܗܘܐ
ܕܐܘܦ ܚ̈ܫܝܢ
ܐܢܬܘܢ ܥܠ ܕܛܒܗ܃

[6]ܕܝ̱ ܕܩ ܗܘ
ܠܘܬ ܐܠܗܐ
ܕܝܦܪܥ ܠܗܠܝܢ
[c]ܕܠܚ̈ܨܝܢ ܠܟܘܢ
ܠܢܝ̈ܚܝܢ܃[c]
[7]ܘܠܟܘܢ ܠܗܠܝܢ
ܕܡܬܠܚ̈ܨܝܢ
ܢܝܚ ܥܡܢ [d]ܒܓܠܝܢܗ
ܕܡܪܢ ܝܫܘܥ
ܡܢ ܓܘ ܫܡܝܐ܃
ܥܡ ܡܠܐ̈ܟܝܐ
ܕܚܝܠܗ܃ [8]ܒܢܘܪܐ
ܕܒܥܪܐ ܝܗܒ
ܢܩܡ[e] ܠܗܠܝܢ
ܕܠܐ ܡܚܟ̈ܝܢ
ܠܐܠܗܐ܃
ܘܠܗܠܝܢ ܕܠܐ
ܡܫܬ̈ܡܥܝܢ
ܠܒܣܘܪܗ
ܕܡܪܢ ܝܫܘܥ
ܡܫܝܚܐ܃ [9]ܐܢܘ̈ܢ
ܕܝܬܦܪ̈ܥܘܢ

MKS IIB, 173: **a** ܠܟܢܫܬܐ / ܐܘܢ ܡܫܬܒܚܝܢ / ܐܢܚ [...] | **c** ܢܝܚܐ ܠܢ̈ܝܚܝܢ / ܕܠܚܨܝܢ ܬܘܢ | **d** omit diacritic | **e** ܢܩܡܐ || **b** The baseline of the *beth* is scarcely visible.

2 Thessalonians 1:9–2:2 F. 29v

ܕܝ ܚܣܝܡ ܕܠܥܠܡ·
ܡܢ ܩܕܡ ܐܦ̈ܘܗܝ
ܕܡܪܝܐ: ܘܡܢ
ܬܫܒܘܚܬܐ
ܕܚܝܠܗ: [10] ܟܕ
ܢܐܬܐ ܕܢܫܬܒܚ
ܒܩܕܝ̈ܫܘܗܝ:·[a]
ܘܢܬܕܡܪ ܒܟܠ
ܗܠܝܢ ܕܡܗ̈ܝܡܢܝܢ:
ܕܐܬܗܝܡܢܬ
ܣܗܕܘܬܢ
ܥܠܝܟܘܢ ܒܗܘ
ܝܘܡܐ: [11] ܒܗܕܐ
ܕܐܘܦ ܐܢܝ
ܡܨ̈ܠܝܢ ܒܟܠ
ܙܒܢ ܥܠ ܕܥܠܝܟܘܢ:
ܕܢܫܘܐ ܢܫܘܝܟܘܢ
ܐܠܗܐ ܩܪ̈ܝܢ
ܒܩܪܝܬܗ:[b]
ܘܢܫܠܐ ܟܠ
ܨܒܝܢ ܕܛܝܒܘ:
ܘܥܒܕܐ ܕܗܝܡܢܘܬܐ
ܒܚܝܠ:

[12] ܠܟܘܠ ܕܢܫܬܒܚ
ܫܡܗ ܕܡܪܢ
ܝܫܘܥ ܒܟܘܢ:
ܘܐܢܬܘܢ ܒܗ:
ܗܝܟ ܛܝܒܘܬܗ
ܕܐܠܗܐ
ܘܕܡܪܢ ܝܫܘܥ·
ܡܫܝܚܐ: [2:1] ܒܥܝܢ
ܐܢܢ ܕܝ ܡܢܟܘܢ
ܐܚ̈ܝܐ· ܥܠܛܠܒ[c]
ܡܐܬܝܬܗ
ܕܡܪܢ ܝܫܘܥ
ܡܫܝܚܐ:
ܘܟܢܘܫܝܐ ܕܝܠܢ
ܕܠܘܬܗ: [2] ܠܟܘܠ
ܕܠܐ ܒܥܓܠ
ܬܗܘܘܢ ܡܕ̈ܪܕܝܢ
ܡܢ ܪܥܝܢܟܘܢ:[d]
ܘܠܐ ܬܗܘܘܢ
ܡܬܪ̈ܗܒܝܢ:
ܠܐ ܒܬܪܥ ܪܘܚ:
ܘܠܐ ܒܬܪܥ

MKS IIB, 174: **a** omit *seyame* | **b** ܕܩܪܝܬܗ | **c** ܥܠ ܛܠܒ | **d** omit diacritic

2 Timothy 1:9–15 F. 58v

ܡܢ ܒܪ ܠܐ
ܐܨ̈ܒܝܗܘܢ
ܕܥܠܡ̈ܝܐ:
[10]ܐܬܓܠܝܬ ܕܝ
ܒܕܘ ܟܥܬܪ ܒ
ܓܠܝܗ ܕܡܚܝܢ
ܝܫܘܥ ܡܫܝܚܐ·
ܕܒܛܠ ܡܢ
ܡܘܬܐ: ܐܢܗܪ
ܕܝ ܚ̈ܝܝܐ:
ܘܠܡܐ[a] ܕܠܐ
ܬܪܦ ܒܬܪܒܗ
ܕܒܣܘܪܐ
ܗܕܝ ܕܐܢܐ
[11]ܐܬܩܝܡܬ
ܠܗ ܡܟܪܙ[b]
ܘܫܠܝܚ ܘܡܠܦ
ܠܚ̈ܢܦܐ: [12]ܠܒܕܝܠ
ܒܕܝ ܗܠܝܢ
ܐܢܐ ܚܫܫ:
ܐܠܐ ܠܝܬܢܐ
ܒܗܬ:

ܝܕܥ ܐܢܐ ܓܝܪ·
ܒܡܢ ܗܝܡܢܬ·
ܘܐܢܐ ܡܦܝܣ
ܕܗܘ ܝܟܠ
ܕܝܛܪ ܦܩܕܘܢ
ܠܗܘ ܝܘܡܐ:
[13]ܕܡܘ ܬܗܐ
ܒܡܢ ܠܡ̈ܠܝܐ
ܚܠܝ̈ܡܬܐ ܗܠܝܢ
ܕܫܡܥܬ ܡܢܝ
ܒܗܝܡܢܘܬܐ
ܘܒܪܚܡܬܐ
ܕܒܝܫܘܥ
ܡܫܝܚܐ:
[14]ܦ̈ܩܕܘܢܐ ܛܒܐ
ܛܪ ܒܬܪܒܗ
ܕܪܘܚܐ
ܕܩܘܕܫܐ
ܗܕܐ ܕܒܕܝܪܐ
ܒܓܘܢ· [15]ܝܕܥ ܐܢܬ
ܗܕܐ ܕܬܒ̈ܥܘ
ܠܗܘܢ ܡܢܝ

MKS IIB, 175: **a** ܘܠܡܚܐ | **b** ܡܟܪܙܝ

2 Timothy 1:15–2:4 F. 58r

ܟܘܠ ܗܠܝܢ
ܕܒܐܣܝܐ: ܦܢ
ܕܗܘ ܦܝܠܝܓܠܘܣ
ܘܐܪܡܘܓܢܝܣ:
16 ܢܬܠ ܐܠܗܐ
ܪ̈ܚܡܝܢ ܠܒܝܬܗ
ܕܐܘܢܣܝܦܘܪܘܣ:
ܕܣܓܝ ܙܒ̈ܢܝܢ
ܐܢܝ ܒܪܘܚܝ:
ܘܒܫܫ̈ܠܬܝ[a]
ܠܐ ܒܗܬ:
17 ܐܠܐ ܟܕ ܐܬܐ
ܠܪܘܡܐ ܒܥܝ ܝܬܝ
ܒܥܐ ܠܝ
ܘܐܫܟܚܢܝ: 18 ܢܬܠ
ܠܗ ܡܪܐ
ܕܝܫܟܚ ܪ̈ܚܡܝܢ
ܡܢ ܠܘܬ ܡܪܐ
ܒܗܘ ܝܘܡܐ:
ܘ̈ܟܘܠ ܡܐ
ܕܫܡܫ ܠܝ
ܒܐܦܣܘܣ

ܛܒܐܝܬ ܐܢܬ
ܝܕܥ: 2:1 ܐܢܬ ܐܘܢ
ܒܪܝ ܐܬܚܝܠ
ܒܚܣܕܐ
ܕܝܫܘܣ
ܡܫܝܚܐ: 2 ܘܡܐ
ܕܫܡܥܬ ܡܢܝ
ܒܬܪܥ ܣܗ̈ܕܝܢ
ܣܓܝ: ܗܠܝܢ
ܗܘܝ ܡܫܠܡ
ܠܒܢܝܫ
ܡܗܝܡܢܝܢ:
ܗܠܝܢ ܕܗ̈ܘܝܢ
ܕܘܡ̈ܠܐܝܢ
ܕܐܘܦ ܠܚܪ̈ܢܝܢ
ܠܡܠܦ: 3 ܐܬܚܫܠ
ܗܝܟ ܦܠܚܗ
ܛܒܐ ܕܝܫܘܣ
ܡܫܝܚܐ: 4 ܐܢܫ
ܠܐ ܗܘܐ[b] ܦܠܚ
ܘܡܬܥܪܟ
ܒܡܦ̈ܩܬܗ ܕܥܠܡܐ:

MKS IIB, 176: **a** omit *seyame* | **b** omit diacritic

2 Timothy 3:2–8 F. 61v

ܕܠܐ ܢܥܢ̈ܝܢ:
[3]ܕܠܐ ܪ̈ܚܡܝܢ:
ܕܠܐ ܝ ܐ̈ܕܝܢ
ܒܪ̈ܡܘܢ:
ܕܠܐ ܡܬܟܒ̈ܫܝܢ:
ܕܠܐ ܪ̈ܚܡܝܢ
ܠܛܒ̈ܬܐ: ܕܠܐ
ܡܫܝ̈ܢܝܢ
ܒܐܬܦ̈ܠܘܬܗܘܢ:*[a]
ܡܫܠ̈ܡ ܒܢܝܢ:
[4]ܡܣܘܪ̈ܝܢ:
ܕܫܒ̈ܚܝܢ: ܢܦܫܝܢ:
ܪ̈ܚܡܝܢ ܡܠܘܢ
ܬܦܢܘܩܬܐ:
ܐܪ̇ ܒܪ ܠܐܠܗܘܬܐ:
[5]ܒܕܡܗܘܢ ܕܕܚܠܬܐ
ܕܝ ܕܡܐ: ܒܚܝܠܗ
ܕܝ ܒܦ̈ܢܝܢ:
ܐܘܦ ܗܠܝܢ
ܗܘܝ ܡܪܚܩ
ܡܢܗܘܢ: [6]ܡܢ ܗܠܝܢ
ܒܪ ܗܘܢ ܗܠܝܢ

ܕܗܘܝܢ ܥܠܝܢ
ܠܒ̈ܬܝܐ: ܘܫܒ̈ܝܢ
ܢܫ̈ܝܢ ܕܐܝ ܢ̈ܝ
ܒܚܛ̈ܝܢ:
ܡܬܕ̈ܒܪܢ
ܒܬܪ̈ܓܢ
ܕܠ̈ܦܫܝܢ
ܣܚ̈ܝܢ: [7]ܘܒܟܘܠ
ܒܪ[b] ܝܠܦܢ: ܘܠܥܠܡ
ܠܡܪܘܬܐ
ܕܩܘܫܛܐ ܠܐ
ܝܟܠܢ ܕܐܬ̈ܝܢ:
[8]ܗܝܟ ܡܐ ܕܝ
ܕܝܢܣ ܘܝܡܒܪܣ
ܩܡܘ ܠܩܘܒܠ
ܡܫܐ: ܗܟܢ
ܐܘܦ ܗܠܝܢ
ܩܝ̈ܡܝܢ ܠܩܘܒܠ
ܩܘܫܛܐ: ܒܢ̈ܝܢܫ
ܕܡܬܚ̈ܒܠܝܢ
ܒܡܕܥ̈ܬܗܘܢ
ܘܦܣܝܠܝܢ ܡܢ

MKS IIB, 177: **a** omit *seyame* | **b** ܒܪ

2 Timothy 3:8–14 F. 61r

ܗܝܡܢܘܬܐ:
9ܐܠܐ ܠܐ
ܡܬܥܒܪ̈ܝܢ*[a] ܥܠ
ܕܝܘܬܪ: ܓܝܪ
ܫܛܝܘܬܗܘܢ
ܓܠܝܐ ܗܘܐ
ܠܟܘܠܐ: ܗܝܟ
ܕܐܘܦ ܗܠܝܢ
ܐܬܥܒܕܬ:[b]
10ܐܢ̇ܬ ܕܝ ܕܒܩܬ[c]
ܠܐܘܠܦܢܝ:
ܠܕܒܪܝ:
ܠܐܬܘܝܬܝ:
ܠܗܝܡܢܘܬܝ:
ܠܐܘܪܟ ܪܘܚܝ:
ܠܚܒܬܝ:
ܠܡܣܝܒܪܢܘܬܝ:
11ܠܪ̈ܕܘܦܝ:
ܠܚ̈ܫܘܫܝ:
ܟ̇ܘܠ ܡܐ
ܕܐܬܥܒܕ ܠܝ
ܒܐܢܛܝܘܟܝܐ:[d]

ܒܐܝܩܘܢܝܐ:
ܒܠܘܣܛܪܐ:
ܗܠܝܢ[e] ܪ̈ܕܘܦܝܢ
ܣܝܒܪܬ:[f] ܘܡܢ
ܟܘܠܗܘܢ ܦܪܩ
ܡܪܐ: 12ܘܐܘܦ
ܟܘܠ ܗܠܝܢ
ܕܨ̈ܒܝܢ ܕܝܚܝܘܢ
ܒܕܚܠܬܗ
ܕܐܠܗܐ.[g]
ܒܝܫܘܥ ܡܫܝܚܐ
ܡܬܪ̈ܕܦܘܢ:
13ܒܝ̈ܫܝܢ ܕܝ ܒܢ̈ܫܝܢ
ܘܡܛܥ̈ܝܢ
ܡܬ̈ܩܕܡܘܢ[h] ܥܠ
ܕܝܘܬܪ
ܒܛ̈ܥܝܬܐ ܛ̈ܥܝܢ
ܘܡܛ̈ܥܝܢ: 14ܐܢܬ
ܕܝ ܟܬܪ
ܒܗܠܝܢ ܕܝܠܦܬ
ܘܐܬܗܝܡܢܬ:
ܝܕܥ ܡܢ ܡ̇ܢ ܝܠܦܬ:

MKS IIB, 178: **a** ܡܬܥܒ̈ܪܝܢ | **b** omit diacritic | **c** ܪܕܦܬ | **d** ܒܐܢܛܝܘܟܝܐ | **e** ܗܢܘܢ | **g** ܕܐܠܗܐ | **h** ܡܬܬܪ̈ܕܦܘܢ || **f** The *yod* appears to be a secondary insertion.

Titus 2:7–12 F. 23r

ܒܟܘܠ ܡ̈ܕܡܢ[a]*
ܚܘ̇ܝ ܗܘܝ[b]
ܗܒ ܕܡܘ
ܠܥ̈ܒܕܝܢ[c] ܛ̈ܒܝܢ:
ܒܐܘܠܦܢܐ
ܕܠܐ ܒܬܪܦܘ:
[d]ܒܪܒܘ: * ܒܢܟܦܘ:
[8]ܒܡܠܐ ܚܠܝܡܐ: *
ܕܠܐ ܒܢܟܦܘܢ:[d]*
ܠܒܥܠ ܕܒܗܕܢ
[e]ܕܩܐܡ ܠܡܘܡܠܐ*
ܢܬܒܗܬ: ܕܠܐ
ܗܘ̇ܐ ܠܗ ܡܠܘܡ
ܒܝܫ ܕܢܡܪ
ܥܠܝܢ:[e] [9]ܥ̈ܒܕܝܐ
ܠܡ̈ܪܝܗܘܢ[f]
ܢܫܬ̈ܥܒܕܘܢ:
ܒܟܘܠ ܡܕܡܐ
ܗܘܢ ܫܦ̈ܝܪܝܢ:
ܘܠܐ ܗܘܘܢ
ܡܣ̈ܪܒܝܢ[g]
ܠܡܘܡܠܗܘܢ: *

[10]ܐܠܐ ܒܟܘܠ[h]
ܗܝܡܢܘ ܛܒܐ
ܗܘܘܢ ܡܚ̈ܘܝܢ:[f]
ܠܒܥܠ[i]
[j]ܕܐܘܠܦܢܗ
ܕܡܚܝܢ ܐܠܗܐ
ܗܘܘܢ ܡܬ̈ܩܢܝܢ
ܒܟܘܠܐ:
ܡܠܝܘܢ ܕܢܘܒ[ܐ]
ܡܨܒܐ ܘܬܢܝܐ
ܕܬܗܘܦܟܝܐ:

[11]ܐܬܓܠܝܬ ܓܝܪ[j]
ܛܝܒܘܬܗ
[k]ܕܐܠܗܐ ܡܚܝܢ
ܠܟܘܠ ܒܢܝ̈ܢܫܐ:[k]
[12]ܕܪܕܝܐ ܠܢ:
ܠܒܥܠ ܕܢܟܦܘܪ
ܒܪܘܫܥܐ[l]
ܘܒܪ̈ܓܝܓܬܗ[f]
ܕܥܠܡܐ:
ܕܒܐܬܝܘܢ

MKS IIB, 185: **a** ܡܕܡܐ | **b** ܢܗܘܐ | **c** ܕܥ̈ܒܕܝܢ | **d–d** ܒܪܒܘ: ܒܢܟܦܘ / ܕܒܡܠܐ ܚܠܝܡܐ: / ܕܠܐ ܒܢܟܦܘܢ | **e–e** ܕܩܐܡ ܠܡܘܡܠܐ / [...] ܡܠܐ / [...] ܠܗ ܡܠܘܡ / ܒܝܫܐ ܕܢܡܪ / [...]: | **f** omit *seyame* | **g** ܡܣܪ̈ܒܝܢ | **h** ܠܟܘܠ | **i** [...] ܠܒܥܠ | **j–j** *nil* | **k–k** ܕܐܠܗܐ [...] / ܠܟܘܠ ܒܢܝ̈ܢܫܐ: | **l** ܒܪܘܫܥܐ || **a** *Prima manu*. Emended by overwriting *nun* with *alaf*.

Titus 2:12–3:3 **F. 23v**

ܘܚܝܢ ܕܝܢ ܘܒܕܚܠܬܐ
ܕܐܠܗܐ ܢܚܐ̇
ܒܗܢܢ ܥܠܡܐ܆
[13] ܡܣܟܝܢ ܠܣܒܪܐ
ܛܒܐ ܘܠܓܠܝܢܐ
ܕܬܫܒܘܚܬܗ
ܕܐܠܗܐ ܪܒܐ܂
ܘܡܚܝܢܢ ܝܫܘܥ
ܡܫܝܚܐ܆ [14] ܗܢܘ
ܕܝܗܒ ܦܓܪܗ
ܚܠ ܕܠܟܝ: ܠܚܕܒܠ
ܕܢܦܪܘܩ ܠܢ
ܡܢ ܟܘܠ ܚܘܠ:
ܘܢܕܟܐ ܠܗ
ܥܡܐ ܠܢܦܫܗ܆
ܡܫܟܚܐ ܒܥ̈ܒܕܝܢ
ܛܒ̈ܝܢ܆ [15] ܗܠܝܢ
ܗܘܝ ܡܡܠܠ
ܘܡܟܣ
ܘܡܚܘܝ ܒܟܘܠ
ܫܘܠܛܢ: ܐܢܫ ܠܐ
ܢܗܐ[a] ܡܫܝܛ ܠܟ:
ܫܠܡ[b]

[3:1] ܗܘܝ ܡܥܗܕ
ܠܗܘܢ ܕܢܗܘܘܢ
ܡܫܬܥ̈ܒܕܝܢ
ܠܪ̈ܫܘܬܐ[c]
ܘܠܫܘ̈ܠܛܢܘܬܐ܆[c]
ܡܬܛ̈ܦܝܣܝܢ
ܠܟܘܠ ܥܒܕ
ܛܒ ܢܗܘܘܢ
ܥܬ̈ܝܕܝܢ܆ [2] ܥܠ
ܐܢܫ ܠܐ ܢܗܘܘܢ
ܡܓ̈ܕܦܝܢ܆ ܘܠܐ
ܢܗܘܘܢ ܝ ܚܪ̈ܝܢ:
ܐܠܐ ܡܬܟ̈ܝܢ܆
ܒܟܘܠ ܡܟܝܟܘ
ܢܗܘܘܢ ܡܚܘ̈ܝܢ
ܠܘܬ ܟܠܗܘܢ
ܒܢ̈ܝܢܫܐ܆ [3] ܗܘܝܢ
ܓܝܪ ܐܦ ܚܢܢ
ܒܙܒܢ ܕܠܐ ܗܘܐ
ܒܝ ܬܪܥܝܬܐ:
ܘܕܠܐ ܡܬܛ̈ܦܝܣܝܢ܆
ܛܥܝܢ ܘܡܫܬܥ̈ܒܕܝܢ

MKS IIB, 186: **a** omit diacritic | **c** omit *seyame* || **b** Rubric indicating the end of the liturgical unit beginning at v. 11 *supra* (f. 23r).

Philemon 11–19 **F. 30r**

[11]ܠܟ ܒܙܒܢ ܦܩܚ:
ܟܕܘ ܕܝ ܠܟ
ܘܠܝ ܗܘ ܕܦܠܚ
ܛܒ: [12]ܗܕܢ
ܕܫܠܚܬ: ܐܢܬ
ܕܝ ܡܩܒܠ ܝܬܗ· *
ܗܢܐ ܕܗܘ
ܠܪ̈ܚܡܝ:·[a]
[13]ܗܕܢ ܕܗܘܝܬ
ܝ ܒܥܐ ܕܐܚܕ ܘܕܝܢܗ
ܠܘܬܝ: ܠܒܪܝܠ
ܕܝܫܡܫܢܝ ܚܠܦܝܟ
ܡܫܡܫ ܠܝ
ܒܐܣܘܪ̈ܝܐ
ܕܣܒܪ̈ܬܐ:
[14]ܠܒܪ ܕܝ ܡܢ
ܡܠܟܝ ܟܠܘܡ ܠܐ
ܝ ܒܥܝܬ ܕܐܥܒܕ:
ܠܒܪ ܕܠܐ
ܗܝܟ ܒܩܛܝ ܘܩܛܪܐ
ܬܗܘܐ ܛܒܬܟ:
ܐܠܐ ܡܢ ܝ ܒܨܘܢ:

[15]ܛܒܐ ܓܪ ܠܒܪܝܠ
ܒܙܢ ܙܥܘܪ ܡܢܟ
ܠܫܥܐ: ܠܒܪܝܠ
ܕܠܥܠܡ ܝܗܐ
ܥܡܟ: [16]ܠܐ ܟܥܒܕ
ܗܝܟ ܥܒܕ: ܐܠܐ
ܡܝܬܪ ܡܢ ܥܒܕ:
ܐܚ ܚܒܝܒ:
ܚܕ ܒܚܕܐ ܠܝ:
ܡܘܬܪ ܕܝ ܠܟ:
ܐܘܦ ܒܒܣܪܐ·
ܘܒܡܪܝܐ: [17]ܐܢ
ܐܝܬ ܐܢܬ ܐܘܢ
ܝ ܚܕ ܠܝ ܫܘܬܦܝܢ
ܡܩܒܠ ܝܬܗ
ܗܝܟ ܕܠܝ:
[18]ܐܢ[b] ܕܝ ܟܠܘܡ
ܛܠܡܟ· ܐܢܐ ܚܝܒ
ܗܘ ܠܟ: ܗܕܐ
ܚܫܒ ܥܠܝ: [19]ܐܢܐ
ܦܘܠܘܣ ܟܬܒܬ
ܒܐܝܕܝ ܕܝܠܝ:

MKS IIB, 192: **a** omit *seyame* | **b** omit diacritic

Philemon 19–25 F. 30v

ܐܢܐ ܦܪܥ܃ ܕܠܐ
ܡܐܡܪ ܠܟ
ܕܐܘܦ ܐܢܬ
ܢܦܫܟ ܡܬܚܝܒ
ܠܝ܃ [20]ܐܝܢ ܐܚܝ܃
ܐܢܐ ܡܬܢܬܦ
ܚܠܦܝܟ ܒܡܪܢܐ܃
ܐܢܝܚ ܪ̈ܚܡܝ
ܒܡܫܝܚܐ܃ [21]ܡܢ
ܪܚܝܨ ܥܠ
ܫܡܘܥܬܟ
ܟܬܒܬ ܠܟ܃
ܝܕܥ ܕܐܘܦ
ܡܘܬܪ ܡܢ
ܡܐ ܕܐܢܐ
ܐܡܪ ܐܬ ܥܒܕ܃
[22]ܟܘܕ ܕܝ ܐܘܦ
ܥܬܕ ܠܝ
ܐܟܣܢܝܐ܃
ܡܣܒܪ ܐܢܐ
ܒܪ ܕܒܝ ܠܨ̈ܠܘܬܟܘܢ[a]
ܐܢܐ ܡܬܝܗܒ
ܠܟܘܢ܃

[23]ܫ̇ܐܠ ܒܫܠܡܟ
ܐܦܦܪܣ ܒܪ
ܫܒܝܬܝ
ܒܝܫܘܥ
ܡܫܝܚܐ܃
[24]ܡܪܩܘܣ܃
ܐܪܣܛܪܟܘܣ܃
ܕܝܡܣ܃ ܠܘܩܣ܃
ܒܢܝ ܒܥܠܡܬܝ܃
[25]ܫܝܢܗ ܕܡܪܢܐ
ܝܫܘܥ ܡܫܝܚܐ
ܥܡ ܪܘܚܟܘܢ
ܐܡܝܢ܃
~~~~~~~~~~~~[b]
ܫܠܡܬ ܐ̇ ܓܪܬܐ
ܕܠܘܬ ܦܝܠܝܡܘܢ
ܘܐܦܝܐ
[... ...]
ܡܢ [...]
ܫܡܥܘܢ [...]
[... ...]
ܐܬܟܬܒܬ[b]

MKS IIB, 193: **a** omit *seyame* | **b–b** *nil*
~~~~~~~~~~~~

Hebrews 2:9–13 F. 25v

9 ܗܕܢ ܕܝ ܕܝܢ ܡܟܝܟ ܙܥܘܪ ܡܢ ܡܠܐ̈ܟܝܐ: ܚܙܝܢܢ ܐܢ ܝܬܗ ܠܝܫܘܥ ܠܒܪܢܫ ܡܚܫܘܫܗ[a] ܕܡܘܬܐ:· ܒܐܝܩܪ ܘܬܫܒܘܚܐ ܡܟܠܠ: ܠܒܪܢܫ ܕܒܛܝܒܘܬܗ ܕܐܠܗܐ ܚܠܦܟ[b] ܒܟܠܐ ܛܥܡܘܢ ܡܘܬܐ:· 10 ܝܐܐ ܓܝܪ ܗܘܐ ܠܗ ܗܕܢ ܕܠܒܪܠܗ ܒܘܠܐ:* ܕܡܢܗ ܒܢ̈ܝܢ[c] ܣܓܝܐܐ[d] ܠܬܫܒܘܚܐ: ܐܪܝܫ ܚܝ̈ܝܗܘܢ ܒܬܪ ܡܚܫ̈ܘܫܝܢ ܡܫܠܡ:

✠ [e]ܘܡܥܠܝܢ ܕܒܪܘܒ[ܬܐ]
[e][… …]

11 ܟܕ ܓܪ ܗܕܢ ܕܡܬܩܕܫ[f] ܘܗܠܝܢ ܕܡܬܩ̈ܕܫܝܢ:[g] ܒܠܗܘܢ ܡܢ ܚܕ:[h] ܠܒܪܢܫ ܒܕܝܢ ܠܐ ܒܗܬ ܩܪܐ[i] ܠܗܘܢ ܐܚ̈ܝܢ: 12 ܐܡܪ ܡܬܢܐ ܐܢܐ ܫܡܟ ܠܐܚ̈ܝ: ܘܒܡܨܥܬ ܒ ܟܢܫܬܐ ܐܢܐ ܡܫܒܚ ܠܟ: 13 ܘܬܘܒ ܐܢܐ ܗܘܐ ܪܚܝܨ ܥܠܘܝ: ܘܬܘܒ[j] ܗܐ ܐܢܐ ܘܛ̈ܠܝܐ ܗܠܝܢ ܕܝܗܒܬ ܠܝ ܐܠܗܐ:·

⸢ܒ⸣

MKS IIB, 202: **a** ܡܚܫܘܫܗ | **b** ܚܠ ܦܟ | **c** omit *seyame* | **d** ܣܓܝܐ | **e–e** *nil* | **g** ܕܡܬܩܕܫܝܢ | **h** ܚܕܐ | **i** omit diacritic | **j** ܘܬܘܒ || **f** MS *sic*; *expectaveris* ܕܡܩܕܫ | Quire number partially visible.

Hebrews 2:14–3:1 F. 25r

14 ܠܒܕܠ ܐܘܢ
ܕܛܠܝ̈ܐ ܐܫܬܘܬܦܘ
ܒܐܕܡܐ ܘܒܒܣܪܐ⁚
ܐܘܦ ܗܘ ܟܢ
ܐܫܬܘܬܦ ܟܡܗܘܢ
ܒܗܘܢ ܒܚ̈ܫܘܫܝܐ⁚ *
ܠܒܕܠ ܕܒܬܪܒܗ
ܕܡܘܬܐ· ܝܒܛܠ
ܠܗܕܝ ܕܒܝܕܗ
ܟ ܫܐܕܗ ܕܡܘܬܐ·
ܟ̇ܢ [a] ܕܗܘ ܣܛܢܐ⁚
15 ܘ̈ܢܦܨܐ ܟܘܠ ܗܠܝܢ ܕܡܢ
ܠܒܕܠ ܕܚܠܬܗ
ܕܡܘܬܐ ܒܟܘܠ
ܒܪ ܚܝ̈ܝܗܘܢ
ܗܘܘ ܡܫܬܥ̈ܒܕܝܢ
ܠܥܒܕܘܬܐ: 16 ܠܐ ܓܪ
ܥܠ ܡܠܐ̈ܟܝܢ ܢܣܒ
ܕܝܬܐ ܐܠܗܐ:
ܐܠܐ ܥܠ ܙܪܥܗ
ܕܐܒܪܗܡ
ܗܘ ܢܣܒ ܕܝܬܐ:

17 ܠܒܕܠ ܟܕܢ ܗܘܐ
ܢܦܠ ܠܗ ܕܒܟܘܠ
ܡܗܡܐ ܢܬܕܡܐ̇
ܠܐܚ̈ܘܝ: [b] ܠܒܕܠ
ܕܪܚܡܢ ܢܬܥܒܕ:
ܘܪܒ ܟܗ̈ܢܝܢ
ܡܗܝܡܢ ܠܘܬ
ܐܠܗܐ⁝ ܕܢܚܣܐ̇
ܥܒܡ ܚܛ̈ܝܬܗ
ܕܥܡܐ⁛ 18 ܒܡܐ
ܓܪ ܕܚܫ ܗܘ
ܘܐܬܢܣܝ: ܝܟܠ
ܗܘ ܐܘܦ ܠܗܠܝܢ
ܕܡܬܢ̈ܣܝܢ ܡܣܥܕ:

✝ [c] ܐ̇ܪܝ ܡܩܠܝܢ [c]

3:1 ܗܘܐ̇ ܐܘܢ ܐܚ̈ܝܐ
ܡܩ̈ܕܫܝܐ ܗܠܝܢ
ܕܫܘܬ̈ܦܝܢ ܠܩܪܝܬܐ [d]
ܕܒܫܡܝܐ: ܐܕ̈ܪܘ
ܠܫܠܝܚܐ ܘܠܪܒ

MKS IIB, 203: **a** omit diacritic | **b** omit *seyame* | **c–c** *nil* | **d** ܩܪܝܬܐ

Hebrews 7:12–20 **F. 28v**

ܠܢܡܘܣܐ[a]
ܡܬܥܒܕܐ
ܚܘܠܦܐ⁖ [13] ܗܕܢ ܓܪ
ܕܡܬܐܡܪ̈ܢ[b] ܥܠܘܝ
ܗܠܝܢ· ܡܢ ܫܒܛ
ܚܘܪܢ ܢܣܒ· ܡܢ
ܗܕܢ ܕܐܢܫ ܡܢܗ
ܠܐ[c]ܐܬܩܪܒ
ܠܡܕܒܚܐ: [14] ܢܗܝܪܐ
ܗܝ ܓܪ ܡܢ
ܡܘܕܥ ܕܡܢ ܝܗܘܕܐ
ܕܢܚ ܡܪܢ:
ܡܐ ܕܥܠ ܫܒܛܗ
ܫܒܛܐ ܟܠܘܡ
ܥܠ ܟܗܢ ܒܗܘ
ܠܐ ܡܠܠ ܡܘܫܐ:
[15] ܘ̈ܥܠ ܕܡܘܬܪ
ܒܘܕ ܢܗܝܪܐ ܗܝ:
ܐܢ ܥܠ ܕܡܘܬܗ
ܕܡܠܟܝܨܕܩ ܩܐܡ
ܟܗܢ ܚܘܪܢ⁖ [16] ܗܕܢ
ܕܠܐ ܒܦܘܩܕܗ
ܕܢܡܘܣܐ

ܕܒܣܪܐ
ܐܬܥܒܕ: ܐܠܐ
ܒܚܝܠܐ ܕܚܝ̈ܐ
ܕܠܐ ܡܫܬܪ̈ܝܢ⁖[d]
[17] ܡ̈ܬܣܗܕ ܥܠܘܝ
ܓܪ ܕܐܢܬ ܟܗܢ
ܠܥܠܡ ܥܠ ܛܟܣܗ
ܕܡܠܟܝܨܕܩ:
[18] ܚܨ ܗܘܢ ܡܢ ܓܪ
ܡܬܥܒܕ ܒܟܐ
ܕܗܘܐ ܦܘܩܕܐ
ܡܢ ܩܘܕܡ ܠܒܛܠ
ܒܐܫܬܘܬܗ· ܘܕܠܐ
ܗܘܐ ܒܗ ܗܢܝܐ:
[19] ܟܠܡ ܓܪ ܠܐ
ܫܠܡ ܢܡܘܣܐ:
ܡܥܘܠ ܕܝ ܗܘܐ
ܕܣܒܪ ܡܝܬܪ:
ܕܒܬܪܒܗ ܐܝܢ
ܡܬܩܪ̈ܒܝܢ
ܠܐܠܗܐ⁝ [20] ܘܗܕܐ
ܕܠܐ ܠܒܪ ܡܢ
ܡܘܡܬܐ:

MKS IIB, 204: **b** ܕܡܬܐܡܪܢ | **d** omit *seyame* || **a** Added secondarily, by the first hand, above the first ruled line. | **c** Secondary marginal insertion, apparently by the same hand.

Hebrews 7:20–27 F. 28r

ܘܠܝܬ ܓܪ ܠܒܪ
ܡܢ ܡܘܡܬܐ
ܗܘܘܢ ܡܬܥ̈ܒܕܝܢ
ܟܗ̈ܢܝܢ܆ [21]ܗܘܕܢ ܕܝ
ܒܡܘܡܬܐ܆ ܠܒܕܝܠ
ܗܘܕܢ ܕܐܡܪ
ܠܘܬܗ܆ ܡܪܝܐ
ܡܪܐ ܘܠܝܬ ܗܘ
ܬܗܘܐ܆ ܕܐܢܬ ܟܗܢ
ܠܥܠܡ܆ [22]ܕܟܘܠ
ܒܕܝܢ ܟܠ ܕܝܬܝܩܐ
ܡܝܬܪܐ ܐܬܥܒܕ
ܝܫܘܥ ܥܪܒ܆
[23]ܘ̈ܗܠܝܢ ܕܗܘܘ ܣܓܝ
ܟܗ̈ܢܝܢ ܒܡ̈ܢܝܢ܆
ܠܒܕܝܠ ܕܗܘܘܢ
ܡܬܟܠܝܢ ܡܢ
ܡܘܬܐ ܕܡܬܪ̈ܘܢ܆
[24]ܗܘܕܢ ܕܝ ܕܗܘܐ
ܡܟܬܪ ܠܥܠܡ܆ ܠܐ
ܥܒܪܐ ܒܟܗܘܢܬܗ܆
[25]ܡܢ ܟܢ ܐܘܦ ܕܝܟܠ[a]

ܗܘ ܝܟܠ ܠܥܠܡ܆
ܠܗܠܝܢ ܕܒܬܪܒܗ
ܡܬܩܪ̈ܒܝܢ
ܠܐܠܗܐ܆ ܕܒܟܘܠ
ܒܪ ܗܘ ܚܝ
ܕܝܗܐ ܒܥܐ ܥܠ
ܕܝܠܗܘܢ܆ [26]ܕ ܟܘܬ
ܒܕܝܢ ܓܪ ܗܘܐ
ܐܘܦ ܥܦܪ ܠܝ ܪܒ
ܟܗܢܝܢ ܚܣܝܕ܆
ܬܡܝܡ܆ ܕܟܝܐ܆
ܦܪܝܫ ܡܢ ܚܛܝܐ܆
ܘܪܡ ܡܢ ܫܡ̈ܝܐ
ܐܬܥܒܕ܆ [27]ܗܘ ܕܝܢ
ܕܠܝܬ ܠܗ ܒܘܝ ܡܢܐ
ܒܟܘܠ ܝܘܡ
ܗܝܟ ܡܢܐ ܕܪ̈ܒܢܐ
ܒܟܗܢܐ܆ ܕܝܩܪܒ
ܢܗܘܢ ܡܩܪ̈ܒܝܢ
ܢܟ̈ܣܝܢ ܥܠܚܛ̈ܐ[b]
ܚܛ̈ܗܝܗܘܢ ܘܡܢ
ܒܬܪ ܒܕܝܢ ܥܠ
ܕܥܡܐ܆

ܪ̇

MKS IIB, 205: **a** omit diacritic | **b** ܥܠ ܚܛ || Side contains quire number.

3. CCR XI: ACTS AND CATHOLIC EPISTLES

To recap: Lewis (1909) originally proposed that CCR II contained Acts, the Pauline Epistles and the Catholic Epistles. This view prevailed for a century; it is reflected in Müller-Kessler's significant re-editing of Codex Climaci Rescriptus (Müller-Kessler and Sokoloff 1998b). In 2014, Dr Suzanna Millar—at the time an undergraduate student at the University of Cambridge—noticed the script differences between the Acts material and the Pauline Epistles material and proposed that 'CCR II' in fact consisted of two separate manuscripts. Recently, Müller-Kessler has made the same claim, pointing (in addition to the different scripts) to certain morphological differences between the two corpora (Müller-Kessler 2023b, 148–49).

Above (§2.1.1.), the quire numbering was used to demonstrate that CCR II originally began at Romans 1:1, and was not preceded by Acts, or any other text. Below (§3.2.1.), it will be demonstrated that the quire numbering of CCR XI is also incompatible with the idea that CCR XI and CCR II are one manuscript. On the other hand, the script comparison below, as well as the paratextual features, clearly demonstrate that the bifolium containing parts of 2 Peter and 1 John originally belonged to the same manuscript as the Acts material. Moreover, the quire numbering points very strongly towards the Catholic Epistles following, rather than preceding, Acts. In both material and canonical terms this finding is gratifyingly unremarkable. Early canon lists

 https://doi.org/10.11647/OBP.0455.03

and manuscripts from the Greek-speaking Eastern church regularly pair up Acts and the Catholic Epistles (almost always in that order).[1] Likewise, codices limited in their contents to the Pauline Epistles are very common (Parker 2008, 256–67).

As for which of the Catholic Epistles are included in CCR XI and in what order, the surviving evidence is, at one and the same time, surprisingly clear, and frustratingly opaque. Only one bifolium is currently known of this part of the manuscript. A rubric at the top of the first column of f. 133r (see *infra*) indicates the end of the first epistle of Peter; this is then followed by the opening twelve verses of 2 Peter. Serendipitously, the conjugate folio contains the end of 2 Peter and the beginning of 1 John. Thus, the sequence: *1 Peter; 2 Peter; 1 John* is secure. What precedes the Petrine epistles, however, is ambiguous (see §3.2.1. *infra* for details).

3.1. Script Comparison between CCR II and CCR XI

The following brief script comparison need carry no probative burden for the question of the division of '*quondam* CCR II' into CCR II and CCR XI. As already mentioned, this issue is settled by the quire numbering. Rather, the discussion below has two other purposes. First, it will show that the Acts script is the same as the Catholic Epistles script, and thus contribute to the claim that CCR

---

[1] For a recent discussion considering both the manuscript evidence and evidence from canon lists and other canon-related discussions, see Nienhuis (2007, 29–98). For a sweeping overview of the manuscript tradition, see Parker (2008, 283–310).

XI was originally an Apostolos manuscript (i.e. Acts + Catholic Epistles). Second, it provides an opportunity to sketch some of the palaeographic features of the CCR II script and the CCR XI script on a comparative basis, rather than on a purely abstract basis.

In general, the CCR II script shows a greater degree of homogeneity than the CCR XI script, which shows considerable variation in letter formation. The CCR II script is squatter than the CCR XI script. It consists mainly of straight strokes, whereas the CCR XI script contains more curved strokes. In CCR II, the ascenders (e.g., *kaf, lamad*) often do not rise very far above the height of the letters with roofs (e.g., *beth, dalath, resh*). This feature is less marked in CCR XI. Many of the ascenders in the CCR XI script are markedly more vertical than their counterparts in the CCR II script.

Here follow the more obviously probative comparisons between individual letter forms.

Table 6: Script comparison chart

Acts	Catholic Epistles	Pauline Epistles
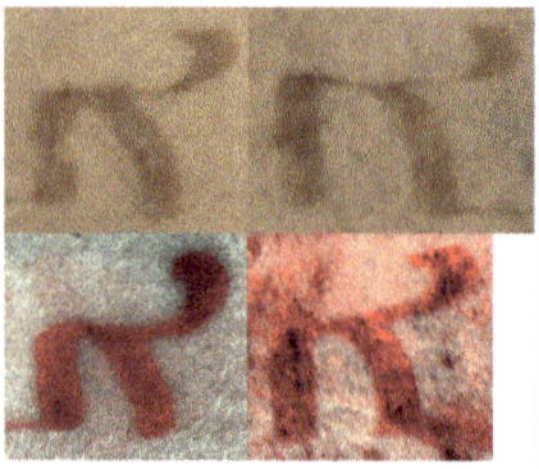		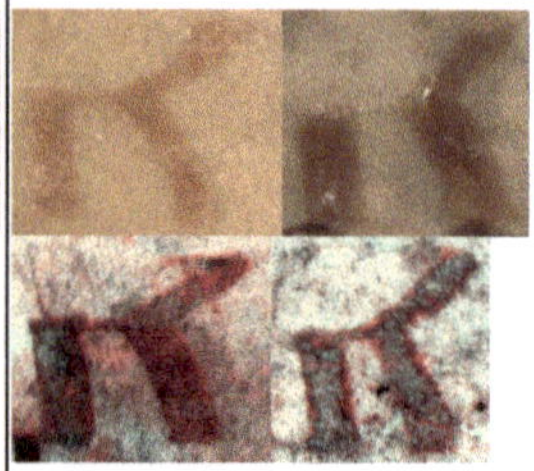
	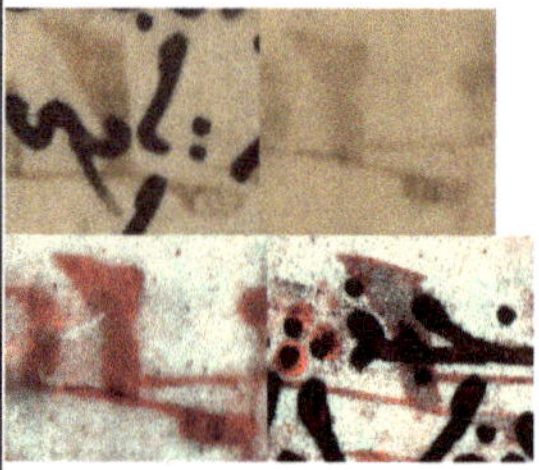	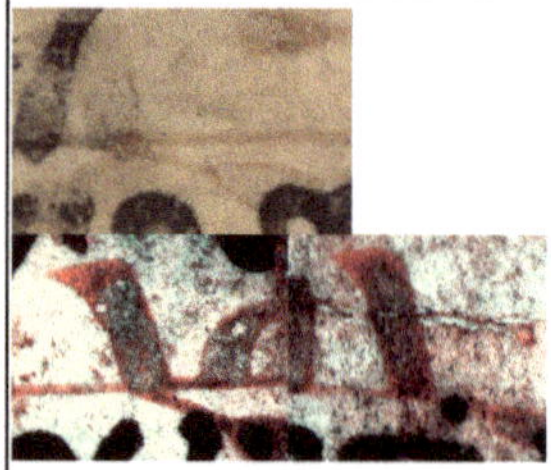
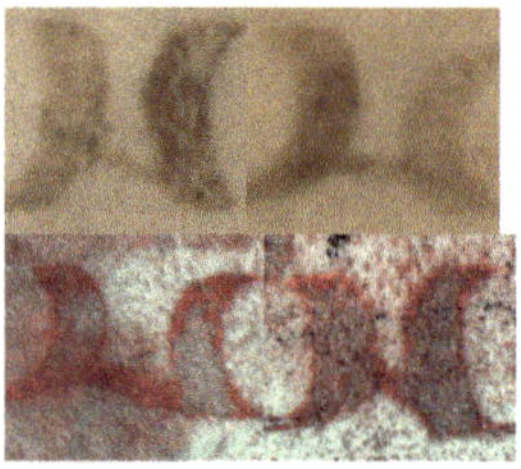	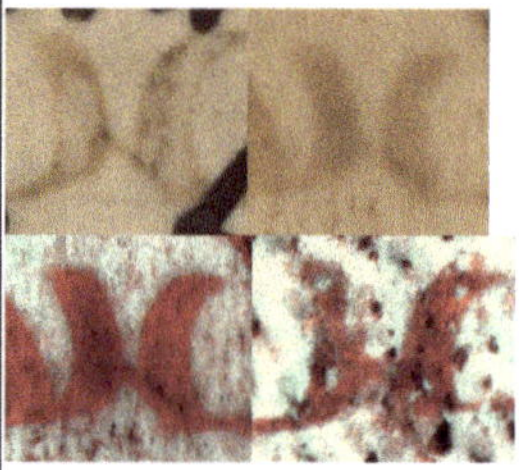	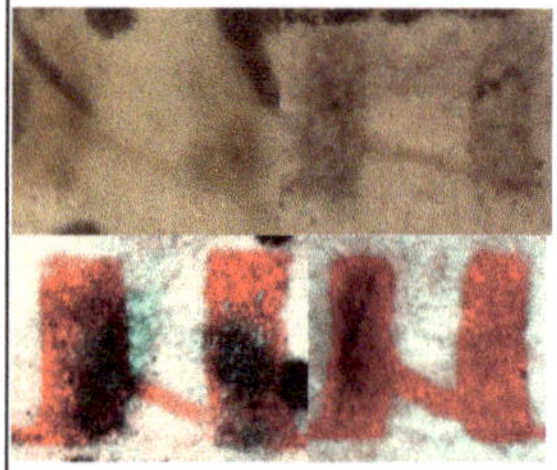
		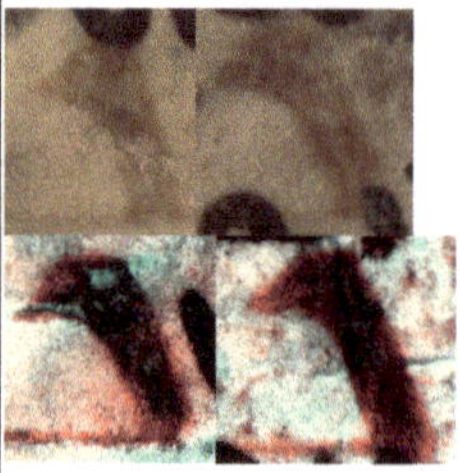
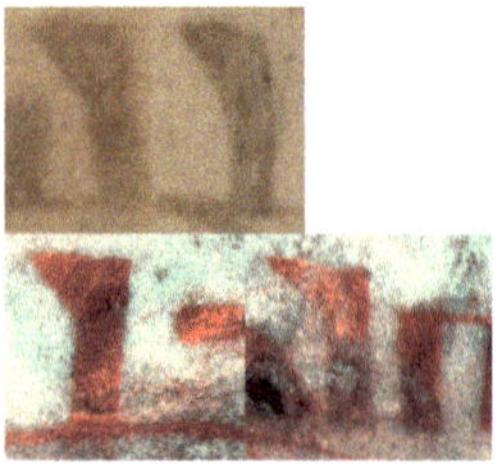		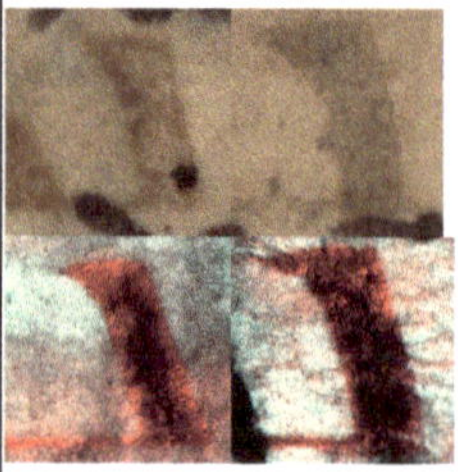

Acts	Catholic Epistles	Pauline Epistles
		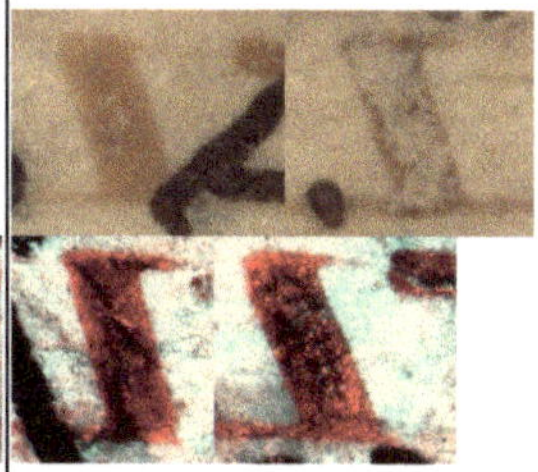
		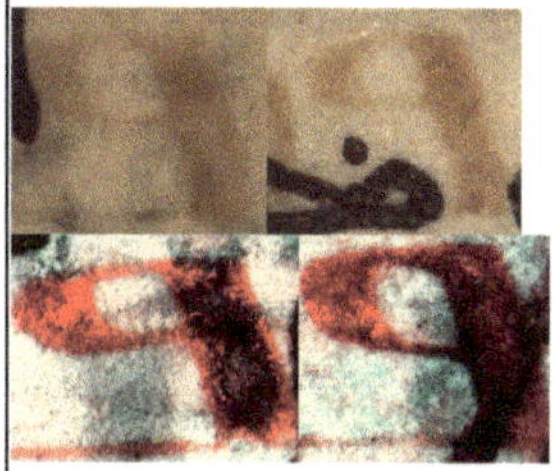
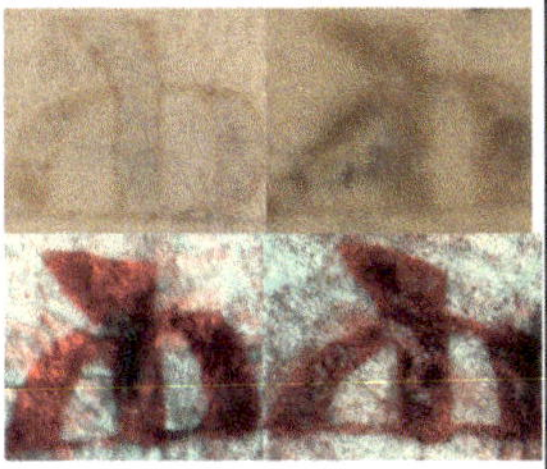	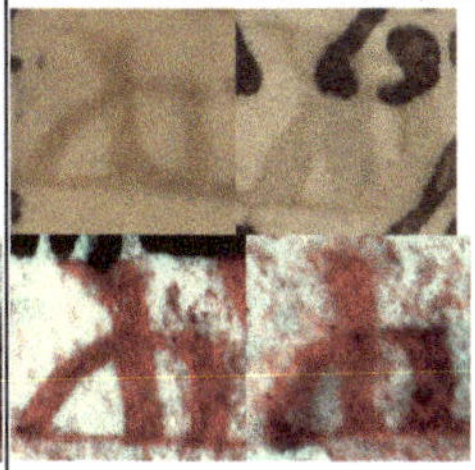	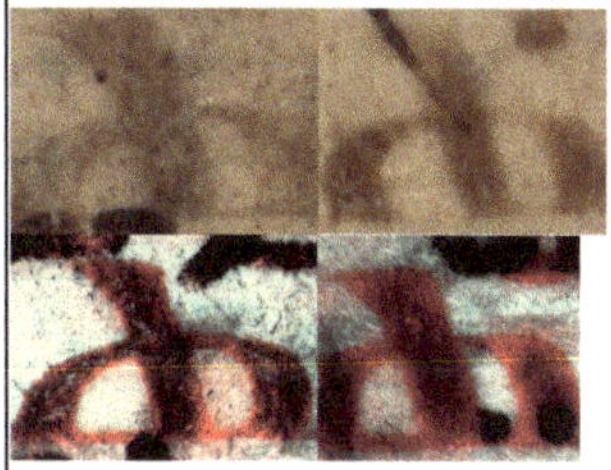

The snippets above uniformly demonstrate that the Acts script and the Catholic Epistles script are from the same hand. Thus, the descriptions below compare the Acts and Catholic Epistles together, against the script of the Pauline Epistles.

Table 7: Comparing scripts; CCR II (Paul) vs CCR XI (Apostolos)

	Acts and Catholic Epistles	Pauline Epistles
ܐ	The arm of the *alaf* is characteristically curved, with substantial shading of the stroke.	The arm of the *alaf* is straight, with little shading and only a small serif.
ܓ	The oblique tail of the *gamal* extends to the left of the ascender as well as to the right. The right-hand baseline joins the *gamal* partway up the ascender.	The baseline to the left of the *gamal's* ascender is nearly horizontal. The right-hand baseline joins the *gamal* at the joint between the tail and the ascender.
ܚ	The arms of the *ḥeth* are curved.	The arms of the *ḥeth* are straight.
ܟ	The ascender of the *kaf* is nearly vertical; the nose consists of a stroke almost perpendicular to the ascender.	The ascender of the *kaf* inclines to the left; the nose is sharply pointed and formed by the shading of a single stroke.
ܠ	The right-hand side of the ascender of the *lamad* is vertical. Shading often extends over half the height of the letter.	The ascender of the *lamad* inclines to the left; shading is limited to the top part of the letter.
ܥ	The arm of the *ʿe* is often nearly vertical, extends well above the height of the roofed letters and usually has a pronounced serif.	The arm of the *ʿe* is consistently oblique, broad and squat. The serif is often less pronounced.
ܦ	The ascender of the *pe* is vertical. The nose is large and semicircular, extending over about two-thirds of the letter height.	The ascender of the *pe* is consistently oblique. The nose is semi-elliptical, extending over less than half of the letter height.
ܬ	The arch of the *tau* is high and skewed to the right. The ascender is near-vertical, with substantial shading at the top of the stroke.	The arch of the *tau* is flattened and skewed to the left. The ascender is consistently oblique, with minimal shading at the top of the stroke.

3.2. CCR XI Codicology

3.2.1. Quire Structure

The limited evidence available suggests that this manuscript was composed largely of quaternions (perhaps with some quinions). As far as can be determined, the quires obeyed Gregory's Rule, flesh side outer, and were mirror-signed.

Twelve folios (six bifolia) of CCR XI are currently known: eleven preserved in the Museum of the Bible collection, and one in the Mingana collection.[2] These six bifolia are distributed across three distinct quires. In only one case (quire ten) has the outer sheet of the quire been preserved (demonstrated by the presence of a quire number and a header on each folio). In the case of two quires (numbers eight and ten), multiple sheets from the same quire have been preserved (two sheets in quire eight, and three sheets in quire ten). Gregory's Rule (flesh–flesh, hair–hair layout) is directly observable in these cases. From the third quire, only one sheet is preserved. On the assumption that this quire is a quaternion, the flesh–hair arrangement of the sheet is consistent with a flesh-outermost quire.

The one outer sheet currently known contains quire numbers on each folio. On the opening side of the quire, the quire

[2] CCR folio 138 (Mingana Syr. MS. 637) is included in the following codicological discussion of CCR XI. The folio has been edited by Duensing (1938), Black (1939) and Müller-Kessler and Sokoloff (1998b, 32–33). I have re-edited the folio from high-quality images, though without the aid of multispectral imaging technology; the text is to be found in Appendix II towards the end of this volume.

number ܝ appears underneath the first column, in the middle of the column. On the closing side, the quire number ܝ appears underneath the second column, in the middle of the column. In accordance with the mirror-signing method of quire numbering, this quire is therefore the tenth quire of CCR XI as a whole.[3] Assuming the whole of Acts was originally included in the manuscript, and that each quire was a quaternion, this gives an average of just under 96 verses per quire, or a little less than 12 verses per folio.[4]

Table 8: Extant quire numbers in CCR XI, quire 10

F. 44r (side 16 of quire)	F. 41v (side 1 of quire)
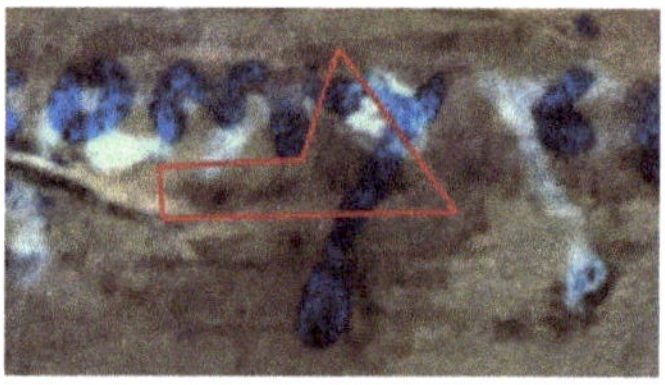	
ܝ	ܝ

The data above permit a relatively secure reconstruction of a three-quire sequence, as follows:[5]

[3] See §2.1.1. for the details of mirror-signing.

[4] The 10 quires contained Acts 1:1–27:27, which consists of 958 verses.

[5] This three-quire sequence has an average of 92 verses per quire, which is rather low, given the average of 96 verses per quire over the first 10 quires. In particular, quire 10 contains an unusually low number of verses (88.5). In terms of words, however, quire 10 is not suspiciously short. To fit Acts 1:1–27:27 into 10 quires means an average of 1756 words per quire (based on the Greek text). Quire 10 contains the equivalent of 1654 Greek words, a deviation of less than 6%. Equally, it is possible that some of the earlier quires were quinions (Desreumaux

Table 9: The quire structure of CCR XI

i. Quire Number *ii. Approx. quire range* *iii. Approx. no. verses* iv. First extant verse v. Last extant verse	Quire Structure
8 *Acts 19:20–21:37* *96* Acts 19:31b Acts 21:26a	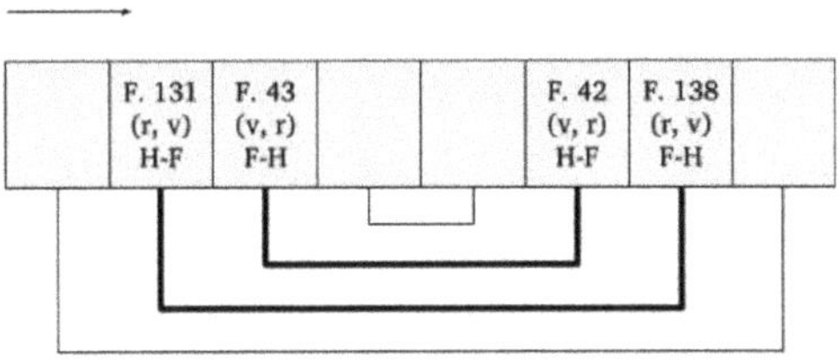
9 *Acts 21:38–24:24* *92* - -	
10 Acts 24:25–27:27a 88.5	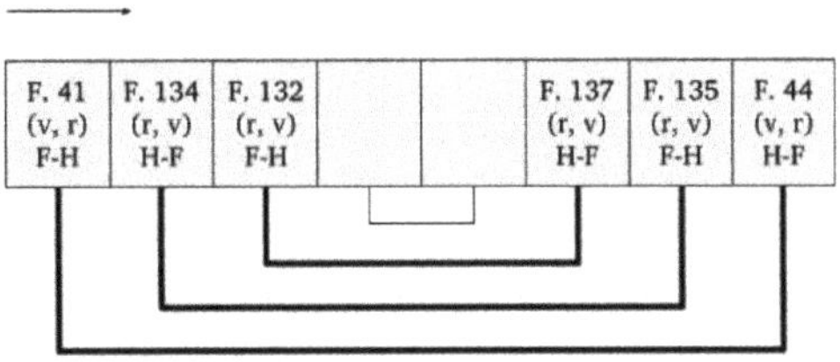

The sixth (and final) bifolium is more difficult to situate. The 46 verses between the end of the first folio and the beginning of the second suggest that there were four folios in between. The flesh–hair arrangement of the bifolium means that, if Gregory's Rule is to be kept, the quire must be a quaternion.

2015, 134). For instance, if two of the earlier quires were quinions, and the first folio of the codex was blank, this would yield just over 11.5 verses per folio, or just over 92 verses per quaternion quire.

Table 10: The Catholic Epistles quire

i. Quire Number *ii. Approx. quire range* *iii. Approx. no. verses* iv. First extant verse v. Last extant verse	Quire Structure
Quire No.? *1 Pet. 5:2–1 John 2:11* *93* 2 Pet. 1:1 1 John 1:9a	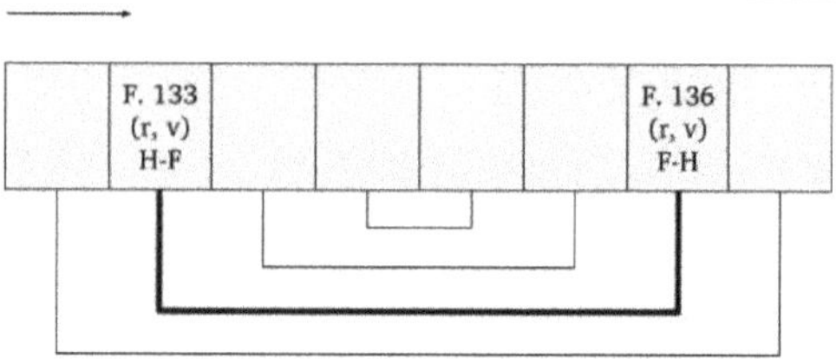

As the quire numbering calculations above demonstrate, the Catholic Epistles must have followed Acts, rather than preceding it. The difficult question to decide is how many quires stand between quire ten and this Catholic Epistles quire. At the very least, the remaining 48 verses of Acts, and the c. 93 initial verses of 1 Peter must stand in between; these 141 verses are too much for one intervening quire (even a quinion), but too little for two. Besides, the virtually unanimous comparative evidence points to the inclusion of the Epistle of James preceding the Petrine Epistles (Nienhuis 2007, 91–93). However, adding the 108 verses of James yields 249 intervening verses. This is now too much for two intervening quires (unless both happened to be quinions, which feels a little too 'neat'), but a little too little for three (83 verses per quire)—even when one allows that there may have been a blank column or so between Acts and the Epistles.

One numerically attractive solution is to posit that both James *and Jude* precede the Petrine epistles. In this case, the intervening material between the end of quire ten and the beginning of our Catholic Epistles quire runs to around 274 verses, or three quires of 91–92 verses each. However, beyond the neat numerical fit, and the attractive idea of placing both epistles written by Jesus' brothers side-by-side, there is little positive evidence for such an arrangement.[6]

3.2.2. Dimensions, Ruling and Mise-en-Page

CCR XI is arranged in portrait format. The average leaf measures approximately 230 × 183mm (though this is dictated largely by the reuse of the parchment for CCR), with a written area of approximately 190 × 140mm. Thus, the written area is slightly larger, on average, than in CCR II (180 × 137mm). As is usual for CPA manuscripts from the early period, the text is laid out in two columns per page. The average column measures approximately 190 × 63mm. Both right and left margins of each column are strictly justified. Justification of the left-hand margin is achieved mainly by adjusting the space between letters and compressing letter width. There is little evidence of dilation of the letters. Each column consists of 22 lines, without deviation. In this, also, CCR XI differs slightly from CCR II, where the scribe occasionally used a twenty-third line. The average height of the letter *beth* is 3–5mm.

---

[6] Wasserman (2006, 106–17) does note a couple of Greek manuscripts, both from the tenth century, in which Jude follows James.

Ruling is performed with a dry point, on the flesh side. It consists of four column-boundary vertical lines, extending over the full height of the sheet. Horizontal lines are drawn for each line of text, and apparently extend across the full width of the bifolium.

3.2.3. Paratextual Features

New paragraphs are usually indicated by ekthesis, and enlargement of the first letter, though sometimes the latter occurs without the former (e.g., f. 131r I.10). Unlike in CCR II, these letters are not ornamented.[7]

In five instances (Acts 20:2; 24:27; 25:23; 27:1; 27:27), the beginning of a larger text unit is marked with the ܪܫ ܡܩܠܝܘܢ rubric. Blank lines are not used to separate these rubrics from the main text, but in each of the five instances a large, ornate cross is collocated with the beginning of the text unit. As in CCR II, where the marginal cross forms an adornment to the text with ekthesis, so too in CCR XI the cross adorns the biblical text itself. In three instances, the first word of the new text unit begins with a *wau*, and the cross appears inside the *wau*, which is significantly enlarged. In the other two instances, the cross appears in the margin, adjacent to the beginning of the text unit.[8]

---

[7] The only exception appears on f. 135r II.6 (Acts 27:7) where, for no obvious reason, an initial enlarged *beth* is adorned with a four-dot diamond very similar to those found regularly in CCR II (see §2.1.3.).

[8] These ornate crosses bear significant stylistic similarities to those documented by Desreumaux (2023, 139) in Sin. syr. NF M56N. Nonethe-

Table 11: The ornamental crosses in CCR XI

Acts 20:2 (F. 43v)	Acts 24:27 (F. 41v)	Acts 25:23 (F. 132r)	Acts 27:1 (F. 137v)	Acts 27:27 (F. 44r)

These rubrics were written using a peculiarly black ink, which in many instances remains easily legible. The same ink was apparently used as one element in the ornamental crosses. Alternatively, it may be that at least some of the original rubrics and ornaments were re-inked at some point in the manuscript's history.

Figure 12: Snippet from f. 131v, showing evidence of re-inking

In region 1 of this snippet, the black four-dot diamond can be seen to have been written over the usual triangle of dots that mark the end of a sentence in this manuscript. In region 2, one sees that although the baseline between the *qof* and the *pe* has

less, these similarities can only be the result of the shared cultural milieu within which both manuscripts were produced and used, rather than pointing to the work of the same scribe; the scripts are markedly different in some respects (e.g. the shape of the *pe*).

been re-inked, the remainder of the baseline up to the *wau* has not been re-inked. Finally, in region 3, the baseline has been re-inked, but poorly; it is just possible to see traces of the original baseline just above the re-inked line.

Between the end of each Catholic Epistle and the beginning of the next, there appears a brief conclusion, ornament, and introduction. Unlike the relatively lengthy conclusions to the Pauline Epistles in CCR II (see §2.1.3.), the concluding formula in CCR XI is simply ܫܠܡܬ ܐܓܪܬܗ ܕ + [name of letter]. The conclusions and introductions are also written in the same unusually black ink as the ܪܝܫ ܦܠܚܘܢ rubrics, and there is the same question of possible reinking.

Figure 13: Snippet from concluding rubric f. 136r

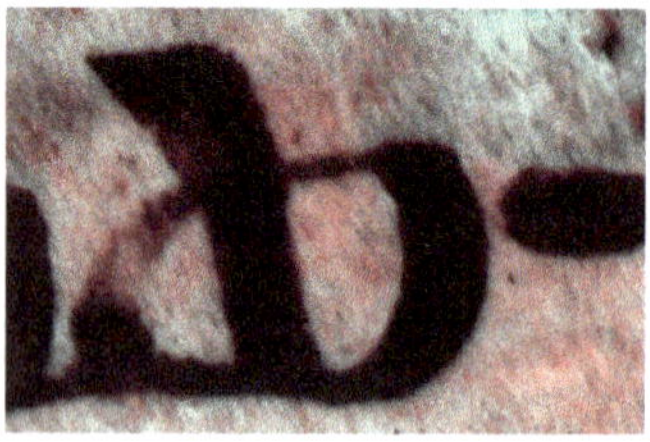

In the small snippet above, from the pseudocolour image of f. 136r, the original *tau* appears in the form of a red 'shadow' to the right of the black re-inking.

Only one outer sheet of a quire is preserved from CCR XI. On both the opening side (f. 41v) and the closing side (f. 44r) the header ܦܪܟܣܝܣ appears.[9] Thus, it appears that CCR XI did not employ running quire headers (at least in the case of the Acts portion

[9] Müller-Kessler (2023b, 149, n. 17), unaware of the quire structure of CCR XI, implies that these headers are added at the beginning of biblical chapters, rather than being codicologically occasioned.

of the manuscript) and used only the short header ܦܪܟܣܝܣ rather than a longer form such as ܦܪܟܣܝܣ ܫ̈ܠܝܚܐ.

3.2.4. Punctuation

In a sample taken across the full range of CCR XI, the three-dot punctuation sign occurred 145 times; the pair of vertically arranged dots occurred 55 times; the single punctuation dot occurred 21 times. The three-dot symbol is obviously the dominant, default punctuation sign in CCR XI. It is even more dominant in CCR XI than was found to be the case in CCR II. To illustrate: in CCR XI the triple-dot sign is nearly three times as common as the double-dot sign, whereas in CCR II it is not even twice as common (see §2.1.4. for details).

Another clear difference between CCR XI and CCR II concerns the positioning of the punctuation dots. In CCR XI, there is a very dominant tendency to place the punctuation dots *low* relative to the letter-position. Frequently, the lower dot of the double- or triple-dot sign falls below the writing base line. This scribal tendency is in clear contradistinction to the tendency in CCR II, in which, usually, the dots are arranged either in line with the mid-height of the letters, or at the height of the top of the roofed letters.

Figure 14: The low placement of the punctuation in CCR XI

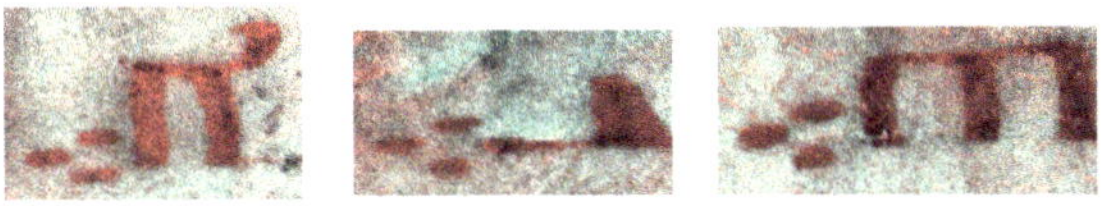

Since the three-dot punctuation sign is so dominant, it is of more interest to inquire whether there is any rationale behind the occasional use of the double-dot or single-dot signs. As was found in CCR II, the entire system of use of the various pausal dots lacks obvious rigour. Nonetheless, as with CCR II, so in CCR XI there is a tendency to reserve the use of the double and single punctuation dots for contexts of minimal semantic or prosodic disjunction. Examples of the use of the single dot include: the disjunction between a main clause and an explanatory phrase (Acts 19:40); the boundary between the end of a restrictive relative clause and the resumption of the main clause (Acts 20:9; 21:10); the minimal boundary between a main clause and an indirect object (Acts 21:11). Examples of the use of the double-dot punctuation sign include: marking the boundary between a fronted temporal phrase and the main clause (Acts 20:1; 21:12); preceding direct speech (Acts 21:11, 13; 26:32; 27:10); between two predicates of a compound sentence (Acts 20:2, 5, 6; 21:3); in general, between clauses with a clear thematic link (Acts 21:7: all the predicates refer to events at Acre; 21:8: all the predicates refer to the arrival at Caesarea). Of course, in most of these cases examples can be found where the default triple-dot sign is used in a parallel grammatical context.

3.3. CCR XI Text

Critical Symbols and Apparatus

[...]	Lacuna
[ܐܒܓ]	Reconstructed text
ܐܒܓ	Uncertain reading
ܐ ܒ ܓ	Supralinear secondary insertion
[a]ܐܒܓ	Word is commented on in the *sub loco* apparatus
[a]ܐܒܓ[a]	Text between the pair of superscript letters is commented on in the *sub loco* apparatus
*ܐܒܓ	Text is commented on in the Textual and Linguistic Commentary at the end of this volume

The critical apparatus is in two parts. The first part compares the present edition to previous editions, principally those of Müller-Kessler and Sokoloff (1997, 1998a, 1998b). For each page, this first apparatus begins with: MKS IIB, [page number(s)], indicating the page(s) of Müller-Kessler and Sokoloff (1998b) corresponding to the particular text at hand.

After this apparatus, and separated therefrom by double vertical lines ||, follows a brief textual apparatus. Substantial issues are reserved for the Textual and Linguistic Commentary at the end of this volume. Textual comments appearing *sub loco* in the second part of the apparatus are limited to minor issues such as the noting of a second hand, or an apparent error in the manuscript.

Acts 19:31–36 F. 131r

ܪ̈ܚܡܘܗܝ: ܫܕܪ̈ܘ
ܠܘܬܗ ܒ̈ܥܝܢ
ܡܢܗ ܕܠܐ ܝܬܠ
ܢܦܫܗ ܠܬܐܛܪܘܢ:
[32] ܣܘ̈ܓܝܢ ܡܢ ܐܘܦ
ܣܘ̈ܓܝܐܢ[a] ܗܘܘ
ܡܢ ܩ̈ܥܝܢ: [b] ܗܘܬ
ܓܪ ܟܢܫܬܐ
ܡܒܪܒܟܐ:
ܘܣܓܝ ܡܢܗܘܢ
ܠܐ ܗܘܘ ܝܕ̈ܥܝܢ
ܒܡܢܐ ܥܠܐ
ܐܬܟܢ̈ܫܘ: [33] ܐܢ̈ܫܝܢ
ܕܝ ܡܢ ܐܘܟܠܘܣܐ
ܒܥܘ̈
ܠܐܠܟܣܢܕܪܘܣ
ܗܕܝ ܕܩܪ̈ܒܘ
ܝܗܘ̈ܕܝܐ: [c]
ܐܠܟܣܢܕܪܘܣ
ܐܘܦ ܐܢܕܕ
ܟܐܝܕܗ ܘܗܘܐ
ܒܥ̇ܐ ܕܝܬܠ

ܐܦܘܠܘ ܓܝܐ
ܠܐܘܟܠܘܣܐ:
[34] ܟܕ ܕܝ ܕܝܕ̈ܥܘ
ܕܗܘ ܝܗܘܕܝ:
ܩܠ ܚܕ ܐܬܥܒܕ
ܡܢ ܟܠܗܘܢ
ܗܝܟ ܚܕ ܬܪ̈ܬܝܢ
ܫ̈ܥܝܢ ܡܢ ܩ̈ܥܝܢ
ܪܒܐ ܗܝ ܐܪܛܡܝܣ
ܕܐܦܣ̈ܝܐ:
[35] ܫܬܩ ܕܝ ܟܠܘܬܟܐ
ܠܐܘܟܠܘܣܐ
ܘܐܡܪ ܠܗܘܢ:
ܓܒ̈ܪܝܐ ܐܦܣ̈ܝܢ[d]
ܡ̇ܢ ܓܪ ܡܢ
ܒܢ̈ܝܫܐ ܠܐ ܡܒܪ
ܕܡܕܝܢܬܗܘܢ
ܕܐܦܣ̈ܝܢ ܗܝ
ܟܡܪܬܐ
ܕܐܪܛܡܝܣ
ܪܒܬܐ ܘܕܕܝܣ:
[36] ܟܕܐ ܐܘܦ ܕܠܝܬ

MKS IIB, 26: **a** ܣܘ̈ܓܝܐܢ | **b** omit *seyame* | **c** omit diacritic | **d** ܐܦܣ̈ܝܢ

Acts 19:36–20:1 **F. 131v**

ܠܗܠܝܢ ܙܗܘܦ
ܢܦܠ ܠܟܘܢ ܕܬܗܘܘܢ
ܫܕܝܟܝܢ ∴ [37] ܐܝܬܝܬܘܢ
ܓܪ[a] ܠܟܐ ܓܒܪ̈ܝܐ
ܗܠܝܢ: ܐܢ̈ܫܝܢ
ܕܠܐ ܚܠܝܢ ܘ
ܝ ܠܗܝܟܠܗܘܢ: ܘܠܐ
ܓܕܦ̈ܘ ܥܠ ܐܠܗܬܟܘܢ ∴
[38] ܐܢ ܕܝ ܠܕܡܝܛܪܝܣ
ܘܠܐܘܡܢ̈ܝܐ
ܗܠܝܢ ܕܥܡܗ
ܐܝܬ ܥܡ ܐܢܫ
ܣܥܡ: ܐܝܬ
ܠܕܝܢ̈ܝܢ[b] ܘܐܘܦ
ܐܢܬܘܦܛ̈ܝܢ ∴
ܢܩܒܠܘܢ ܠܗܘܢ
ܗܠܝܢ ܥܠ ܗܠܝܢ ∴
[39] ܐܢ ܕܝ ܥܠ
ܥܠܡ ܐܚܪܢ
ܐܬܘܢ ܡܬܒ̈ܥܝܢ
ܒܟܢܫܬܐ ܕܢܡܣ
ܢܡܘܣܐ ܗܘ

ܡܫܬܪܐ ∴ [40] ܠܒܕܢ
ܕܗܐ ܐܢܗ ܒܒܪ
ܡܬ̈ܚܡܝܢ ܕܢܬܫܐܠ·
ܡܢ ܛܒ ܚܘܪܒܬܐ
ܕܐܬܥܒܕܬ
ܝܘܡܢ ∴ ܕܥܠܐ
ܠܝܬ ܠܢ ܕܒܬܪܗ
ܢܟܠ ܕܢܬܠ
ܐ ܓܒܗ ܚܠܛܒ[c]
ܒܢܫܐ ܗܕܢ ∴
[41] ܘܟܕܐ ܕܐܡܪ
ܗܠܝܢ ܦܛܪܬ* ܟܢܫܬܐ ∴
[20:1] ܘܡܢ ܒܬܪ ܕܫܠܝܬ[d]
ܚܘܪܒܬܐ:
ܩܪܐ ܦܘܠܘܣ
ܠܬܠܡ̈ܝܕܝܐ ∴
ܘܟܕܐ ܕܢܣܒ
ܬܗܘܢ ܫܐܠ
ܒܫܠܡܗܘܢ
ܘܢܦܩ ܕܢܐܙܠ
ܠܡܩܕܘܢܝܐ ❖[e]
ܪܫ ܡܩܠܘܢ ∴

MKS IIB, 27: **b** ܠܕܝܢ̈ܝ, | **c** ܚܠ ܛܒ | **d** omit diacritic || **a** marginal addition, apparently by the same hand | **b** The final *nun* was already predicted by Schulthess (1910, 52). | **e** See §3.2.3.

Acts 20:2–7 **F. 43v**

[2]ܘܟܕ[a] ܚܓܠ ܦܘܠܘܣ
ܬܚܘܡܝ ܐܬܪ̈ܝܐ.*
ܒܡܠܐ ܣܓܝ.
ܐܬܐ ܠܗܠܣ:
[3]ܘܥܒܕ ܬܡܢ
ܬܠܬܐ ܝܪ̈ܚܝܢ:
ܒܥܐ ܕܝ
ܕܐܬܥܒܕ ܠܗ
ܚܒܠܐ ܡܢ ܝܗ̈ܘܕܝ[b]
ܐܬܐ̇[c] ܕܢܦܪܘܫ
ܠܣܘܪܝܐ: ܐܬܡܠܟ
ܕܢܬܘܒ ܠܗ ܥܠ
ܕܡܩܕܘܢܝܐ:
[4]ܗܘܘ ܕܝ ܚ̈ܓܠܝܢ
ܥܡܗ ܣܘܦܛܪܘܣ
ܒܪܗ ܕܦܘܪܘܣ
ܡܢ ܒܪܘܝܐ: ܡܢ
ܬܣܠܘܢܝܩܝ̈ܐ ܕܝ:
ܐܪܝܣܛܪܟܘܣ
ܘܣܩܘܢܕܘܣ
ܘܓܐܝܘܣ ܡܢ ܕܪܒܐ.[b]
ܘܛܝܡܬܝܘܣ:

ܡܢ ܐܣܝܐ ܕܝ
ܛܘܟܝܩܘܣ:
ܘܛܪܘܦܝܡܘܣ:
[5]ܗܠܝܢ ܕܝ ܩܕܡܘ:
ܘܗܘܘ ܡܣܟܪ̈ܝܢ
ܠܢ ܒܛܪܘܐܣ:
[6]ܘܐܢܢ ܦܪ̈ܫܢܢ
ܡܢ ܒܬܪ ܝܘ̈ܡܝܐ
ܕܦܛܝܪ̈ܐ ܡܢ
ܦܝܠܝܦܘܣ:
ܘܐܬܝܢܢ ܠܘܬܗܘܢ
ܠܛܪܘܐܣ
ܠܚ̈ܡܫܐ ܝܘ̈ܡܝܢ:*
[7]ܒܝܘܡܐ ܕܝ ܕܚܕ
ܒܫܒܐ ܗܘܝܢ
ܡܟܢ̈ܫܝܢ ܕܢܩܨ ܐ
ܠܚܡܐ: ܘܦܘܠܘܣ
ܗܘܐ ܡܡܠܠ
ܠܗܘܢ ܐܬܐ̇ ܕܢܦܘܩ
ܒܝܘܡܐ ܕܡܚܪ:
ܦܫܛ ܡܠܬܐ
ܥܕ ܡܨ̇ܥܬ ܠܠܝܐ

MKS IIB, 28: **b** omit *seyame* | **c** omit diacritic || **a** Initial *wau* contains ornate cross. See §3.2.3.

Acts 20:7–14

F. 43r

ܕܠܝܠܝܐ: [8] ܘܗܘܘ ܕܝ
ܠܡܦ̈ܕܝܢ ܣܓܝܢ
ܒܥܠܝܬܐ ܗܝ
ܕܗܘ̈ܝܢ ܡܟܢܫܝܢ:
[9] ܘܥܠܝܡ ܚܕ ܕܗܘܐ
ܫܡܗ ܐܘܛܝܟܘܣ·
ܗܘܐ ܝܬܒ
ܒܟܘܬܐ ܫܟܒ
ܕܝ ܒܫܢܐ ܒܥܡܘܩܐ:
ܘܟܡܐ ܕܗܘܐ
ܦܘܠܘܣ ܡܡܠܠ.
ܥܠ ܕܣܓܘܬ̈ ܛܒ
ܒܫܢܬܐ: ܘܢܦܠ ܡܢ
ܬܠܬܐ ܕܪ̈ܓܝܢ ܠܪ̈ܥ:
ܘܐܪ̈ܡܘܗ ܡܝܬܗ
ܡܝܬ: [10] ܘܢܚܬ
ܦܘܠܘܣ ܘܢܦܠ
ܥܠܘܝ ܘܓܦ ܠܗ:
ܘܐܡܪ ܠܐ
ܬܕܚܠܘܢ ܢܦܫܗ
ܓܪ ܒܓܘܗ ܐܝܬ
ܗܝ: [11] ܘܣܠܩ

ܘܩܨ ܐ ܠܚܡܐ
ܘܐܟܠ: ܥܠ ܕܢܗܪ
ܕܝ ܡܠܠ ܥܕ ܡܛܠܐ
ܕܢܓܗܬ· ܘܒܟܢ
ܢܦܩ: [12] ܐܝܬܝܘ[a] ܕܝ
ܛܠܝܐ ܒܚܝܝܢ:
ܘܐܬܢܝܚܘ̈
ܘܠܐ ܝ ܡܚܣܪ:
[13] ܐܢܢ ܕܝ ܐܙ̈ܠܢ
ܠܗ ܒܐܠܦܐ:
ܘܦܪ̈ܫܢܗ
ܠܐܣܘܣ: ܕܡܢ
ܬܡܢ ܗܘܝܢ ܐܙ̈ܠܝܢ
ܕܢܣܒ ܠܦܘܠܘܣ:
ܗܟܢ ܓܪ ܐܬܦܩܡ
ܥܡܢ ܗܘ ܐܬܐ
ܗܘ ܕܢܗܠܟ:
[14] ܒܡܟܐ ܕܝ ܕܦܓ̈ܥܢ
ܥܡܢ ܒܐܣܘܣ:
ܢܣܒܢ ܝܬܗ
ܘܐܬܝܢ
ܠܡܛܝܠܝܢܐ: [b]

MKS IIB, 29: **a** ܐܝ̈ܬܝܘ || **b** MS *sic; expectaveris* ܠܡܝܛܝܠܝܢܐ

Acts 21:3–8 F. 42v

ܠܣܘܪܝܘܣ ܀
ܘܢܚܬܢ ܠܬܗ̇[a]
ܠܬܡܢ: ܘܗܘܝܢ
ܦܪܩܝܢ ܠܛܥܘܢܐ ܀
ܘܡܛܝܢ ܠܨܘܪ :
ܬܡܢ ܓܝܪ ܗܘܐ
ܐܠܦܐ[a] ܦܪܩ ܛܥܢܗ ܀
[4]ܘܐܫܟܚܢܢ
ܬܠܡܝܕܝܐ ܀
ܘܟܬܪܢ ܬܡܢ[b]
ܫܒܥܐ ܝܘܡܝܢ ܀
ܗܠܝܢ ܕܝ ܗܘܘ
ܐܡܪܝܢ ܠܦܘܠܘܣ
ܒܪܘܚܐ ܕܠܐ
ܢܣܩ ܠܝܪܘܫܠܡ ܀
[5]ܘܟܕ ܐܬܟܡܠ ܠܢ
ܕܫܠܡ ܝܘܡܝܐ
ܢܦܩܢ ܐܙܠܢ ܀
ܘܗܘܘ ܡܠܘܝܢ
ܠܢ ܟܠܗܘܢ ܥܡ
ܢܫܝܗܘܢ ܘܒܢܝܗܘܢ
ܥܕ ܡܢ[a] ܠܒܪ

ܡܢ ܡܕܝܢܬܐ ܀
ܘܩܒܕܢܗ
ܐܪܟܒܬܢ[c]
ܥܠ ܣܦܪ ܝܡܐ
ܘܨܠܝܢ ܀ ܘܫܠܡܢ[c]
ܟܠܢ ܠܟܠܢ : [6]ܘܣܠܩܢ
ܠܐܠܦܐ ܀ ܗܠܝܢ
ܕܝ ܬܒܘ ܠܗܘܢ
ܠܒܝܬܗܘܢ ܀ [7]ܘܐܢܚܢ
ܫܠܡܢܢ[d] ܦܪܘܫܐ[e]
ܡܢ ܨܘܪ ܀ ܘܡܛܝܢ
ܠܥܟܘ ܀ ܘܫܐܠܢ
ܒܫܠܡܗܘܢ
ܕܐܚܝܐ: ܘܝܬܒܢ
ܠܘܬܗܘܢ ܚܕ ܝܘܡ ܀
[8]ܘܒܝܘܡܐ ܕܒܬܪ
ܢܦܩܢ ܘܐܬܝܢܢ
ܠܩܣܪܝܢ ܘܥܠܢ
ܠܒܝܬܗ ܕܦܝܠܝܦܘܣ
ܡܒܣܪܐ ܗܘ ܕܝ
ܕܗܘܐ ܡܢ ܫܒܥܬܐ ܀
ܘܝܬܒܢ ܠܘܬܗ:

MKS IIB, 30: **a** omit diacritic | **c** omit *seyame* | **d** ܫܠܡܢܗ | **e** omit *seyame* (MS *sic*) || **b** MS *sic*; *expectaveris* ܬܡܢܘܢ or ܬܡܢܢ

Acts 21:9–14 F. 42r

9 ܗܘܐ ܕܝ ܠܗܕܢ
ܐܪܒܥ ܒܢ̈ܢ ܒܬܘܠܢ
ܡܬܢܒ̈ܝܢ܀ 10 ܟܡܐ
ܕܝ ܕܟܪ̈ܝܢ [a]
ܬܡܢ ܝܘ̈ܡܝܢ
ܡܚܬܪ ܢܚܬ
ܢܒܝܐ [b] ܚܕ ܡܢ
ܝܗܘܕܝܐ
ܕܫܡܗ ܐ ܓܒܘܣ.
11 ܘܐܬܐ ܠܘܬܢ܀
ܘܢܣܒ ܙܘܢܪܐ
ܕܦܘܠܘܣ. ܘܟܦܬ
ܐܝ̈ܕܘܗܝ ܘܪ̈ܓܠܘܗܝ [c]
ܕ ܓܪܡܗ ܘܐܡܪ܀
ܗܟܢ ܐܡܪܬ
ܪܘܚܐ ܕܩܘܕܫܐ.
ܠܓܒܪܐ ܗܕܢ
ܕܙܘܢܪܐ ܗܕܐ
ܕܝܠܗ܀ ܗܟܢ
ܢܟܦܬܘܢ ܝܬܗ
ܝ̈ܗܘܕܝܝܢ ܒܐܘܪܫܠܡ܀
ܘܢܫܠܡܘ°ܢܗ [d] ܝܬܗ
ܠܓܘ ܐܪ̈ܡܝܘܢ
ܕܡܫܬܡܥܐ܀ 12 ܟܕ ܕܝ
ܫܡܥ̈ܢܢ ܗܠܝܢ܀
ܗܘܝܢ ܒܥ̈ܝܢ
ܡܢܗ ܐܢܗ
ܘܒ̈ܢܝ ܐܬܪܐ
ܕܠܐ ܢܣܩܘܢ
ܠܐܘܪܫܠܡ܀
13 ܘܒܟܝ ܐ ܓܢܒ
ܦܘܠܘܣ ܘܐܡܪ܀
ܡܢܐ ܐܬܘܢ
ܥܒ̈ܕܝܢ ܒܟ̈ܝܢ
ܘܡܫܚܩܝܢ*
ܝܬܗ ܠܠܒܝ܀
ܐܢܐ ܓܪ ܠܐ
ܒܠܚܘܕ ܕܐܬܟܦܬ [e]
ܐܠܐ ܐܘܦ ܕܐܡܘܬ
ܒܐܘܪܫܠܡ
ܥܬܝܕ ܐܢܐ ܟܠ
ܫܡܗ ܝܫܘܥ [f]
14 ܟܡܐ ܕܝ ܕܠܐ
ܗܘܐ ܡܬܦܝܣ܀

MKS IIB, 31: **a** ܕܒܬܪ̈ܝܢ | **b** ܢܒܝܐ | **c** ܘܪ̈ܓܠܘܗܝ | **d** ܘܢܫܠܡ(ܘ)ܢܗ (MS *sic*) | **e** omit diacritic || **a** MS *sic*; *expectaveris* ܕܬܪ̈ܝܢ. *Kaf* was originally a *tau*, subsequently emended. | **e** The diacritic over the *tau* is often found in a range of morphological forms of this root. | **f** MS *sic*; *expectaveris* ܕܝܫܘܥ

Acts 24:25–25:3 **F. 41v**

ܦܪܟܣܝܣ

[25]ܟܕܟܐ ܕܝ ܕܗܘܐ
ܡܡܠܠ ܥܠܝܗ[a]
ܙܕܟܐ ܘܥܠܝܗ[b]
ܕܟܝܢܘܬܐ ܘܕܝܢܐ
ܕܥܬܝܕ: ܐܬܕܚܠ
ܕܝ ܦܝܠܟܤ
ܒܕܚܠܬܐ.. ܘܐܡܪ ܠܗ[c]
ܟܕܘ ܐܙܠ ܠܟ: ܘܡܟܐ[d]
ܕܗܘܐ ܡܢܪܗ[e]
ܐܢܐ ܡܩܪܐ ܒܬܪܟ.:
[26]ܐܘܦ ܗܕܐ
ܡܣܟܐ ܕܡܬܝܗܒ
ܗܘܠ ܠܗ ܦܘܠܘܤ:
ܘܠܡܘܠ ܗܕܐ
ܐܘܦ ܐܢ ܡܣܟܢܬ
ܗܘܐ ܡܩܪܐ
ܒܬܪܗ
ܘܡܡܠܠ ܥܡܗ:
ܐܝܟ ܡܥܠܝܐ
✝ [27]ܟܕܟܐ ܕܝ
ܕܐܬܡ̈ܠܝܐ[f]
ܬܪܬܝܢ ܫܢܝܢ.
:ܠ:[g]

ܢܣܒ ܦܝܠܝܟܤ
ܣܠܝܦܘܗܝ[f]
ܠܦܘܪܩܝܘܤ
ܦܣܛܘܤ.:
ܟܕ ܐܬܐ ܕܝ ܦܝܠܝܟܤ
ܕܢܥܒܕ ܛܝܒܘ
ܠܝܗ̈ܘܕܝܐ ܥܒܕ
ܦܘܠܘܤ ܟܦܝܬ.:
[25:1]ܦܣܛܘܤ ܕܝ ܐܬܐ
ܥܠ ܠܗܦܪܟܝܐ.:
ܘܡܢ ܒܬܪ ܬܠܬܐ
ܝܘ̈ܡܝܢ ܣܠܩ ܡܢ
ܩܣܪܝܐ
ܠܐܘܪܫܠܡ.:
[2]ܐܘܕܥܘ ܠܗ ܕܝ
ܪܝܫ[f] ܟܗܢܐ.
ܘܪܒܪܒܢܝܗܘܢ
ܕܝܗܘ̈ܕܝܐ.:[h] ܥܠ
ܦܘܠܘܤ: ܘܗܘܘ
ܒܥܝܢ ܡܢܗ
[3]ܛܝܒܘ ܥܠܘܗܝ ܠܡܫܕܪ
ܕܢܝܬܐ ܠܗ

MKS IIB, 34: **a** ܥܠ ܥܠܝܗ | **b** ܘܥܠ ܥܠܝܗ | **c** ܘܐܡܪ ܠܗ | **d** ܘܡܟܐ | **e** ܡܙܘܢܐ | **f** omit *seyame* || **g** Quire number (see §3.2.1.) | **h** *Dalath* is a marginal addition, apparently by the same hand.

Acts 25:3–9 F. 41r

ܠܝܪܘܫܠܡ܀
ܟܡܝܢ ܠܗ ܒܡܟܡܢ
ܕܝܩܛܠܘܢ ܝܬܗ
ܒܐܘܪܚܐ܀
[4] ܦܝܣܛܘܣ ܐܘܢ
ܐ ܥܢܐ ܘܐܡܪ:
ܡܬܢܛܪ ܗܘ
ܦܘܠܘܣ ܒܩܣܪܝܢ܀
ܥܠ ܥܝܪܗ ܕܝ
ܐܡܪ ܕܗܘ
ܥܬܝܕ ܒܩܪܝܒ
ܕܐܦܩܘܣ܀ [5] ܘܐܡܪ
ܗܠܝܢ ܐܘܢ ܕܒܟܘܢ
ܚܝܠܝܢ· ܢܚܬܘܢ܀
ܘܒܗ ܕܐܢܬ
ܒܓܒܪܐ ܥܠܐ
ܢܛܪܘܢ ܒܗ [a] ܝܬܗ܀
[6] ܒܬܪ ܕܝ ܕܥܒܕ
ܥܡܗܘܢ ܝܘܡܝܢ:
ܠܐ ܝܬܝܪ
ܡܢ ܬܡܢܝܐ ܐܘ
ܥܣܪܐ: ܢܚܬ

ܠܩܣܪܝܢ܀
ܘܒܝܘܡܐ ܕܡܚܪ
ܝܬܒ ܥܠ ܒܝܡܐ:
ܘܐܡܪ ܕܝܝܬܘܢ [b]
ܠܦܘܠܘܣ܀ [7] ܟܕ
ܕܝ ܐܬܐ ܩܪܒܘ
ܝܬܗ ܝܗܘܕܝܐ
ܗܠܝܢ ܕܢܚܬܘ [c]
ܡܢ ܝܪܘܫܠܡ:
ܘܩܡܘ ܥܠܝܢ ܡܫܢܝܐ [c]
ܗܘܘ ܡܬܢܛܝܢ ܥܠܘܝ:
ܗܠܝܢ ܕܠܐ ܗܘܘ
ܝܟܠܝܢ ܡܚܘܕܝܢ
[8] ܕܗܘܐ ܦܘܠܘܣ
ܡܗܒ ܐܦܣܘ:
ܕܠܐ ܒܢܡܘܣܗܘܢ
ܕܝܗܘܕܝܐ:
ܘܠܐ ܥܠ ܗܝܟܠܐ.
ܘܠܐ ܥܠ ܩܣܪ
ܐܣܟܠܬ ܟܠܘܡ܀
[9] ܦܝܣܛܘܣ ܕܝ
ܒܥܐ ܕܝܥܒܕ

MKS IIB, 35: **b** ܕܝܬܘܢ | **c** omit *seyame* || **a** MS *sic*; *expectaveris* ܢܛܪܘܢ ܒܗ

Acts 25:9–14 — F. 134r

ܛܒܘ ܠܝܗ̈ܘܕܝ܇
ܐܬ ܥܢܝ ܘܐܡܪ
ܠܦܘܠܘܣ܇ ܨܒܐ
ܐܬ ܕܬܣܩܘܡ
ܠܝܪܘܫܠܡ:
ܘܬܡܢ ܥܠܠܒ[a] ܗܠܝܢ
ܬܬܕܝܢ ܩܘܕܡܝ܀
[10] ܦܘܠܘܣ ܕܝ
ܐܡܪ ܩܘܕܡ
ܒܝܡܐ ܕܩܝܣܪ
ܐܢܐ ܩܐܡ܇ ܗܢ
ܕܝܠ[b] ܠܝ ܕܐܬܕܝܢ܀
ܠܝܗ̈ܘܕܝ ܟܠܘܡ
ܠܐ ܛܠܡܬ ܗܘܝ
ܟܡܐ ܕܐܘܦ ܐܬ
ܛܒܐܝܬ ܐܬ
ܝܕܥ܇ [11] ܐܢ ܕܝ
ܐܝܬ ܐܢܐ ܛܠܡ
ܘܥܒܕ ܟܠܘܡ
ܕܫܘܐ[c] ܠܡܘܬܐ.
ܠܝܬ ܐܢܐ ܦܫܠ
ܕܝܡܘܬ܀ ܐܢ ܕܝ

ܟܠܘܡ ܠܝܬ ܗܘ
ܡܢ ܗܐ ܕܗܠܝܢ
ܡܩܛܪ̈ܓ ܒܝ ܠܝ:
ܐܢܫ ܠܐ ܝܟܠ
ܕܝܬܠ ܝܬܝ ܠܗܘܢ
ܡܬܘܗܒܐ. ܠܩܝܣܪ
ܐܢܐ ܩܪܐ܀
[12] ܘܒܟܢ ܦܝܣܛܘܣ
ܡܠܠ ܥܡ ܒܪ
ܡܠܟܗ ܘܐ ܥܢܝ:
ܠܩܝܣܪ ܩܪܝܬ
ܠܘܬ ܩܝܣܪ ܬܐܙܠ܀
[13] ܒܡܐ ܕܝ ܕܐܥܒܪܘ
ܝܘ̈ܡܝܢ܀ ܐ ܓܪܝܦܣ
ܡܠܟܐ ܘܒܪܢܝܩܐ
ܢܚܬܘ ܠܩܝܣܪ̈ܝܢ
ܕܝܫܐܠܘܢ
ܒܫܠܡܗ
ܕܦܝܣܛܘܣ܀
[14] ܘܟ̈ܕܘ ܬܡܢ
ܝܘ̈ܡܝܢ ܡܣܓܝܬ܀
ܦܝܣܛܘܣ ܕܝ

MKS IIB, 36: **a** ܥܠ ܠܒ | **c** omit diacritic || **b** *Dalath* is a marginal addition, apparently by the same hand.

Acts 25:14–19 F. 134v

ܐܘܕܥ ܠܡܠܟܐ
ܥܠ ܕܝܠܗ ܕܦܘܠܘܣ
ܘܐܡܪ: ܓܒܪ
ܚܕ ܐܝܬ ܠܝ
ܕܐܫܬܒܩ ܡܢ
ܦܝܠܝܟܣ ܟܦܝܬ ܀
[15]ܘܥܠ ܕܝܠܗ ܕܗܘܝܬ
ܟܕ ܗܘܝܬ[a]
ܒܐܘܪܫܠܡ ܀
ܐܘ̈ܕܥܘ ܠܝ ܪ̈ܫܝ
ܟܗ̈ܢܝܐ
ܘܣ̈ܒܝܗܘܢ
ܕܝ̈ܗܘܕܝ· ܫܐ̈ܠܝܢ
ܥܠܘܝ ܚܝܘܒ ܀
[16]ܐܢܐ ܕܝ ܐ ܠܝܒܢܬ
ܬܡܗܘܢ: ܕܠܝܬ
ܢ̈ܡܘܣܝ ܐܠ̈ܦܝܢ
ܡ̈ܫܒܩܝܢ ܒܡܬܘܢܐ
ܒܪܢܫ ܟܕ ܡܠܟܐ
ܕܝܗܒ̈ ܠܗܘܢ
ܕܡܬܦܘܝܢ ܠܝ
ܡܘܕܝܢ ܐܦܘ̈ܝ ܀

ܗܠܝܢ[b] ܕܡܬܦܘܝܢ ܠܝܢ
ܠܗ: ܕܝܗܒ
ܐܬܪ ܠܐܦܩܘܣ
ܚܠܦ[c] ܒܣܘܣܗ:
[17]ܒܟܢܐ ܐܘ ܕܐܬ̈ܘ
ܠܟܐ: ܐܘܦ ܠܐ
ܣܕܐ ܠܬܐܘܢ[d]* ܠܐ
ܒܒܕܬ: ܐܠܐ
ܠܝܘܡܐ ܚܘܪܢܐ
ܝܬܒܬ ܥܠ ܒܝܡܐ:
ܘܐܡܪܬ ܕܝܬ̈ܠܘܢ
ܝܬܗ ܠܓܒܪܐ ܀
[18]ܘܩ̈ܡܘ ܩܛܝ̈ܓܪܘ
ܘܥܠ[e] ܕܝܠܗ[f] ܐܘܦ
ܠܐ ܣܕܐ ܥܠܐ
ܠܐ ܗܘܘ ܡ̈ܝܬܝܢ
ܡܢ ܗܠܝܢ ܕܗܘܝܬ[g]
ܗܒܪ ܐܢܐ ܒܝܫܐ:
[19]ܒܥܘ̈ܬܝܢ ܕܝ ܣܘ̈ܪܝܢ
ܚܠܦ[c] ܕܝܠܬܗܘܢ
ܗܘܐ ܠܗܘܢ
ܠܦܘܠܘܣ ܀ ܘܥܠ

MKS IIB, 37: **a** ܕܗܘܝܬ | **b** ܗܢܝܢ | **c** ܚܠܦ ܥܠ | **d** ܦܬܐܘܢ following Schulthess (1924, 114) | **e** ܥܠ | **f** ܕܝܠܗ | **g** ܕܗܘܝܬ || **d** MS *sic* | **f** MS *sic*; *expectaveris* ܕܝܠܗ

Acts 25:19–24 F. 132r

ܥܠ ܚܕ ܝܫܘܥ:*
ܗܕܝ ܕܗܘܐ
ܦܘܠܘܣ ܐܡܪ
ܥܠܘܝ ܕܗܘ ܚܝܐ܁
[20] ܒܡܐ ܕܝ ܐܢܐ[a]
ܠܐ ܗܘܝܬ ܝܕܥ
ܥܠܠܒ[b] ܗܠܝܢ
ܒܒܥܝܢܐ: ܗܘܝܬ
ܐܡܪܬ ܠܗ ܐܢ ܐܝܬ
ܗܘ ܨܒܐ ܕܝܐܙܠ
ܠܐܘܪܫܠܡ
ܘܬܡܢ ܝܬܕܝܢ
ܥܠܠܒ[b] ܗܠܝܢ܁
[21] ܗܘ ܕܝ ܦܘܠܘܣ
ܒܥܐ ܕܝܬܢܛܪ
ܕܝܫܬܒܩ[c] ܠܗ
ܡܠܟܐ܁ ܐܘܦ
ܐܢܐ ܐܡܪܬ[d]
ܕܝܬܢܛܪ ܒܕܝܢܐ
ܕܝܫܕܪ ܝܬܗ
ܠܘܬ ܩܣܪ܁
[22] ܐܓܪܝܦܘܣ ܕܝ

ܐܡܪ ܠܦܝܣܛܘܣ
ܨܒܐ[e] ܗܘܝܬ
ܕܐܘܦ ܐܢܐ
ܡܫܡܥ ܝܬܗ
ܠܗܕܝ ܒܪܢܫܐ:
ܘܐܡܪ ܡܚܪ
ܐܬ ܫܡܥ ܠܗ܀[f]
ܪܫ ܡܥܠܝ܁
✝ [23] ܒܘܡܐ ܐܘܢ
ܕܡܚܪ ܐܬܐ
ܐܓܪܝܦܘܣ
ܘܒܪܢܝܩܐ ܥܡ
ܬܫܒܘܚܬܐ ܣܓܝ:
ܘܥܠ ܠܒܝܬ ܡܫܡܥܘܬܐ
ܥܡ ܪܫ ܐܠܦ̈ܐ:
ܘܥܡ ܓܒܪ̈ܝܐ
ܗܠܝܢ ܕܗܘܘ
ܪ̈ܫܝܗ[e] ܕܡܕܝܢܬܐ:
ܘܒܡܐ ܕܐܡܪ
ܦܝܣܛܘܣ܁
ܐܬܝܘ ܠܦܘܠܘܣ:
[24] ܘܐ ܓܒܪ[g] ܦܝܣܛܘܣ

MKS IIB, 38: **a** ܕܐܢܐ | **b** ܥܠ ܠܒ | **d** omit diacritic | **e** omit diacritic | **g** ܐ ܓܒܪ || **c** MS *sic*; *expectaveris* ܕܝܫܬܒܩ | **d** MS *sic*; *expectaveris* ܐܡܪܬ | **f** Re-inking. See §3.2.3.

Acts 25:24–26:1 **F. 132v**

ܘܐܡܪ ܡܠܟܐ
ܐ ܓܪܝܦܐ ܘܟܘܠ
ܓܒܪ̈ܝܐ ܗܠܝܢ
ܕܓܒܢ ܚܙ̈ܘ
ܠܗܕܢ ⁖[a] ܗܕܢ ܕܟܠ
ܕܥܠܗ ܟܘܠ
ܥܡ ܝܗܘܕܝ
ܕܒܥܘ̈ ܡܢܝ
ܠܝ ܒܝܪܘܫܠܡ
ܘܗܟܐ ܡܟܢ ܘܬܡܢ :
ܕܠܐ ܝܘܠ ܠܗ
ܕܝܚܐ ܥܘܕ ⁖
[25] ܐܢܐ ܕܝ ܚܡܝܬ.
ܘܐܫܟܚ* ܝܬܗ[b]
ܕܠܘܡ ܠܐ
ܚܒܪ ܕܡܘܬܐ̇[c]
ܥܒܕܬ ⁖ ܗܘ
ܕܝ ܗܕܢ ܩܪܐ
ܠܡܠܟܐ ⁖ ܘܫܡܥܬ[d]*
ܕܫܕܪ ܝܬܗ ⁖
[26] ܘܥܠ ܕܥܠܗ
ܠܝܬ ܠܝ ܡܕܡ

ܕܐܟܬܘܒ
ܫܪܝܪܐܝܬ
ܠܡܪܝ ⁖ ܠܒܕܝܠ
ܟܕܢ ܐܦܩܬ ܝܬܗ
ܠܩܕܡܟܘܢ :
ܚܕ ܒܟܐ ܘܩܕܡܝܟ
ܡܠܟܐ ܐ ܓܪܝܦܐ :
ܕܒܟܐ ܕܫܐܠܬܐ
ܡܬܟܬܒܐ
ܝܗܐ ܠܝ ܡܕܡ
ܕܐܟܬܘܒ ⁖ [27] ܠܝܬ
ܗܕܐ ܓܪ ܫܦܝܪܐ
ܘܕܡܝ ܕܫܕܪ
ܐܢܫ ܟܦܝܬ
ܘܠܐ ܢܘܕܥ*[e] ܥܠ̈ܝܐ
ܕܒܬܪܗ
[26:1] ܐ ܓܪܝܦܘܣ ܕܝ
ܐܡܪ ܠܦܘܠܘܣ
ܫܠܝܛ ܐܢܬ
ܕܬܐܡܪ
ܥܠܛܠ[f] ܓܪܡܝܟ ⁖
ܘܟܕܢ ܦܘܠܘܣ

MKS IIB, 39: **b** ܘܐܫܟܚܬܗ | **c** omit diacritic | **d** ܘܫܡܥܬ | **f** ܥܠ ܛܠ || **a** *lamad* is a marginal addition, apparently by the same hand | **b** MS *sic* | **d** MS *sic* | **e** MS *sic*

Acts 26:23–29 **F. 137r**

ܠܥܡܐ ܘܠܥܡ̈ܡܝܐ ׃ [a]
÷24 ܗܟܐ [b] ܕܝ ܕܗܘܐ
ܡܦܩ ܒܡܠܝܢ ׃
ܦܣܛܘܣ ܐܡܪ
ܒܩܠ ܪܒ ׃ ܡܫܬܛܛ
ܐܬ ܦܘܠܘܣ ׃
ܣܘ ܓܝܗܘܢ
ܕܟܬ̈ܒܝܐ ܠܛܦܫܘ
ܗܦܟܝܢ ܠܟ ׃
25 ܘܦܘܠܘܣ ܐܡܪ ׃
ܠܝܬܢܐ ܡܫܬܛܛ
ܣܘܠܛܐ ܦܣܛܘܣ ׃ [c]
ܐܠܐ ܡ̈ܠܝܢ ܕܩܘܫܛ
ܘܕܫܦܪ ܐܢܐ
ܡܡܠܠ ׃ 26 ܝܕܥ ܗܘ
ܓܪ ܡܠܟܐ ܥܠܝܗܝܢ [d]
ܗܠܝܢ ׃ ܗܕܝ
ܕܐܢܐ ܡܡܠܠ
ܠܘܬܗ ܒܡܝܢ ܚܝܘ ׃
ܠܝܬ ܐܢܐ ܓܪ
ܡܬܦܝܣ ܕܟܠܘܡ
ܡܢ ܗܠܝܢ ܛܡܝܪ

ܡܢܗ ׃ ܠܝܬܘܝ
ܓܪ ܗܕܝ ܒܘܝ
ܒܚܒܝ ׃ 27 ܡܗܝܡܢ
ܐܬ ܡܠܟܐ
ܐ ܓܪܦܐ ܠܢܒ̈ܝܝܐ ׃
ܝܕܥ ܐܢܐ ܕܐܬ
ܡܗܝܡܢ ׃
28 ܐ ܓܪܦܣ ܕܝ
ܐܡܪ ܠܦܘܠܘܣ
ܒܙ ܒܚܒܝ ܐܬ
ܡܦܝܣ ܠܝ
ܕܬܥܒܕ ܠܝ
ܟܪܣܛܝܢܐ ׃
29 ܘܦܘܠܘܣ ܐܡܪ ׃
ܡܢ ܠܐ ܐܢܐ
ܠܐܠܗܐ [e] ܕܒܙ ܒܚܒܝ
ܘܒܣܓܝ ׃....
ܠܐ ܒܠܚܘܕ ܠܟ
ܐܠܐ ܐܘܦ ܠܟܠ
ܗܠܝܢ ܕܫܡ̈ܥܝܢ
ܠܝ ܝܘܡܢ ׃ ܕܬܗ̈ܘܘܢ
ܒܕܝ ܗܟܢ ܗܟܐ

MKS IIB, 40: **a** omit *seyame* | **c** ܦܣܛܘܣ | **d** ܥܠ ܐܠܝܢ | **e** ܠܐܠܗܐ || **b** Interlinear *paragraphos* sign. See 44r I.3–4 for another instance.

Acts 26:29–27:3 F. 137v

ܕܐܝܟܐ ܗܘ ܠܒܪ
ܡܢ ܗܠܝܢ ܒܩ̈ܬܐ܀
30 ܘܟܕ ܡܟ ܠܗ
ܡܠܟܐ ܘܗܓܡܘܢܐ
ܘܒܪܢܝܩܐ[a]
ܘܗܠܝܢ ܕܗܘܘ
ܝܬ̈ܒܝܢ ܥܡܗܘܢ[b]܀ *
31 ܘܗܢܝܢ ܕܗܘܘ
ܐܙ̈ܠܝܢ ܗܘܘ ܡܡ̈ܠܠܝܢ
ܦܠܓܗܘܢ ܠܦܠܓ
ܘܐܡܪ̈ܝܢ܀ ܕܟܠܘܡ
ܫܘܐ̇ ܒܡܘܬ
ܐܐ̇ ܒܒܩ̈ܬܝܢ:
ܠܝܬ ܗܕܢ ܒܪܢܫܐ
ܚܐܒ܀ 32 ܐܓܪܝܦܘܣ
ܕܝ ܐܡܪ̇
ܠܦܣܛܘܣ:
ܡܫܠ ܗܘܐ
ܗܕܢ ܒܪܢܫܐ
ܕܝܬܦܛܪ ܐܠܘ
ܠܐ ܕܩܪܐ ܠܩܣܪ:[c]
ܢܫ ܡܩܠܝܗ܀

27:1 ܘܟܕܡܐ[d] ܕܝ ܕܐܬܝܢ
ܕܢܦܘܩ[e] ܠܐܝܛܠܝܐ.
ܗܘܘ ܡܫܪ̈ܝܢ
ܝܬܗ ܠܦܘܠܘܣ
ܘܠܐܢܫ̈ܝܢ
ܣܘ̈ܪܝܢ ܒܩ̈ܬܝܢ:
[f]ܠܩܢܛܪܘܢ ܚܕ[f]
ܕܫܡܗ ܝܘܠܝܣ܀
ܡܢ ܡܣܛܪܐ
ܕܣܒܣܛܐ̇܀
2 ܘܣ̈ܠܩܢܗ
[g]ܒܐ̇ܠܦ ܡܢ[g]
ܐܕܪܡܛܘܣ[h]
ܕܗܘܐ ܐܬܐ̇
ܕܢܦܘܩ
ܠܐܬܪ̈ܝܐ
ܕܐܣܝܐ܀ ܘܦܪ̈ܫܢ
ܘܗܘܐ ܥܡܢ
ܐܪܝܣܛܪܟܘܣ
ܡܩܕܘܢܝܐ ܕܡܢ
ܬܣܠܘܢܝܩܐ̇:[a]
3 ܘܠܝܘܡܐ ܬܢܝܢܐ

MKS IIB, 41: **a** omit diacritic | **b** ܠܗܘܢ | **f–f** ܠܩܢܛܪܘܢܐ | **g–g** ܒܐ̇ܠܦܐ ܕܡܢ | **h** ܐܕܪܡܛܘܣܐ || **b** *beth* added supralinearly, apparently by the same hand | **c** Possible reinking. See §3.2.3. | **d** Initial *wau* contains ornate cross. See §3.2.3. | **e** MS *sic*; *expectaveris* ܕܢܦܪܩ

Acts 27:3–9 F. 135r

ܢܚܬ̈ܝܢ ܠܨܝܕܢ :
ܒܚܪܘ ܕܝ
ܐܬܦܠܚ
ܝܘܠܝܣ ܥܡ
ܦܘܠܘܣ :
ܘܫܒܩ ܝܬܗ
ܕܢܐܙܠ ܠܘܬ
ܒܚܒ̈ܪܗ
ܘܕܢܬܒܥܪ ܥܠ
ܚܙܡܗ : * [4] ܘܡܢ
ܬܡܢ ܦܪ̈ܫܢ
ܘܒܚܪ̈ܝܗ
ܩܦܪܘܣ :
ܠܒܕܠ ܕܗܘܘ
ܪ̈ܘܚܝܐ ܠܩܘܒܠܢ : [a]
[5] ܘܡܥܒܪܬܢܐ
ܕܐܪܥܐ
ܕܩܝܠܝܩܝܐ
ܘܕܦܡܦܘܠܝܐ :
ܘܦܪ̈ܫܢܗ
ܘܢܚܬ̈ܝܢ ܠܡܝܪܐ
ܕܠܘܩܝܐ : [6] ܘܡܢ

ܬܡܢ ܐܫܟܚ
ܩܢܛܪܘܢܐ ܐܠܦ
ܐܠܟܣܢܕܪܐܝ
ܦܪܫ ܠܐܝܛܠܝܐ :
ܘܐܣܩ ܝܬܢ ܠܗ :
[7] ܒܝ̈ܘܡܐ ܕܝ ܕܗ̈ܘܝܢ
ܡܒܬ̈ܝܢ ܣܓ̈ܝܢ
ܥܡ ܒܦܘܫܐ :
ܘܒܩܘܫܝ ܐܬ̈ܝܢ
ܠܩܘܒܠ ܩܢܝܕܘܣ :
ܕܠܐ ܗܘܐ ܪܘܚܐ
ܫܒܩ ܠܢ : ܒܒ̈ܪܝܗ
ܦܪ̈ܫܢ ܩܪܝܛܐ
ܠܩܘܒܠ ܣܠܡܘܢܐ:
[8] ܘܠܘܬܗ ܒܩܘܫܝܐ
ܥܒ̈ܪܢ : ܘܐܬ̈ܝܢ
ܠܐܬܪ ܚܕ
ܕܡܬܩܪܐ
ܠܡܝ̈ܢܐ ܛܒ̈ܝܐ :
ܘ ܩܪܝܒܗ ܕܝ ܗܘܬ [b]
ܡܕܝܢܐ ܐܠܣܐ :
[9] ܒܬܪܐ ܕܝ ܕܥܒܪ

MKS IIB, 42: **a** omit *seyame* | **b** omit diacritic

Acts 27:9–13 **F. 135v**

ܐܚܪܘܢ ܗܘܘ:
ܘܥܒܪ ܗܘܐ
ܦܘܨܚܐ ܕܨܘܡ:
ܠܒܪ ܕܐܘܦ
ܝܘܡܐ ܗܘܐ
ܒܒܪ ܕܒܒܪ:.
ܘܗܘܐ ܦܘܠܘܣ
ܡܠܝܦ ܠܗܘܢ
[10]ܘܐܡܪ: ܓܒܪ̈ܝܐ.
ܚܙܝܐ ܐܢܐ
ܕܒܥܨܪ ܚܘܣܪܢ
ܘܒܥܠ ܦܫܪ:
ܠܐ [a]ܒܠܚܘܕ
ܕܛܥܘܢܐ[*a] ܕܐܠܦܐ.
ܐܠܐ ܐܘܦ
ܕܢܦܫ̈ܬܢ ܐܦ̈ܐ
ܦܘܨܚܐ ܕܚܝܐ.
[11]ܡܛܪܘܢܐ ܕܝ
ܠܡܒܪܛܐ
ܘܠܡܪܗ[b] ܕܐܠܦܐ
ܗܘܐ ܡܬܛܦܣ
ܡܠܝ ܐܢܐ[c] ܠܡܠܐ

ܕܗܘܐ ܦܘܠܘܣ
ܐܡܪ:…
[12]ܒܡܠܐ ܕܝ
ܕܠܐ ܗܘܐ
ܠܡܝܢܐ ܡܬܩܢ
ܕܢܣܬܐ ܬܡܢ.
ܗܘ ܓܒܘܗܘܢ
ܝܗ̈ܒܘ ܡܠܟܘܢ
ܕܢܦܪ̈ܩܘܢ ܡܢ
ܬܡܢ: ܕܡܐ ܝܟܘܠܘܢ
ܡ̈ܛܝܢ ܠܦܝܢܩܐ:
ܘܢܫ̈ܬܘܢ ܬܡܢ
ܒܠܡܝܢܐ ܕܟܪܝܛܐ.
ܕܫܡܗ ܒܝܢ
ܡܢܒܥܐ
ܠܕܘܪܒܐ:
[13]ܒܡܠܐ ܕܝ ܕܢܦܫ
ܪܘܚܐ ܕܕܪܘܡܐ:
ܘܣܒܪܘ ܕܝ ܕܬ
ܢܥܒܕܘܢܗܘܢ:
ܘܐܬܘ ܠܐܣܘܣ
ܘܗܘܘ ܡܥܒܪ̈ܝܢ

MKS IIB, 43: **a–a** ܒܠܚܘܕ ܡܢ / ܡܛܥܘܢܐ | **b** omit diacritic | **c** omit first diacritic

Acts 27:13–20 **F. 44v**

ܠܩܪܛܐ܂ [14] ܡܢ
ܒܬܪ ܕܝ ܙܥܝܪ
ܪܡܐ ܥܠܝܗ[a]
ܪܘܚ ܢܦܘܚ ܗܕܝ
ܕܡܬܩܪܝܐ
ܐܘܪܩܠܝܘܢ
[15] ܘܐܬܚܛܦܬ ܐܠܦܐ
ܘܠܐ ܗܘܐ ܝܟܠ
ܕܝܕܡܐ ܠܩܘܒܠ
ܪܘܚܐ܂ ܘܫܒܩܢ[b]
ܐܢ̈ܕܝܐ ܘܒܕܝ
ܗܘܝܢ ܐܙ̈ܠܝܢ܂
[16] ܒܡܐ ܕܝ ܕܪܗܛܢ[a]
ܚܠ ܢܣܘܣܘ
ܚܕܐ ܡܬܩܪܝܐ
ܩܠܘܕܐ܂ ܒܡܘܥܐ
ܝܟܠܝܢ ܕܢܠܒܘܢ
ܩܝܦܐ܂ [17] ܘܒܕ
ܢܣܒܘ ܝܬܗ܂
ܗܘܘ ܡܣܬܥܕܝܢ
ܘܣܩܝܢ ܐܠܦܐ܂
[ܕ]ܢܠܝܢ ܕܠܐ

ܢܦܠܘܢ ܠܚܘܠܐ*
ܣܘܪܛܘܣ܂
ܘܐܪ̈ܡܘ* ܡܠܐ܂
ܘܒܕܝ ܗܘܘ ܐܙ̈ܠܝܢ܂
[18] ܒܡܐ ܕܝ ܕܗܘܐ
ܡܥܘܠܐ[c] ܒܪܐ
ܥܠܝܗ ܠܣܓܝܐ܂
ܒܥܘܠܐ ܣܓܪܐ
ܗܘܘ ܫܕܝܢ[a] ܠܡܝܐ܂
[19] ܘܒܝܘܡܐ ܬܠܝܬܝܐ
ܗܢܘܢ ܒܐܝܕܝܗܘܢ
ܫܒܠܝܠܗ ܕܐܠܦܐ
ܫ̈ܕܘ܂ [20] ܠܐ ܕܝ
ܫܡܫܐ ܘܠܐ
ܟܘܟܒܝܢ ܗܘܘ
ܡܬܚܙܝܢ
ܒܕ ܡܛܐ ܠܝܘ̈ܡܝܢ
ܣܓܝ̈ܢ܂ ܘܡܥܘܠܐ[c]
ܕܝ ܗܘܐ ܥܠܝܢ
ܘܠܐ ܙܥܝܪ܂
ܘܟܕܘ ܐܬܦܣܩ
ܟܠ ܣܒܪܝ ܕܐܚܝܗ

MKS IIB, 44: **a** add *seyame* | **b** omit *seyame* || **c** MS *sic*; *expectaveris* ܡܥܘܠܐ

Acts 27:20–27 F. 44r

<u>ܦܪܟܣܝܣ</u>

ܡܫܬܘܙܒܝܢ܀
[21]ܐܡܪ ܕܝܢ ܡܛܠ
ܠܐ ܗܘܐ ܐܟܠ܀
ܩܳܡ ܦܘܠܘܣ ܡܢ
ܒܡܨܥܬܗܘܢ
ܘܐܡܪ܆ ܘܠ ܗܘܐ
ܗܘܐ ܗܘ ܠܓܒܪܐ
ܕܬܬܬܦܝܣܘܢ[a] ܠܝ
ܘܠܐ ܬܬܪܦܘܢ[b]
ܡܢ ܩܪܝܛܐ܆[c]
ܘܬܬܠ ܓܪܡܢ ܗܕܐ
ܚܘܣܪܢܐ ܘܗܕܐ
ܦܣܝܕܐ܆ [22]ܘܐܦ
ܗܫܐ ܕܝܢ ܡܦܝܣܢ[d]
ܐܢܐ ܠܟܘܢ ܕܬܬܠܒܒܘܢ܀
ܐܝܟܢ ܓܝܪ ܠܐ
ܗܘܐ܆ ܐܦܠ
ܠܐ ܠܚܕܐ ܢܦܫ
ܡܢ ܕܝܠܟܘܢ ܠܒܪ
ܡܢ ܐܠܦܐ܆ [23]ܗܢ
ܓܝܪ ܠܠܝܐ[e] ܕܗܢܐ
ܠܘܬܝ ܡܠܐܟܗ

ܕܐܠܗܐ ܗܘ ܕܝ
ܕܐܢܐ ܕܝܠܗ.
ܘܠܗ ܦܠܚ܀ [24]ܐܡܪ
ܠܝ ܠܐ ܬܕܚܠ
ܦܘܠܘܣ܆ ܩܕܡ
ܩܝܣܪ ܠܟ
ܕܬܩܘܡ܆ ܘܗܐ
ܡܘܗܒܐ ܝܗܒ
ܠܟ ܐܠܗܐ ܟܠ
ܗܠܝܢ ܕܪܕܝܢ
ܥܡܟ܆ [25]ܡܛܠ
ܗܢܐ ܐܬܠܒܒܘ
ܓܒܪܐ ܡܗܝܡܢ
ܐܢܐ ܓܝܪ ܒܐܠܗܐ܆
ܕܗܟܢ ܢܗܘܐ[c] ܐܝܟ
ܡܐ ܕܐܬܡܠܠ ܠܝ܀
[26]ܠܢܣܘܣ ܕܝܢ ܚܕܐ
ܗܐ[f] ܠܝ ܕܢܦܠ܀
[g]ܐܝܟ ܡܫܠܡܝܢ܀[g]
[27]ܘܟܕ[h] ܗܘܐ ܠܝ
[i]ܐܪܒܥܬܥܣܪ
ܠܠܝܐ ܡܕܪܕܪܝܢ*[i]
[j]܀ ܕ ܀

MKS IIB, 45: **a** omit *seyame* | **b** ܬܬܦܪܩܘܢ | **c** omit diacritic | **d** ܡܦܝܣ | **e** ܠܠ | **f** ܗܐ | **g–g** *nil* | **i–i** ܐܪܒܥܬܥܣܪ / ܠܠܝܐ ܡܕܪܕܪܝܢ || **b** *wau* inserted beneath roof of *resh*, apparently by the same hand | **h** Initial *wau* contains ornate cross. See §3.2.3. | **j** Quire number (see §3.2.1.)

2 Peter 1:1–5 F. 133r

ܕܦܛܪܘܣ ܩܕܡܝܬܐ

~~~~~~~~~~~~~~~~~~

ܐܓܪܬܐ ܬܢܝܢܬܐ ܕܦܛܪܘܣ
[1:1] ܫܡܥܘܢ ܦܛܪܘܣ
ܥܒܕܗ ܘܫܠܝܚܗ
ܕܝܫܘܥ ܡܫܝܚܐ .:
ܠܗܠܝܢ ܕܫ̈ܘܘ
ܒܗܝܡܢܘܬܐ
ܡܝܩܪܬܐ .: ܥܡ̈ܢ
ܠ ܒܝ ܕܗܘ ܕܐܠܗܢ :
ܘܕܡܚܝܢܢ
ܝܫܘܥ ܡܫܝܚܐ .:
[2] ܚܣܕܐ ܠܟܘܢ :
[a]ܘܫܝܢܐ ܣܓܝܬ ܠܟ .:[a]
ܒܐܟܪܘܬܗ
ܕܐܠܗܐ ܘܕܝܫܘܥ
ܡܫܝܚܐ ܡܪܢ .:
[3] ܗܟܡܐ ܕܟܘܠܐ
ܡܢ ܚܝܠܐ
ܕܐܠܗܘܬܗ
ܐܬܝܗܒ ܠܢ ܠܚܝܝܢ

ܘܠܕܚܠܐ ܕܐܠܗܐ .:
ܒܐܟܪܘܬܗ
ܕܕܝ ܕܩܪܐ ܠܢ
ܒܬܫܒܚܬܗ
ܘܒܪܟܘܬܗ :
[4] ܗܠܝܢ ܕܒܗ̈ܘܢ
ܡܢ ܡ̈ܢ ܐܬܐ
ܪܒܪ̈ܒܬܐ
ܘܡܫܘܪ̈ܬܐ
ܝܗܒ ܠܢ ܠܒܕܝܠ
ܕܒܗܠܝܢ ܬܬܚ̈ܒܪܘܢ
ܫܘܬܦܝܢ ܠܟܝܢܗ
ܕܐܠܗܘܬܐ :
ܕܒܪ̈ܘܬܘܢ ܡܢ
ܬܚܒܘܠܬܐ
ܘܬܪܓܘܬܐ*
ܕܒܥܠܡܐ .: [5] ܘܐܬܘܢ
ܕܝ ܒܗܠ ܡܢ ܗܘ
ܐܚ̈ܠܘ ܘܣܦ̈ܩܘ
ܒܗܝܡܢܘܬܟܘܢ
ܠܬܫܒܚܬܐ :
ܒܬܫܒܚܬܐ ܕܝ

MKS IIB, 214: **a–a** ܘܫܝܢܐ ܐܣܓܝܬ ܠܟ
~~~~~~~~~~~~~~~~~~

2 Peter 1:5–12

F. 133v

ܠܐܒܪܘܬܐ܀
ܒܐܒܪܘܬܐ[a][6] ܕܝ
ܠܚܟܡܘܬܐ.*
ܒܚܟܡܘܬܐ ܕܝ[a]
ܠܡܣܒܪܢܘܬܐ:
ܒܡܣܒܪܢܘܬܐ
ܕܝ ܠܕܚܠܬܗ
ܕܐܠܗܐ
[7]ܒܕܚܠܬܗ ܕܝ
ܕܐܠܗܐ ܠܚܒܬܐ[b]
ܕܐܚ̈ܝܐ܆ ܒܚܒܬܐ
ܕܝ ܕܐܚ̈ܝܐ
ܠܚܒܬܐ: [8]ܟܕܐ ܓܪ
ܕܗܘܝܢ ܠܟܘܢ
ܗܠܝܢ ܘܡܬܝܬܪ̈ܢ:
ܠܐ ܒܛ̈ܠܝܢ ܘܠܐ[c]
ܦܬ̈ܝܢ ܦܢ̈ܝܢ.
ܡܫܬ̈ܟ ܠܟܘܢ
ܠܚܟܡܬܗ
ܕܡܪܢ ܝܫܘܥ
ܡܫܝܚܐ܆ [9]ܠܕܝܢ
ܓܪ ܕܠܝܬ ܠܗ

ܗܠܝܢ ܡܒܘܪ ܗܘ
ܘܡܥܒܕ܆ ܘܦܠܐ
ܕܒܡܫ̈ܝܚ ܕܡܫܠܡܬܗ[d]
ܡܚܘܝܬܐ: [10]ܠܒܕܝܠ
ܒܕܝܢ ܡܠܝܢ ܐܚ̈ܝܐ.
ܚܝ ܦ̈ܘܩ[e] ܕܒܡܒ̈ܕܝܐ
ܠܒ̈ܢܝܐ ܘܢܬܪܒܘܢ
ܥܢܢܐ ܘܒܚܝܪܐ
ܬܗܘܢ ܒܒ̈ܕܝܢ܀
ܗܠܝܢ ܓܪ ܒܕ
ܬܗܘܢ ܒܒ̈ܕܝܢ.
ܠܬܬܘܢ ܥ̈ܒܕܝܢ
ܠܚܠܡ܆ [11]ܒܕܝܢ ܓܪ
ܚܬܪܐܝܬ.
ܡܬܦܫܩܐ ܠܟܘܢ
ܡܥܠܬܐ ܠܡܠܟܘܬܐ
ܕܠܚܠܡ܆ ܕܡܪܢ
ܘܡܚܝܢ ܝܫܘܥ
ܡܫܝܚܐ܆ [12]ܠܟܢ
ܐܢܐ ܚܝ ܦ ܕܒܡܒܠ
ܒܪ ܗܘܐ ܐܢܐ
ܡܕܒܪ ܠܟܘܢ

MKS IIB, 215: **a** ܒܚܟܡܬܘܬܐ ܕܝ / ܠܚܟܡܬܘܬܐ / ܒܐܒܪܘܬܐ | **b** ܚܒܬܐ | **c** ܘܐ | **d** ܕܗܫܠܡܬܗ | **e** omit *seyame*

2 Peter 3:16–18; 1 John 1:1–3 F. 136r

ܡܢ ܕܗܠܝܢ ܕܠܐ
ܝܠܦܝܢ ܘܠܐ ܡܫܪܪܝܢ
ܡܗܦܟܝܢ܆ ܗܝܟ
ܕܐܘܦ ܫܪܟܬ
ܟܬܒܝܐ ܠܡܘܒܠ
ܐܒܕܢܗܘܢ܆
[17] ܐܢܬܘܢ ܕ݁ ܚܒܝܒܝܐ
ܕܝܕܥܬܘܢ ܡ̈ܩܕܡܬܘܢ·
ܛܪܘ ܢܦܫܟܘܢ܆
ܕܠܐ ܒܛܘܥܝܬܐ
ܕܫܝܛܝ̈ܐ
ܬܬܓܪܒܘܢ ܘܬܦܠܘܢ
ܡܢ ܫܪܝܪܘܬܟܘܢ܆
[18] ܗܘܘ ܕ݁ ܪܒܝܢ
ܒܛܝܒܘܬܗ
ܘܒܝܕܥܬܗ
ܕܡܪܢ ܘܡܚܝܢ
ܝܫܘܥ ܡܫܝܚܐ܆
ܠܗ ܬܫܒܘܚܬܐ
ܐܘܦ ܟܕܘ
ܘܠܝܘܡ ܕܠܥܠܡ
ܠܥܠܡܝܢ ܐܡܝܢ܆

ܫܠܡܬ[a] ܐ ܓܪܬܗ
ܕܦܛܪܘܣ ܬܢܝܢܬܐ܆[b]
~~~~~~~~~~~~~~~

ܐ ܓܪܬܗ ܕܝܘܚܢܢ
ܡܫܠܝܚܐ܆
[1:1] ܡܢ ܕܗܘܐ ܡܢ
ܪܫ ܡܢ ܕܫܡܥܢܢ
ܘܡܢ ܕܚܙܝܢܢ
ܒܥܝܢܝܢ܆ ܡܢ
ܕܚܙܝܢܗ ܘܐܝܕܝܢ
ܦܫܫܘ܆ ܥܠܘܝ[c]
ܡܠܬܐ ܕܚܝܝܐ܆
[2] ܘܚܝܝܐ ܐܬܓܠܝܘ܀
ܘܚܙܝܢܢ ܘܐܝܢ
ܡܣܗܕܝܢ܆[d] ܘܐܝܢ
ܡܟܪܙܝܢ ܠܟܘܢ
ܚܝܝܐ ܕܠܥܠܡ܆
ܗܠܝܢ ܕܗܘܘ ܠܘܬ
ܐܒܐ ܘܐܬܓܠܝܘ
ܠܝ܆ [3] ܡܢ ܕܚܙܝܢܢ
ܘܫܡܥܢܢ ܐܝܢ

MKS IIB, 216: **a** omit diacritic | MKS IIB, 217: **c** ܥܠܘܝ ܥܠ | **d** omit *seyame* || **b** MS *sic*; *expectaveris* ܬܢܝܢܬܐ
~~~~~~~~~~~~~~~

1 John 1:3–9 F. 136v

ܡܫܘܬܦܝܢ ܐܘܦ
ܠܟܘܢ ⁖ ܠܒܕܝܠ
ܕܐܘܦ ܐܢܬܘܢ
ܫܘܬܦܘ ܬܗܘܐ̇
ܠܟܘܢ ܥܡܢ ⁖
ܘܫܘܬܦܘܬܢ
ܕܝܠܢ ܥܡ ܐܒܐ
ܘܥܡ ܒܪܗ
ܝܫܘܥ ܡܫܝܚܐ ⁖
[4] ܘܗܠܝܢ ܐܢܚܢ
ܟܬܒܝܢ ܠܟܘܢ ܠܒܕܝܠ
ܕܚܕܘܬܟܘܢ
ܬܗܘܐ̇ ܡܫܠܡܐ:
[5] ܘܗܝ ܗܕܐ
ܗܝ ܗܝ ܬܐ
ܗܕܐ ܕܫܡ̈ܥܢܢ
ܡܢܗ ⁖ ܘܐܡܢ
ܡܫ̈ܡܥܝܢ ܠܟܘܢ ⁖
ܕܐܠܗܐ ܢܘܗܪ̇
ܐܝܬ ܗܘ: ܘܚܫܘܟ
ܠܝܬ ܒܗ ܐܘܦ
[a]ܠܐ ܚܕ ⁖[a] [6] ܐܢ

ܢܐܡܪ ܕܫܘܬܦܘ
ܐܝܬ ܠܢ ܥܡܗ
ܘܒܚܠܡܐ[b] ܢܗܐ̇
ܡܗܠܟܝܢ ⁖ ܡܕܓ̈ܠܝܢ
ܐܢܢ ܘܠܐ ܥܒ̈ܕܝܢ
ܩܘܫܛܐ ⁖ [7] ܐܢ ܕܝ
ܒܢܘܗܪܐ ܢܗܐ̇
ܡܗܠܟܝܢ. ܗܝܟ
ܕܗܘ ܐܝܬܘܗܝ
ܒܢܘܗܪܐ
ܫܘܬܦܘ ܐܝܬ ܠܢ
ܥܡ ܐܠܗܐ ⁖
ܘܐܕܡܗ ܕܒܪܗ
ܝܫܘܥ ܡܫܝܚܐ:
ܡܕܟܝ ܠܢ ܡܢ
ܟܘܠ ܚܛܝܐ ⁖
[8] ܐܢ ܢܐܡܪ ܕܠܝܬ
ܠܢ ܚܛܝܐ. ܓܪܡܢ
ܐܢܚ ܡܛܥܝܢ:
ܘܩܘܫܛܐ ܠܝܬ
ܗܘ ܒܓܘܢ ⁖ [9] ܐܢ[c]
ܢܗܐ̇ ܡܘܕܝܢ

MKS IIB, 218: **a–a** ܝ ܚܣܕ | **b** ܘܒܚܫܘܟܐ | **c** ܐܢ || **b** MS *sic; expectaveris* ܘܒܚܫܘܟܐ

4. TEXTUAL AND LINGUISTIC COMMENTARY

Entries in this brief commentary are arranged in the order Acts, Catholic Epistles, Pauline Epistles, in imitation of the usual order found in New Testament manuscripts. As the title to this chapter implies, the commentary includes both textual and linguistic issues. Textually, the CPA was read alongside the 28th edition of Nestle-Aland (Aland et al. 2012). This commentary does not pretend to be a full collation; only the most obvious semantic divergences between the Greek and CPA were taken into account. Where relevant, textual variants within the Greek tradition are brought to bear.[1] Where no Greek variants are explicitly mentioned, the reader can assume that—at least in the judgement of the author—none of the known variants are relevant to the discussion at hand. Linguistically, the commentary presents all the instances known to the author where the reading of the new edition contributes to our understanding of CPA grammar and lexicography.

In each instance, the relevant Greek and CPA text is cited, with some context. Where the issue concerns a particular word or phrase within the CPA, this is <u>underlined</u> to assist the reader.

[1] These variants were gathered from the Nestle-Aland apparatus and the collation of Von Soden (1913).

 https://doi.org/10.11647/OBP.0455.04

4.1. CCR XI: Acts and Catholic Epistles

Acts 19:40 (F. 131v)

καὶ ταῦτα εἰπὼν ἀπέλυσεν τὴν ἐκκλησίαν

ܘܟܕܐ ܕܐܡܪ ܗܠܝܢ <u>ܦܛܪܬ</u> ܟܢܝܫܬܐ

The transitive construction found in the Greek ('he dismissed the crowd') does not appear to be so rendered in the CPA. As it stands, the CPA appears to read 'the crowd dispersed'. This reading parses the verb ܦܛܪܬ as a 3fs *peʿal* intransitive. The *peʿal* of this root, with the sense 'depart', is known in Syriac and Qumran Aramaic, but until now the root has only appeared in CPA as a transitive *paʿel* ('to send away/divorce'). Sokoloff (2014, 327) assumes textual corruption, and emends to: ܦܛܪ ܝܬ ܟܢܝܫܬܐ, understanding ܦܛܪ as a transitive *paʿel.*[2] Corruption is certainly plausible, especially given the many other *lapsus calami* in this MS, and Sokoloff's emendation would draw the CPA rendering back close to the Greek, to which it usually adheres closely. However, the reconstruction of ܝܬ in his proposal is untenable: this accusative particle only appears with pronominal suffixes in CPA (Sokoloff 2014, 168). Moreover, since the seven clear occurrences of the *paʿel* in CPA refer to a man divorcing his wife, this may help tip

---

[2] Müller-Kessler (2019a, 160 n. 18) chooses not to make reference to Sokoloff's dictionary on account of its having been withdrawn from sale over a legal dispute. While sympathising with the sentiment, I continue to refer to the work inasmuch as the volume remains readily accessible, and represents far and away the most up-to-date lexicographical treatment of the dialect.

the balance in favour of the prima facie reading of ܦܠܓܬ as 3fs *peʿal* intransitive ('the crowd dispersed').[3]

Acts 20:2 (F. 43v)

Διελθὼν δὲ τὰ μέρη ἐκεῖνα καὶ παρακαλέσας αὐτοὺς λόγῳ πολλῷ ἦλθεν εἰς τὴν Ἑλλάδα

ܘܟܕ: ܣܚܠ ܦܘܠܘܣ ܬܗܘܢ ܐܬܪ̈ܝܐ. ܒܡܠܐ ܣܓܝ. ܐܬܐ ܠܗܠܣ

The CPA appears to read: 'And when Paul had gone around those places, with many word(s), he came to Greece.' Thus, the phrase *καὶ παρακαλέσας αὐτούς* 'having encouraged them' is not represented in the CPA. This could be simple haplography; alternatively, it could possibly be related to the Greek text found in Codex Bezae (*prima manu*): *διελθων δε παντα τα μερη εκεινη και χρησαμενος λογω πολλω* '...having used (i.e., spoken) many words'.

Acts 20:6 (F. 43v)

καὶ ἤλθομεν πρὸς αὐτοὺς εἰς τὴν Τρωάδα ἄχρι ἡμερῶν πέντε οὗ διετρίψαμεν ἡμέρας ἑπτά

ܘܐܬܝܢܗ ܠܘܬܗܘܢ ܠܛܪܘܐܣ ܠܚܡܫܐ ܝܘ̈ܡܝܢ

The CPA reads: 'We came to them at Troas in five days.' The phrase *οὗ διετρίψαμεν ἡμέρας ἑπτά* is not represented in the CPA. In this case, homoioteleuton is most easily explained if the scribe is copying from an extant CPA *Vorlage*, rather than translating directly from the Greek. In CPA the 'missing' phrase could be rendered ܘܒܬܪ̈ܗ ܬܡܢ ܫܒܘܥܐ ܝܘ̈ܡܝܢ. Parablepsis from the first ܝܘ̈ܡܝܢ to the second would explain the relevant omission.

---

[3] The lack of diacritic over the *tau* is a blow to this possibility, though hardly a fatal one.

Acts 21:13 (F. 42r)

τί ποιεῖτε κλαίοντες καὶ συνθρύπτοντές μου τὴν καρδίαν;

ܡܢܐ ܐܬܘܢ ܥ̈ܒܕܝܢ ܒ̈ܟܝܢ ܘܡܦܫܪ̈ܝܢ ܠܗ ܠܠܒܝ

The CPA ‘melting’ does not suit *συνθρύπτοντές* ‘breaking to pieces’. Consequently, Müller-Kessler and Sokoloff (1998b, 31) mention Schulthess’ emendation of ܘܡܦܫܪ̈ܝܢ to ܘܡܦܫܪ̈ܘܢ. However, *συνθρύπτω* is a *hapax* in the entire Greek Bible, and the *afʿel* of ܦܫܪ may constitute a rather fitting contextual interpretation: ‘What are you doing, weeping and melting my heart?’

Acts 25:17 (F. 134v)

ἀναβολὴν μηδεμίαν ποιησάμενος

ܐܘܦ ܠܐ ܚܕܐ ܠܬܐܘܢ ܠܐ ܥܒܕܬ

The form ܠܬܐܘܢ has proved troublesome. In this instance, the text itself is clear, while the interpretation of the CPA word is not. Quite possibly the text is corrupt. Schulthess (1924, 114) emends the form to ܦܬܐܘܢ without comment. Presumably he supposes a nominal form from the widespread Aramaic root ܦܬܝ ‘to be broad/wide’, with a semantic extension from a spatial to a chronological sense: breadth → delay. Müller-Kessler and Sokoloff (1998b, 37) adopt this reading. However, elsewhere in Aramaic this root and its various derivatives appear to be used exclusively in a spatial sense. Thus, the proposed CPA noun ܦܬܐܘܢ/ܦܬܘܢ ‘delay’ that has made its way into the lexicon (Sokoloff 2014, 345) is not only based on a conjectural emendation, but also relies on a semantic extension without near parallel.

The Syriac idiom ܕܠܐ ܬܘܗܝܐ 'without delay' may suggest a more helpful direction. This idiom, occurring *ad loc.* in the Peshitta, and elsewhere, relies on the secondary meaning of the root ܬܗܝ 'to delay'. The noun ܬܗܘ 'delay' is itself attested elsewhere in CPA. Possibly, therefore, the form ܬܐܚܘ is simply a by-form of this same noun, though with the exchange of gutturals so characteristic of CPA. On this reading, the *lamad* is presumably to be understood as an error.

Acts 25:19 (F. 132r)

καὶ περί τινος Ἰησοῦ τεθνηκότος, ὃν ἔφασκεν ὁ Παῦλος ζῆν

ܘܥܠ ܚܕ ܝܫܘܥ: ܗܕܢ ܕܗܘܐ ܦܘܠܘܣ ܐܡܪ ܥܠܘܗܝ ܕܗܘ ܚܝܐ,

The participle τεθνηκότος is not represented in the CPA. Again, if the haplography occurred during the copying of this particular MS, it is easier to explain if the scribe was copying from a CPA *Vorlage*, rather than translating directly from the Greek. If the Greek participle was translated using the common CPA correlative ܗܕܢ ܕ, i.e., ܗܕܢ ܕܡܝܬ, *parablepsis* from the first ܗܕܢ to the second would explain the omission.[4]

Acts 25:25a (F. 132v)

ἐγὼ δὲ κατελαβόμην μηδὲν ἄξιον αὐτὸν θανάτου πεπραχέναι

ܐܢܐ ܕ، ܐܫܟܚܬ. ܘܐܫܟܚ ܠܗ ܕܚܠܦ ܠܐ ܥܒܕ ܕܢܬܩܛܠ ܒܡܘܬ.:

Müller-Kessler and Sokoloff (1998b, 39) read the underlined words as a single word: ܘܐܫܟܚܬܗ. This is a particularly difficult

---

[4] In this case, understanding the omission as intentional—theologically motivated—also seems rather plausible.

case to judge. As can be seen in the image, the *yod* is clear, and there is no trace of a baseline between the *ḥeth* and the *yod.*

Figure 15: Snippet from f. 132v

It is possible—scarcely—that the superior text has obscured the baseline. However, the relative positioning of the letters on this line also clearly favours reading two words (ܘܐܫܟܚܝ ܬܗ) rather than one (ܘܐܫܟܚܝܬܗ). If two words are read here, one must assume a *lapsus calami.* Perhaps the scribe's *Vorlage* read one word, which he misinterpreted as two, or perhaps a *tau* suffix was omitted from the first word.

This reading has grammatical significance. Müller-Kessler (1991, 259–60) collects all the examples of verbs with object suffixes from the early period CPA sources. She finds only two examples of a suffix on the 1cs/1cpl perfect verb: the supposed reading in this verse, and one other in 1 Cor. 15:3 ܩܒܠܬܗ. This latter example, too, turns out to be a will-o'-the-wisp (see *ad loc.* f. 22r). Moreover, Müller-Kessler's only example of a suffix on a 2nd person perfect is also a red herring. Thus, it seems that in the extant corpus there are no examples whatsoever of an object suffix on the 1st or 2nd perfect verb; the phenomenon is limited to the 3rd person.

Acts 25:25b (F. 132v)

αὐτοῦ δὲ τούτου ἐπικαλεσαμένου τὸν Σεβαστὸν ἔκρινα πέμπειν

ܗܘ ܕܝ ܗܕܢ ܩܪܐ ܠܡܠܟܐ: ܘܫܡܥܬ ܕܐܫܕܪ ܠܗ:

Müller-Kessler and Sokoloff (1998b, 39) read ܘܫܡܠܬ and posit metathesis of the *mim* and the *lamad*. However, the thin backstroke at the top of the *ʿe* is clearly visible in the pseudocolour image. The text can be understood as it stands: 'He himself appealed to the emperor, so I understood that I should send him.' More likely, though, is that the word ܫܡܬ 'I decided' was intended here.[5] Once again, this error is more plausible on the assumption that the scribe was copying out a CPA *Vorlage* (and misread the *yod* as an *ʿe*) than on the assumption that he was translating directly from a Greek *Vorlage*.

Acts 25:27 (F. 132v)

μὴ καὶ τὰς κατ' αὐτοῦ αἰτίας σημᾶναι

ܘܠܐ ܢܕܘܥ ܥܠܠܐ ܕܒܬܪܗ

This appears to be a genuine case of metathesis: ܢܘܕܥ 'one should make known' is a more likely translation of σημᾶναι 'to make known'.

---

[5] Acts 21:25 furnishes another instance where *κρίνω* is translated by the root ܫܘܡ.

Acts 26:30 (F. 137v)

Ἀνέστη τε ὁ βασιλεὺς καὶ ὁ ἡγεμὼν ἥ τε Βερνίκη καὶ οἱ συνκαθήμενοι αὐτοῖς·

ܘܩܡ ܡܢ ܠܗ ܡܠܟܐ ܘܗܓܡܘܢܐ ܘܒܪܢܝܩܐ ܘܗܠܝܢ ܕܗܘܘ ܝܬ̈ܒܝܢ ܥܡܗܘܢ܀

The *beth* was added supralinearly, not obviously by a second hand. Müller-Kessler and Sokoloff (1998b, 41) read ܠܗܘܢ, which Sokoloff (2014, 169) interprets as the ingressive *lamad* accompanying a passive participle. Contextually, the ingressive sense does not suit: the attending audience has already sat through a long speech by Paul. Moreover, the use of the passive participle would be unexpected in an ingressive context, and Sokoloff offers only this text as an example. The updated reading therefore solves this particular grammatical puzzle.

Acts 27:3 (F. 135r)

ἐπέτρεψεν πρὸς τοὺς φίλους πορευθέντι ἐπιμελείας τυχεῖν.

ܘܫܒܩ ܠܗ ܕܝܐܙܠ ܠܘܬ ܒܢ̈ܝ ܥܡܗ ܘܡܬܕܒܪ ܥܠ ܢܦܫܗ܀

Usually, the CPA cleaves to the Greek closely. Here, however, the clause 'he permitted him to go to his people *and to live by himself*' is an odd rendering of ἐπιμελείας τυχεῖν 'he permitted him to go to his friends *to obtain care*'. Solely based on this verse, Sokoloff (2014, 314) proposes an idiom ܕܒܪ ܥܠ ܢܦܫ- 'to obtain care for oneself'. However, given the lack of parallels for such an idiom, either within CPA itself or in related dialects, a textual explanation seems more plausible than a linguistic one. Possibly this passage has suffered contamination from Acts 28:16: ἐπετράπη τῷ Παύλῳ μένειν καθ' ἑαυτὸν 'it was permitted to Paul to stay by himself'. The use of ἐπιτρέπω in both verses could have triggered this kind of transfer, though whether the confusion occurred as the scribe was copying this manuscript, or whether it was already in this manuscript's *Vorlage* is impossible to discern.

Acts 27:10 (F. 135v)

ܠܐ ܒܠܚܘܕ ܕܛܥܘܢܐ ܕܐܠܦܐ.

Müller-Kessler and Sokoloff (1998b, 43) misread this as ܡܛܥܘܢ, and thereby generated a ghost-word appearing only here. For now, therefore, it should be excised from the CPA lexicon. By contrast, the noun ܛܥܘܢܐ 'cargo' appears also in Acts 21:3 (f. 42v).

Acts 27:17 (F. 44v)

μὴ εἰς τὴν σύρτιν ἐκπέσωσιν

ܕܠܐ ܢܦܠܘܢ ܠܓܘܢܐ ܣܘܪܛܝܣ.:

The CPA text is legible; its meaning is opaque. Müller-Kessler and Sokoloff (1998b, 44) echo Schulthess' suggestion to emend to ܠܘܙܐ 'shallows'. Sokoloff (2014, 70) suggests emending to ܠܓܘܒܐ 'into the chasm'. In either case, the *status emphaticus* of the word in question, and the lack of genitive particle on the next word, are troubling. If this manuscript really was copied from a CPA *Vorlage*, the present text may conceivably represent a misconstrual of ܠܓܘ ܐܣܘܪܛܝܣ (though, without a consonant cluster in the Greek σύρτις, it is not clear why the word would have attracted a prosthetic *alaf*).

Acts 27:17 (F. 44v)

ἣν ἄραντες βοηθείαις ἐχρῶντο ὑποζωννύντες τὸ πλοῖον· φοβούμενοί τε μὴ εἰς τὴν σύρτιν ἐκπέσωσιν χαλάσαντες τὸ σκεῦος, οὕτως ἐφέροντο.

'Having raised [the lifeboat], they used rope-supports to brace the ship; then, afraid they might fall foul of the Syrtis they let down the gear, and in this way they were carried along.'

ܘܟܕ ܢܣܩܘܗ ܠܗ̇ܘ܆ ܗܘܘ ܡܫܩܕܝܢ ܘܣܘܩܝܢ ܐ̱ܠܦܐ: [ܕ]ܕܚܠܝܢ ܕܠܐ ܢܦܩܠܘܢ ܠܓܘܡܐ
ܕܣܘܪܛܝܣ܆ ܘܐܫܪܝܬܘ ܡܠܚܐ. ܘܟܕܢ ܗܘܘ ܐܙܠܝܢ:

'And when they had lifted it [i.e., the lifeboat] up, they set about supporting and fastening the ship, afraid they might fall foul of the shallows (?) of Syrtis. And they lowered the sail, and thus proceeded.'

The clause division in the CPA does not match the Greek. In the Greek, the conjunctive particle τε (not to mention the raised dot punctuation), indicates a semantic division after τὸ πλοῖον 'the ship'. In turn, this indicates that the explanatory clause about fear of running aground on the Syrtis refers cataphorically to the lowering of the gear. The punctuation of the CPA, by contrast, as well as the additional conjunctive *wau* on 'they lowered', indicates that the explanatory clause was understood to refer *anaphorically* to the strengthening of the ship.

Acts 27:27 (F. 44r)

ܘܟܕ ܗܘܐ ܠܝ ܐܪܒܥܬܥܣܪ ܠܠܝܐ ܡܛܪܛܠܝܢ

Müller-Kessler and Sokoloff (1998b, 45) read ܡܬܛܪܕܝܢ *ad loc*. This passage is the only instance recorded in Sokoloff (2014, 185) as evidence of *Ithpe/a* ܛܪܕ in the sense 'to be driven about'. This rather ill-fitting sense may thus be excised from the CPA lexicon.

On the other hand, this passage does furnish the first attestation in CPA of the *Ithpalpel* of ܝܠܠ.

2 Peter 1:4 (F. 133r)

ἀποφυγόντες τῆς ἐν τῷ κόσμῳ ἐν ἐπιθυμίᾳ φθορᾶς

ܕܥܪ̈ܩܬܘܢ ܡܢ ܬܐܘܬܐ ܘܬܪܦܘܬܐ ܕܒܥܠܡܐ ܀

The CPA ‘you have fled from the desire and corruption that are in the world’ reflects an alternative Greek text at this point, already attested in Von Soden’s collation (Von Soden 1913, *ad loc.*): ἀποφυγόντες τῆς ἐν τῷ κόσμῳ ἐπιθυμίας καὶ φθορᾶς.

2 Peter 1:6 (F. 133v)

ἐν δὲ τῇ γνώσει τὴν ἐγκράτειαν, ἐν δὲ τῇ ἐγκρατείᾳ τὴν ὑπομονήν

ܒܝܕܥܬܐ ܕܝ، ܠܚܝܡܘܬܐ. ܒܚܝܡܘܬܐ ܕܝ، ܠܡܣܝܒܪܢܘܬܐ ܀

Twice in this verse, the Greek ἐγκράτεια ‘self-control’ is translated by the previously unattested ܚܝܡܘܬܐ. Müller-Kessler and Sokoloff (1998b, 215) read ܚܠܡܘܬܐ in both occurrences *ad loc.* This new reading thus represents a new addition to the CPA lexicon, and a concomitant simplification: ܚܠܡܘܬܐ apparently need only mean ‘healing’ rather than both ‘healing’ and ‘soundness’ (see Sokoloff 2014, 130).

4.2. CCR II: Pauline Epistles

Romans 6:21 (F. 1v)

⌈ܗ⌉ ܠܡ ܕܒܗܘ ܐܬܘܢ ܡܬܒܗ̈ܬܝܢ ܒܗܘܢ ܀

Müller-Kessler and Sokoloff (1998b, 60): ܡܬܒܗ̈ܬܝܢ. Sokoloff (2014, 41) cites only this location for the supposed occurrence of the *Ithpeal* of ܒܗܬ. Therefore, unless or until other examples can be adduced, the *Ithpeal* of ܒܗܬ should be removed from the CPA lexicon.

Romans 9:33 (F. 40v)

τίθημι ἐν Σιὼν λίθον προσκόμματος καὶ πέτραν σκανδάλου, καὶ ὁ πιστεύων ἐπ᾽ αὐτῷ οὐ καταισχυνθήσεται.

ܐܢܐ ܡܩܝܡ ܒܨܝܘܢ ܟܐܦ ܕܬܘܩܠܐ· ܘܫܥܝ ܕܡܟܫܘܠ: ܘܡܢ ܕܡܗܝܡܢ ܒܗ̇ ܠܐ ܝܒܗܬ:

Müller-Kessler and Sokoloff (1998b, 65) omit the diacritic on ܒܗ̇. In this case, the presence of the diacritical dot has a measure of exegetical significance. Since ܟܐܦ and ܫܥܝ are both feminine, if the suffixed pronoun was indeed ܒܗ—masculine—this would have implied that the translator had shown a degree of exegetical licence (presumably to make explicit the Christological referent): ‘the one who believes in *him*…’.

1 Corinthians 1:17 (F. 21v)

ἐν σοφίᾳ λόγου

ܒܚܟܡܬܐ ܕܡܠܬܐ

Müller-Kessler and Sokoloff (1998b, 70) read ܕܡܠܝܐ ‘of words’. The letter-spacing clearly points to the singular reading, though there are traces of what might possibly be a secondarily inserted *yod*. Significantly, the Peshitta has a plural at this point, as does one sixth-century Greek papyrus (𝔓[11]).

1 Corinthians 4:8 (F. 10v)

Ἤδη κεκορεσμένοι ἐστέ, ἤδη ἐπλουτήσατε, χωρὶς ἡμῶν ἐβασιλεύσατε·
ܟܒܪ ܣܒܥܬܘܢ: ܠܒܪ ܡܢ ܡܠܟܬܘܢ:

The Greek ἤδη ἐπλουτήσατε 'already you have become rich' is not represented in the CPA text. Müller-Kessler and Sokoloff (1998b, 73) posit that ܟܒܪ ܥܬܪܬܘܢ were omitted by homoioteleuton. They thus imply that they understand this to be an inner-Aramaic *lapsus calami*. This is certainly possible, though in this particular instance the Greek sentence seems just as ripe for haplography as the CPA.

1 Corinthians 13:4 (F. 19r)

Ἡ ἀγάπη μακροθυμεῖ, χρηστεύεται ἡ ἀγάπη
ܚܒܬܐ ܡܓܪܐ ܪܘܚܐ ܘܒܣܝܡܐ܀

There is a great deal of flux within the Greek tradition as to the second occurrence of ἡ ἀγάπη 'love' in the citation above. The CPA sides with the textual witnesses that omit it.

1 Corinthians 13:4 (F. 19r)

οὐ ζηλοῖ ἡ ἀγάπη, οὐ περπερεύεται, οὐ φυσιοῦται
ܚܒܬܐ ܠܐ ܡܩܢܝܐ: ܠܐ <u>ܡܬܒܠܛܐ</u>܀ ܠܐ ܡܬܢܦܚܐ܀

The CPA rendering of περπερεύεται 'to boast' is extremely difficult. Müller-Kessler and Sokoloff (1998b, 75) read ܡܬܒܛܠܐ 'is anulled'. Even if this were a fitting translation, there is little evidence of the descender loop beneath the middle radical. Our suggestion, ܡܬܒܠܛܐ 'make oneself prominent', is far from certain. Nonetheless, there are traces of what may be a descender loop beneath the third radical, and ܒܠܛ 'to protrude' is well-established in post-biblical Hebrew, Syriac and Jewish Aramaic.

1 Corinthians 13:7 (F. 19r)

πάντα ὑπομένει

ܟܘܠܐ ܗܝ ܡܣܝܒܪܐ:·

This is apparently the first appearance of the *paʿel* ܣܝܒܪ 'to endure' in CPA.

1 Corinthians 13:8 (F. 19r)

εἴτε γνῶσις, καταργηθήσεται

ܘܐܢ ܐܒܪ̈ܘܐܢ ܒܛܠ:·

This short clause has both textual and grammatical significance. Among the Greek witnesses to this verse there is a degree of uncertainty as to whether the singular should be read here (as above) or the plural: εἴτε γνώσεις, καταργηθήσονται. The CPA evidence should be added to the witnesses for the latter.

In terms of morphology, the form ܐܒܪ̈ܘܐܢ appears to represent the first secure attestation in CPA of the plural of an abstract feminine noun in -*ū*.

1 Corinthians 13:11 (F. 19r)

ἐφρόνουν ὡς νήπιος

ܗܝܟ ܛܠܝܐ ܗܘܝܬ ܡܬܦܟܣܢ:·

Müller-Kessler and Sokoloff (1998b, 75) read the final verb as ܡܬܪܥܐ. The root ܦܟܣ is attested in CPA in the nominal forms ܦܟܝܣ 'wise/prudent', ܦܟܝܣܐܝܬ 'clearly' and ܦܟܝܣܘ 'prudence'. The first is sometimes used to translate φρονιμός (e.g., Matt. 24:45 in CCR I;

see Phillips 2024, *ad loc.*). The third can translate φρόνησις. Nonetheless, the occurrence in the text above is apparently the first verbal attestation of the root in CPA, translating ἐφρόνουν.

1 Corinthians 14:3 (F. 19v)

ܘܬܝܢܚܘܡܗܘܢ

The *yod* here is uncertain (Müller-Kessler and Sokoloff 1998b, 76 omit it). If correct, it would be a rare example of the a>i shift occurring outside of a sibilant context in CPA (Müller-Kessler 1991, 62, 96–99).

1 Corinthians 15:42 (F. 18v)

ܡܙܕܪܥ ܗܘ ܒܬܪܦܘ:

Instead of ܒܬܪܦܘ, Müller-Kessler and Sokoloff (1998b, 86) read ܒܚܒܠܐ. Sokoloff (2014, 117) gives only this supposed occurrence *ad loc.* as evidence for the noun ܚܒܠ 'perishability', which should therefore be excised from the CPA lexicon.

1 Corinthians 15:45 (F. 18v)

ܐܕܡ ܒܬܪܝܐ ܠܪܘܚ ܡܚܝܢ:

This clause apparently represents the first occurrences of the adjectival forms ܒܬܪܝ 'last' (well attested in many other Aramaic dialects, including Galilean and Samaritan) and ܡܚܝܢ 'life-giving' (apparently unique to CPA).

1 Corinthians 15:48 (F. 18v)

οἷος ὁ χοϊκός, τοιοῦτοι καὶ οἱ χοϊκοί, καὶ οἷος ὁ ἐπουράνιος, τοιοῦτοι καὶ οἱ ἐπουράνιοι· καὶ καθὼς ἐφορέσαμεν

ܗܟܢ ܕܝ ܕܡܢ ܪܘܚܢܝܐ· ܗܟܢܝ ܐܘܦ ܗܠܝܢ ܕܡܢ ܪܘܚܢܝܐ܀
ܘܗܟܢ ܗܟܐ ܕܠܒ̈ܫܢ

The Greek *καὶ οἷος ὁ ἐπουράνιος, τοιοῦτοι καὶ οἱ ἐπουράνιοι* is not represented in the CPA. The CPA rendering would presumably be: ܘܗܟܢ ܕܝ ܕܡܢ ܫܡ̈ܝܐ· ܗܟܢܝ ܐܘܦ ܗܠܝܢ ܕܡܢ ܫܡ̈ܝܐ. Note that in the Greek, the opening phrase of the missing unit, *καὶ οἷος*, is distinct from the opening phrase of the next sentence, *καὶ καθώς*. This is not so in the CPA: both opening phrases are rendered by ܘܗܟܢ. Thus, once again, this haplography is easier to explain on the assumption that it occurred when copying from a CPA *Vorlage* than from a Greek *Vorlage*: the repetition of the phrase ܘܗܟܢ in the CPA is a ready opportunity for *homoioarcton*.

1 Corinthians 16:20 (F. 20r)

ܫܐ̈ܠܘ ܒܫܠܡܐ ܕܦܠܓܗܘܢ ܕܦܠܓ:

Here, and at Eph. 4:25 (f. 56r), Müller-Kessler and Sokoloff (1998b, 87) read ܒܦܠܓ. The phrase ܦܠܓ ܕܦܠܓ thus needs to be added to the CPA lexicon.

2 Corinthians 2:1 (F. 17r)

ἔκρινα γὰρ ἐμαυτῷ τοῦτο
ܗܕܐ ܓܪ ܕܝܢܬ ܒܢܦܫܝ:

Müller-Kessler and Sokoloff (1998b, 95) read the verb here as ܪܝܢܬ. There does appear to be a diacritical dot over the first consonant. However, it is lower than the usual height of the diacritical dot over a *resh*. The dot is rather to be understood as residue from the superior text, which has been largely obliterated in the first part of this line, leaving only faint ink traces of similar colour to the undertext. Moreover, in CPA ܕܘܢ is regularly used to translate forms of *κρίνω* (e.g., 1 Cor. 4:5; 5:12; 10:15; Col. 2:16) and thus suits the *Vorlage* at this point. Since this verse was the only supposed instance of ܪܘܢ in the CPA corpus to date, it should now be excised from the CPA lexicon.

2 Corinthians 5:1 (F. 3r)

ܒܐܝ ܕܠܐ ܒܥܒܕ ܒܐܝ̈ܕܝܢ

Among the various Aramaic dialects, there is a lot of variability in the spelling of the absolute form of the common lexeme 'house'. Nonetheless, now that the occurrence here is found to be ܒܐܝ rather than ܒܝ, the various CPA witnesses are entirely consistent in spelling the word with *alaf*.

2 Corinthians 6:4 (F. 6r)

ἐν θλίψεσιν, ἐν ἀνάγκαις, ἐν στενοχωρίαις

ܒܠܚ̈ܨܝܢ܇ ܒܚܩ̈ܝܢ: ܒܥܩ̈ܬܝܢ܇

Müller-Kessler and Sokoloff (1998b, 99) read the final word in this list as ܒܚܢܩ̈ܝܢ. However, the verb ܚܢܩ in CPA is limited in meaning to the restriction of the breath by choking, strangulation or drowning. Thus, ܚܢܩ̈ܝܢ as a gloss for *στενοχωρίαις* 'straits, distress' is rather unexpected. Since the present context is its only supposed occurrence, it is presumably another ghost word. The updated reading, by contrast, is already part of the CPA lexicon.

2 Corinthians 7:5 (F. 2v)

ἀλλ’ ἐν παντὶ θλιβόμενοι

ܐܠܐ ܒܟܘܠܐ ܡܬܚܨܝܢ:

The verb form here is presumably an error for ܡܬܠܚܨܝܢ.[6] The phrase ἐν παντὶ θλιβόμενοι also occurs at 2 Cor. 4:8, where it is likewise translated ܒܟܘܠܐ ܡܬܠܚܨܝܢ (Müller-Kessler and Sokoloff 1998b, 106). Müller-Kessler and Sokoloff’s (1998b, 102) reading ܐܬܐܠܝܢ here at 2 Cor. 7:5 was, to date, the only supposed evidence of the use of the root ܐܠܝ in CPA. For now, then, the root should be excised from the CPA lexicon.

2 Corinthians 7:7 (F. 2v)

ܕܗܝܟ ܡܠܘܢ ܚܕܝܐ

Sokoloff (2014, 100) records the adverbial idiom ܗܝܟ ܠܐ ܡܠܘܢ ‘how much more’, to which can now be added ܗܝܟ ܡܠܘܢ with the same meaning. Although, given that both ‘idioms’ are simply word-by-word glosses of their Greek *Vorlagen* (πῶς οὐχὶ μᾶλλον and ὥστε… μᾶλλον respectively), one wonders whether they really ought to be classified as CPA idioms at all.

Galatians 1:13 (F. 130r)

ὅτι καθ’ ὑπερβολὴν ἐδίωκον

ܕܟܠ ܕܠܚܕܝܐ ܗܘܝܬ ܪܕܦ

In place of ܕܠܚܕܝܐ, Müller-Kessler and Sokoloff (1998b, 109) read ܕܡܘܬܪ. This appears to be the first attestation of the phrase ܟܠ

[6] There may be traces of a supralinear *lamad* between the ascender of the *tau* and the *seyame*.

ܕܠܚܕܐ ‘extremely’ in CPA, though ܥܠ ܕܝܬܝܪ and ܥܠ ܕܡܘܬܪ, both similar in meaning, are common.

Galatians 1:14 (F. 130r)

ܝܬܝܪ ܡܢ ܣܓܝ ܒܢ̈ܝ ܓܝܠܝ

Instead of ܓܝܠܝ, Müller-Kessler and Sokoloff (1998b, 109) read ܓܢܣܝ. The word ܓܝܠܝ occurs in Samaritan Palestinian Aramaic, but this appears to be the first attestation of the word in CPA. Its appearance in the phrase ܒܢ̈ܝ ܓܝܠܝ ‘those of [my] own age/those in [my] circle’ is strikingly similar to the use of the same phrase in Mishnaic Hebrew (e.g., b. Ned. 39b).

Galatians 3:21 (F. 39r)

τῶν ἐπαγγελιῶν τοῦ θεοῦ

ܡܝ ܡܝ ܬܗ ܕܐܠܗܐ:

Müller-Kessler and Sokoloff (1998b, 111) mark a *seyame* over the first word, matching the plural ‘promises’ in the Greek. Despite the limitations imposed by the superior text, in this instance the supra-linear space above ܡܝ ܡܝ ܬܗ is quite visible. If the lack of *seyame* is anything more than a simple *lapsus calami*, it might perhaps be explained as harmonisation towards the many instances of the singular ἐπαγγελία in the surrounding verses (e.g., vv. 14, 17, 18, 19, 22).

Galatians 4:23 (F. 125v)

κατὰ σάρκα γεγέννηται

ܒܕܒܣܪܐ ܗܘܐ ܝܠܝܕ܀

Instead of ܒܕܒܣܪܐ, Müller-Kessler and Sokoloff (1998b, 114) read ܒܝܕ ܒܣܪܐ, and thereby generated an otherwise unattested meaning for ܒܝܕ 'according to', rather than its common meaning 'through/ by means of'. This sense can therefore be excised from the CPA lexicon.

Galatians 5:3 (F. 128r)

ܕܚܝܒ ܗܘ ܕܝܥܒܕ ܟܘܠ ܢܡܘܣܐ܀

Instead of ܕܚܝܒ, Müller-Kessler and Sokoloff (1998b, 115) read ܕܚܝܘܒ, which was interpreted by Sokoloff (2014, 126) as a *qāṭōl* adjectival form, existing alongside the nominal *qiṭṭūl* form ܚܝܘܒ 'condemnation'. No other instances of the *qāṭōl* adjectival form are currently attested, so this word, too, can be excised from the CPA lexicon.

Ephesians 5:18 (F. 59r)

ܘܠܐ ܬܗܘܘܢ ܪܘܝܢ ܒܚܡܪܐ ܗܕܢ ܕܒܗ ܒܚܫܘܬܐ܀

Müller-Kessler and Sokoloff (1998b, 133) read ܪܓܫܘܬܐ. In CPA, the root ܪܓܫ means 'to break out/burst; to make war against' (Sokoloff 2014, 406). The only occurrence of the putative noun form ܪܓܫܘܢ in CPA is here at Eph. 5:18, CCR II. The noun does occur once in Jewish Palestinian Aramaic, apparently referring to clamour or noise: אלה עבר ברעשון (Sokoloff 2002, 845). Neither the verb in CPA nor the noun form in JPA closely supports CPA

ܙܢܝܘܬܐ as a translation of *ἀσωτία* 'debauchery, prodigality', as required here at Eph. 5:18. Moreover, since our re-reading of CCR II, Müller-Kessler (2021) has subsequently confirmed the existence of both the noun ܡܣܚܦܘܬܐ and the related noun ܡܣܚܦܘ in texts apart from CCR.

2 Timothy 3:3 (F. 61v)

ἄστοργοι, ἄσπονδοι, διάβολοι, ἀκρατεῖς, ἀνήμεροι, ἀφιλάγαθοι

ܕܠܐ ܪ̈ܚܡܝܢ: ܕܠܐ ܐ̈ܚܕܝܢ ܠܢܦܫܗܘܢ: ܕܠܐ ܡܬܬ̈ܟܢܝܢ: ܕܠܐ ܪ̈ܚܡܝܢ ܠܛܒܬܐ:

ܕܠܐ ܡܩ̈ܒܠܝܢ ܟܐܬܩܘܢܘܬܗܘܢ: ܡܟܠ̈ܝ ܩܪܨܝܢ:

There has been some sort of interference between the Greek text and its CPA counterpart in verse 3. *Pace* Müller-Kessler and Sokoloff (1998b, 221), each descriptor in the CPA does have a counterpart in the Greek text; it is simply that the order of the elements differs. Arranging the Greek text in its canonical order, but right to left, the elements align as follows:

ἀφιλάγαθοι	ἀνήμεροι	ἀκρατεῖς	διάβολοι	ἄσπονδοι	ἄστοργοι
ܕܠܐ ܪ̈ܚܡܝܢ	ܕܠܐ	ܕܠܐ ܐ̈ܚܕܝܢ	ܡܟܠ̈ܝ ܩܪܨܝܢ	ܕܠܐ ܡܩ̈ܒܠܝܢ	ܕܠܐ ܪ̈ܚܡܝܢ
ܠܛܒܬܐ	ܡܬܬ̈ܟܢܝܢ	ܠܢܦܫܗܘܢ		ܟܐܬܩܘܢܘܬܗܘܢ	

The phrase ܕܠܐ ܡܩ̈ܒܠܝܢ ܟܐܬܩܘܢܘܬܗܘܢ, previously thought to lack a corresponding element in the Greek, in fact corresponds nicely to the Greek *ἄσπονδοι*, which carries the idea of 'refusal to make a truce/treaty'.

Comparing the lists, one sees that elements two and three in the Greek have become elements five and six in the CPA. Such rearrangements could easily happen in either language. Nonetheless, if the rearrangement is to be explained by human error, parablepsis when working from a CPA *Vorlage* is strikingly plausible. In this scenario, the scribe's eye skipped from the first element ending in ܝܢ, i.e., ܪ̈ܚܡܝܢ, to the only other element in the list with the same ending: ܡܣܠ̈ܝ ܠܚܡܝܢ. In each case, the element ending in ܝܢ is then followed by a three-word element with the structure ܕܠܐ + [participle] + [noun] + ܗܘܘ. Thus, prompted by these similarities, the scribe skipped straight from element one to element four; becoming aware of his error, he then copied out the missing elements at the end of the verse.

2 Timothy 3:9 (F. 61r)

ἀλλ' οὐ προκόψουσιν

ܐܠܐ ܠܐ ܡܬܒܟܪ̈ܝܢ

Here, and in verse 13 on the same page, προκόπτω 'to advance, progress' is translated by the *Ithpeʿal* of ܒܟܪ. Both instances were misread in previous editions. The *peʿal* of ܒܟܪ can be used in CPA with the sense 'to progress', so the use of the root in the *Ithpeʿal* here requires no semantic gymnastics, despite its not previously being attested in this sense. In the one other extant occurrence of a translation of προκόπτω in the CPA corpus from the early period (Gal. 1:14), ܐܬܝܬܪ is used.

Titus 2:7 (F. 23r)

περὶ πάντα

ܒܟܘܠ ܬ̈ܚܘܡܝܢ

A relatively clear instance of scribal correction. The original text read the plural ܬ̈ܚܘܡܝܢ as above. At some point thereafter, this was emended to the singular by adding an *alaf* to the end of the word. It is clear that the emendation was in this, rather than the opposite, direction; there is ample space between the second *mim* and the end of the line to write an *alaf*. Instead, the baseline has been extended, such that the head of the *nun* aligns perfectly with the left-hand margin. The corrector apparently preferred not to write the *alaf* on top of this inked baseline. Instead, he aligned the right-hand leg of the *alaf* to overlap the head of the quondam *nun*, with the result that the majority of the *alaf* extends beyond the left-hand margin.

This correction may give an insight into the translator's mindset. Generally, the CPA cleaves tightly to the Greek *Vorlage*. It may be that on this occasion the desire to replicate the plural found in the Greek initially trumped the use of the common, though singular, idiom ܒܟܘܠ ܙܒܢܐ. At Heb. 2:17, on the other hand, the idiomatic singular ܒܟܘܠ ܙܒܢܐ trumped the Greek's plural: κατὰ πάντα.[7]

Titus 2:7 (F. 23r)

ἐν τῇ διδασκαλίᾳ ἀφθορίαν, σεμνότητα

ܒܐܘܠܦܢܐ ܕܠܐ ܒܬܪܘܦܘ: ܒܪܒܝܘ: ܒܢܟܦܘ:

This small section is of textual and lexicographical significance. Müller-Kessler and Sokoloff (1998b, 185) misread ܒܪܒܝܘ as ܒܪܝܘ. The ghost-word ܒܪܝܘ 'gravity, seriousness' should therefore be removed from the CPA lexicon.

Textually, Von Soden (1913, *ad loc.*) lists various Greek witnesses that add ἁγνείαν 'purity' after ἀφθορίαν. It seems that the

---

[7] These comments have no bearing on the question of whether the scribe who wrote CCR II was translating directly from a Greek *Vorlage*, or copying an existing CPA text.

CPA, too, had this longer reading, to which the phrase ܒܪܒܘ corresponds nicely. If this is the case, then ܒܚܣܝܘ 'in purity' corresponds to σεμνότητα 'solemn dignity, holiness'. Indeed, Sokoloff (2014, 290) notes that at Phil. 4:8 σεμνός is rendered by ܚܣܝ. See further, *infra* (on Tit. 2:7–8).

Titus 2:7–8 (F. 23r)

ܒܪܒܘ: ܒܚܣܝܘ: ܒܡܠܐ ܫܠܝܡܐ:·

Müller-Kessler and Sokoloff (1998b, 185) read ܕܡܠܐ. Consequently, Sokoloff (2014, 291) parses the text as a phrase modifying the previous noun: ܒܚܣܝܘ ܕܡܠܐ ܫܠܝܡܐ 'in the purity of sound speech', which he understands as representing the Greek λόγον ὑγιῆ. In our text, both the *beth* on ܒܡܠܐ and the punctuation following ܒܚܣܝܘ militate against such a reading.

Titus 2:8 (F. 23r)

ἀκατάγνωστον

ܕܠܐ ܒܒܣܪܘܢ

Müller-Kessler and Sokoloff (1998b, 185) omitted the final *nun*, and thus generated a ghost word which should be corrected. The form ܒܣܪܘܢ and its cognate form ܒܘܣܪܢ are also attested in Qumran Aramaic, Galilean Aramaic, and the Aramaic of Onkelos and Jonathan.

Titus 2:8 (F. 23r)

ἵνα ὁ ἐξ ἐναντίας

ܠܒܕܠ ܕܗܘܢ ܕܐܡܪ ܠܡܘܒܠܐ

Müller-Kessler and Sokoloff (1998b, 185): ܠܡܘܒܠ.

The use of the preposition ܠܩܘܒܠ with personal suffixes modifying the verb ܩܘܡ is well attested in CPA. Likewise, the compound adverb ܡܢ ܠܩܘܒܠܐ 'opposite' is attested. However, this appears to be the first attestation of the form ܠܩܘܒܠܐ being used independently as an adverb.

Titus 2:10 (F. 23r)

μὴ ἀντιλέγοντας, μὴ νοσφιζομένους, ἀλλὰ πᾶσαν πίστιν

ܘܠܐ ܗܘܝܢ ܡܣܪ̈ܒܝܢ ܠܩܘܒܠܗܘܢ܇ ܐܠܐ ܟܘܠ ܗܝܡܢܘ

The CPA does not seem to have an equivalent for *μὴ νοσφιζομένους* 'not pilfering'. If the CPA equivalent were ܘܠܐ ܗܘܝܢ ܠܓܢ̈ܒܝܢ, this would invite parablepsis either backwards to the previous ܘܠܐ ܗܘܝܢ or forwards, with a confusion between ܘܠܐ and ܐܠܐ. In this instance, the Greek offers slightly less fertile ground for parablepsis.

Philemon 12 (F. 30r)

ὃν ἀνέπεμψά σοι αὐτόν, τοῦτ' ἔστιν τὰ ἐμὰ σπλάγχνα

ܗܕܢ ܕܫܠܚܬ: ܐܢܬ ܕܝ ܩܒܠ ܝܬܗ · ܗܢܐ ܕܗܘ ܠܫܝ̈ܢܐ:·

The addition in the CPA: ܐܢܬ ܕܝ ܩܒܠ ܝܬܗ 'but you—receive him!' apparently reflects an alternative Greek *Vorlage* that appears in quite a few early witnesses (see Nestle-Aland 2012, *ad loc.* for details).

Hebrews 2:10 (F. 25v)

δι' ὅν τὰ πάντα καὶ δι' οὗ τὰ πάντα

ܗܕܢ ܕܠܒܕܠܗ ܟܠܐ: ܕܗܘ̈ܝ

The phrase *καὶ δι' οὗ τὰ πάντα* 'and through whom [are] all things' is not represented in the CPA. This seems to be a straightforward case of haplography. The equivalent CPA phrase would presumably be ܘܗܕܢ ܕܒܥܪܬܗ ܟܠܐ, or perhaps ܘܗܕܢ ܕܒܐܝܕܗ ܟܠܐ. In both CPA and Greek, the omitted phrase is very similar to the preceding phrase.[8] Therefore, this *lapsus calami* (if this is what it is) could have occurred equally easily whether the scribe behind CCR II was translating directly from a Greek *Vorlage*, or simply copying an extant CPA *Vorlage*.

Hebrews 2:14 (F. 25r)

καὶ αὐτὸς παραπλησίως μετέσχεν τῶν αὐτῶν

ܐܦ ܗܘ ܒ ܐܫܬܬܦ ܒܗܘܢ ܒܗܘܢ ܒܚܫܘܫܝܐ:

The CPA adds the word ܒܚܫܘܫܝܐ 'sufferings'. The Greek text of Codex Claromontanus (*prima manu*) reflects the same tradition, adding *παθηματων* 'sufferings' to the end of the clause.

[8] This is particularly true when one remembers that in the CPA script *ʿe* and *lamad* are graphically very similar, as are *resh* and *dalath*. Hence, ܕܠܒܕܠܗ and ܕܒܥܪܬܗ are relatively easy to confuse.

APPENDIX I: IS SIN. SYR. NF M64N PART OF CCR II?

In her recent publication of the missing quire from CCR, Müller-Kessler (2023b) makes the claim that a bifolium of Sin. syr. NF M64N, which contains two leaves of Hebrews from early period CPA as its undertext, is none other than another bifolium from CCR II. However, the codicological and palaeographic results of the present study render this claim highly improbable.

Script Comparison

Table 12: Script comparison chart between CCR II and Sin. syr. NF M64N

Letter	Sin. syr. NF M64N	CCR II
ܐ		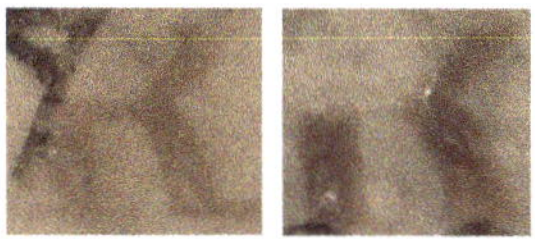
ܡ	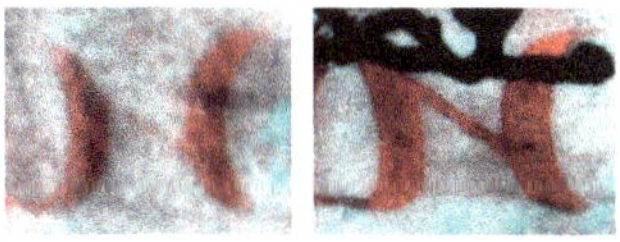	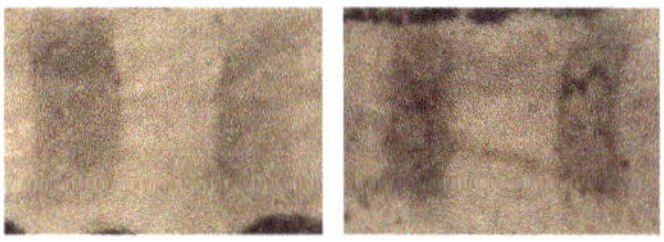
ܠ	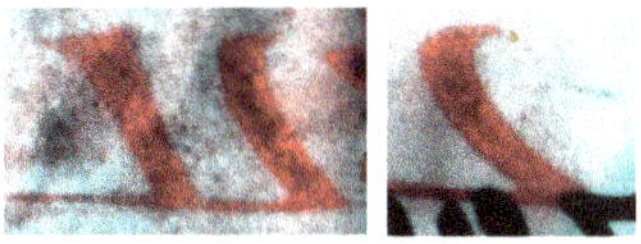	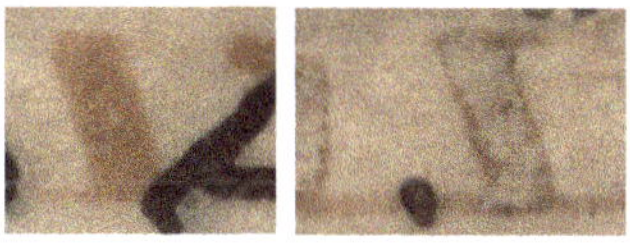
ܬ	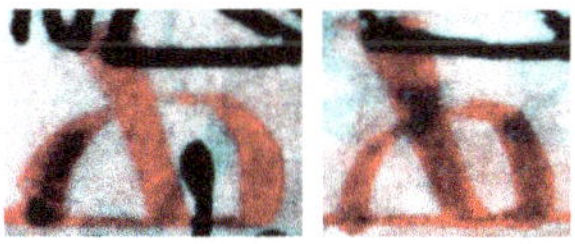	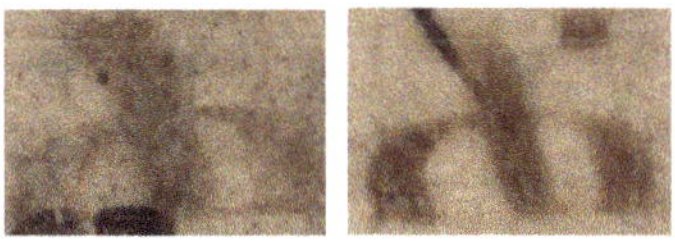

Table 13: Comparing scripts; CCR II vs Sin. syr. NF M64N

	Sin. syr. NF M64N	CCR II
ܐ	The arm of the *alaf* begins horizontal, then curves upwards, with substantial shading of the stroke.	The arm of the *alaf* is straight and oblique, with little shading and only a small serif.
ܚ	The arms of the *ḥeth* are curved. The crossbar joins the left arm towards the top.	The arms of the *ḥeth* are straight. The crossbar joins the left arm towards the bottom.
ܥ	The arm of the *ʿe* has a pronounced curve.	The arm of the *ʿe* is consistently oblique, broad and straight.
ܬ	The arch of the *tau* is high and skewed to the right.	The arch of the *tau* is flattened and skewed to the left.

The script comparison chart above is very limited, and several highly distinctive letter forms could have been added (e.g., the shape of the *gamal*, the final *kaf* and final *nun*). Nonetheless, the material above is more than sufficient to demonstrate that the scripts of the two manuscripts are far from identical.

Quire Arrangement

The details of the Sin. syr. NF M64N CPA bifolium are as follows (Desreumaux n.d.):[1]

[1] N.B. the flesh-hair orientation of F. 2 appears to have been mis-typed on the website.

Figure 16: Structure of bifolium Sin. syr. NF M64N

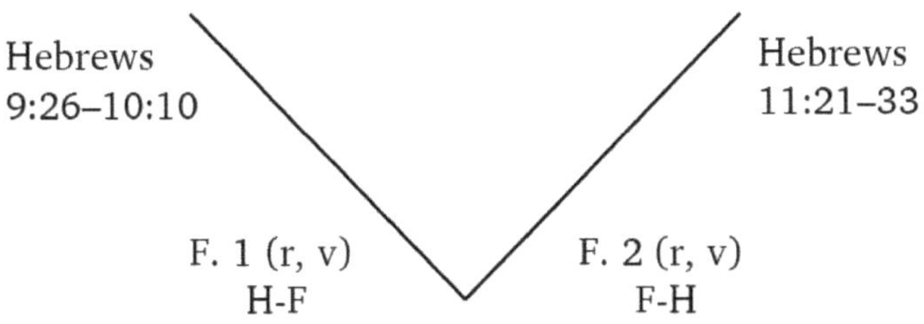

Each folio contains approximately 12 verses. This suggests that the approximately 49 intermediate verses were contained in four folios.[2] Thus, assuming that the quire from which this sheet derives was a quaternion, that quire would have been constructed thus:

Figure 17: Structure of the quire containing bifolium Sin. syr. NF M64N

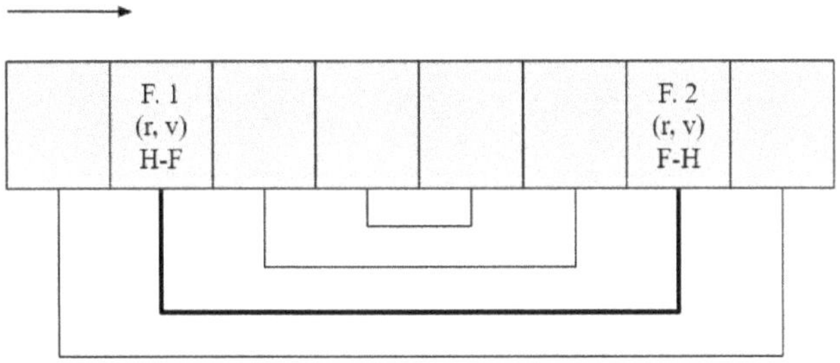

Note that the flesh-hair orientation of the surviving sheet is consistent with a quaternion obeying Gregory's Rule, with flesh side outermost.

This quire reconstruction simply does not fit with the quire reconstruction of CCR II. The final extant folio from CCR II (F. 28, v–r) ends at the close of Heb. 7:27, and comprises the final folio of quire 23 of CCR II as a whole:

[2] Desreumaux (n.d.) arrived at the same conclusion.

Figure 18: Quire structure of CCR II quire 23

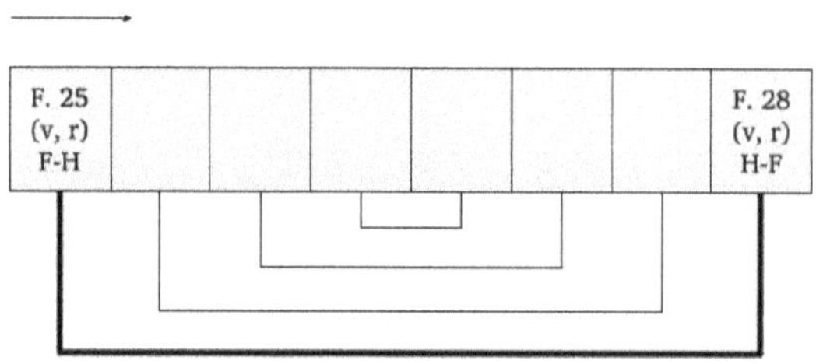

Note that it is quite certain that F. 28 is the final folio of the quire, thanks to the presence of a quire number.

Thus, approximately 39 verses separate the end of CCR II F. 28r and the beginning of Sin. syr. NF M64N (i.e. Heb. 7:29–9:25). Clearly this number of verses is far too low to posit an entire intervening quire between CCR II quire 23 and the Sin. syr. NF M64N quire; rather, CCR II quire 23 and the Sin. syr. NF M64N quire must be contiguous. However, the only way these 39 intervening verses could be incorporated is if there were three folios between CCR II F.28 and Sin. syr. NF M64N F.1. This would require the Sin. syr. NF M64N quire to be a senion—an unprecedented quire structure not only in CCR II, but in all known CPA codices from the early period.

Thus, on the basis of the different scripts and the incompatible quire data, we conclude that the CPA bifolium underlying Sin. syr. NF M64N did not originally derive from CCR II.

APPENDIX II: MINGANA SYR. MS. 637

Acts 21:14–21 **F. 138r**

ܫܬܩܢ ܘܐܡܪܢ
ܨܒܝܢܗ ܕܡܪܢ
ܢܬܥܒܕ܀
ܪܫ ܡܦܠܣܘܢ܀
[15] ܘܡܢ ܒܬܪ ܗܠܝܢ
ܡܛܝܒܐ ܐܬܥܒܕ
ܠܢ ܕܢܣܩ
ܠܐܘܪܫܠܡ܀
[16] ܘܐܬܘ ܥܡܢ ܡܢ
ܬܠܡܝܕܝܐ ܗܠܝܢ
ܕܡܢ ܩܣܪܝܐ܀
ܘܕܒܪܝܢ ܥܡܢ
ܡܢ ܕܢܩܒܠܢ܀
ܠܡܢܐܣܘܢ ܚܕ
ܩܦܪܐܝ ܡܢ
ܬܠܡܝܕܝܐ ܩܕܡܝܐ܀
[17] ܘܟܕ ܕܝ ܐܬܝܢ
ܠܐܘܪܫܠܡ
ܒܟܠ ܚܕܘܐ
ܩܒܠܘ ܠܢ ܐܚܝܐ܀
[18] ܘܠܝܘܡܐ ܚܘܪܢܐ
ܥܠ ܦܘܠܘܣ ܥܡܢ
ܠܘܬ ܝܥܩܘܒ܀
ܘܟܠܗܘܢ ܩܫܝܫܝܐ
ܐܬܘ܀ [19] ܘܫܐܠ
ܒܫܠܡܗܘܢ
ܘܬܢܝ ܠܗܘܢ
ܟܘܠ [ܚ]ܕܐ
ܘܚܕܐ [ܡܢ ܡ]ܐ
ܕܥܒܕ ܐܠܗܐ
ܒܥܡܡܝܐ
ܒܬܪܥܗ
ܕܫܡܫܘܬܗ܀
[20] ܗܢܘܢ ܕܝ ܫܡܥܘ
ܘܫܒܚܘ ܠܐܠܗܐ
ܘܐܡܪܘ ܠܗ
ܚܙܝ ܐܬ ܐܚܘܢ
ܟܡܐ ܪܒܘܐܢ
ܗܢܘܢ ܕܗܝܡܢܘ
ܡܢ ܝܗܘܕܝ
ܘܟܠܗܘܢ
ܡܩܢܝܢ ܠܢܡܘܣܐ܀
[21] ܫܡܥܘ ܕܝ ܥܠ
ܕܠܟܘܢ ܕܐܬ ܡܠܦ

Acts 21:21–26 F. 138v

ܦܩ̈ܕܝܢ ܗܠܝܢ
ܕܟܝܢ ܡܫ̈ܢܝܐ
ܕܢܬ̈ܘܒܘܢ
ܡܢ ܢܡܘܣܗ
ܕܡܘܫܐ. ܐܡܪ
ܠܗ[ܘܢ] ܕܠܐ
ܢܗܘܢ ܓܙ̈ܪܝܢ
ܒܢܝܗܘܢ: ܘܕܠܐ
ܢܗܘܢ ܡܗ̈ܠܟܝܢ
ܒܥܝܕܝܗܘܢ:
[22] ܡܐ ܐܘܢ ܢܗܐ.
ܫܠܘܦ ܠܗ
ܐܘܠܒܘܦ
ܕܐܬܒܥ ܥܡ̈ܡܝܢ
ܗܘܢ ܓܪ ܕܐܬܝܬ:
[23] ܗܕܐ ܐܘܢ ܥܒܕ:
ܡܐ ܕܐܢܐ ܐܡ̈ܪܝܢ
ܠܟ: ܐܝܬ ܠܢ
ܐܪ̈ܒܥܐ ܓܒܪܝܢ
ܕܠܗܘܢ ܢܕܪ ܐ
ܥܠ ܓܪܡܝܗܘܢ:
[24] ܗܠܝܢ ܐܘܢ ܕܒܪ

ܘܐܬܕܟܝ ܥܡܗܘܢ:
ܘܐܦܩ ܥܠܝܗܘܢ
ܕܝܓܪ̈ܥܘܢ ܪ̈ܫܝܗܘܢ:
ܘܝ̈ܕܥܘܢ ܟܠܗܘܢ
ܕܡܐ ܕܫ̈ܡܥܘ
ܥܠ ܕܝܠܟ ܠܝܬ
ܗܘ ܥܠܡ:
ܐܠܐ ܕܐܘܦ
ܐܢܬ ܫܠܡ ܠܗܘܢ
ܡܛܪ ܢܡܘܣܐ:
[25] ܥܠ ܥܡ̈ܡܐ ܓܪ ܗܠܝܢ
ܕܗܝܡܢܘ ܡܢ
ܡܫܠܚܐ ܐܢܚܢ
ܫܕ̈ܪܢ ܘܟܬܒܢ
ܠܗܘܢ ܕܝܗܘܢ
ܡܛ̈ܪܝܢ ܓܪ̈ܡܝܗܘܢ
ܡܢ ܕܒܚܬ̈ܗ
ܕܝ ܠܛܥܐ. ܘܡܢ
ܐܕܡܐ. ܘܡܢ
ܗܕܐ ܕܚܢܝܩܐ.
ܘܡܢ ܙܢܘܬܐ:
÷[26] ܩ̈ܕܡ ܫܘܠܒܘܦ

BIBLIOGRAPHY

Aland, Barbara, Kurt Aland, Johannes Karavidopoulos, Carlo M. Martini, and Bruce Metzger, eds. 2012. *Novum Testamentum Graece: Begründet von Eberhard Und Erwin Nestle*. 28th ed. Stuttgart: Deutsche Bibelgesellschaft.

Bar-Asher, Moshe. 1977. *Palestinian Syriac Studies: Source-Texts, Traditions and Grammatical Problems*. Jerusalem: Hebrew University.

Bausi, Alessandro, ed. 2015. *Comparative Oriental Manuscript Studies: An Introduction*. Hamburg: Tredition.

Black, Matthew. 1939. 'A Palestinian Syriac Palimpsest Leaf of Acts XXI:14–26'. *Bulletin of the John Rylands Library* 23: 201–14.

Brock, Sebastian. 1999. 'Fragments of Ps-John Chrysostom, Homily on the Prodigal Son, in Christian Palestinian Aramaic'. *Le Muséon* 112: 335–62.

———. 2012. 'Ktabe Mpassqe: Dismembered and Reconstituted Syriac and Christian Palestinian Aramaic Manuscripts: Some Examples, Ancient and Modern'. *Hugoye* 15 (1): 7–20.

Capron, Laurent. 2016. 'La ponctuation dans les manuscrits en araméen christopalestinien: Quelle importance?' *L'information philologique*. Last accessed 28 August 2024. https://iphi.hypotheses.org/446

Davies, Helen, and Alexander J. Zawacki. 2019. 'Making Light Work: Manuscripts and Multispectral Imaging'. *Journal of the Early Book Society*: 177–93.

Desreumaux, Alain. 2010. 'Les manuscrits araméens christo-palestiniens du nouveau fonds du monastère de Sainte-Catherine du Sinaï (Note d'information)'. *Comptes rendus des séances de l'Académie des inscriptions et Belles-Lettres* 154 (3): 1317–28.

———. 2015. 'Codicology: Christian Palestinian Aramaic Manuscripts'. In *Comparative Oriental Manuscript Studies: An Introduction*, edited by Alessandro Bausi, 132–36. Hamburg: Tredition.

———. 2023. 'Le palimpseste Sin. syr. NF M56N du nouveau fonds de Sainte-Catherine: Son apport à la codicologie araméenne christo-palestinienne, aux versions anciennes des textes bibliques et à l'histoire de la liturgie'. In *New Light on Old Manuscripts: The Sinai Palimpsests and Other Advances in Palimpsest Studies*, edited by Claudia Rapp et al., 131–45. Österreichische Akademie der Wissenschaften Philosophisch-historische Klasse Denkschriften 547. Vienna: Austrian Academy of Sciences.

———. n.d. 'Sinai Syriac NF 64: Hebrews. New Testament'. Sinai Palimpsests Project, a publication of St Catherine's Monastery of the Sinai in collaboration with EMEL and UCLA. https://sinai.library.ucla.edu, accessed 7 March 2024.

Duensing, Hugo. 1906. *Christlich-palästinisch-aramäische Texte und Fragmente*. Göttingen: Vandenhoeck und Ruprecht.

———. 1938. 'Zwei christlich-palästinisch-aramäische Fragmente aus der Apostelgeschichte'. *Zeitschrift für die Neutestamentliche Wissenschaft* 37: 42–46.

Easton, Roger L. 2017. 'Multispectral and Hyperspectral Imaging of Cultural Heritage'. *Rochester Cultural Heritage Imaging, Visualisation and Education.* Unpublished lecture slides.

Easton, Roger L., and David Kelbe. 2014. 'Statistical Processing of Spectral Imagery to Recover Writings from Erased or Damaged Manuscripts'. *Manuscript Cultures* 7: 35–46.

———. 2023. 'Multispectral Image Collection and Statistical Processing of Palimpsests at St. Catherine's Monastery'. In *New Light on Old Manuscripts: The Sinai Palimpsests and Other Advances in Palimpsest Studies*, edited by Claudia Rapp et al., 407–18. Österreichische Akademie der Wissenschaften Philosophisch-historische Klasse Denkschriften 547. Vienna: Austrian Academy of Sciences.

Géhin, Paul. 2017. *Les manuscrits syriaques de parchemin du Sinai et leurs membra disjecta.* Corpus Scriptorum Christianorum Orientalium 665. Leuven: Peeters.

Gysembergh, Victor, Peter J. Williams, and Emanuel Zingg. 2022. 'New Evidence for Hipparchus' Star Catalogue Revealed by Multispectral Imaging'. *Journal for the History of Astronomy* 53 (4): 383–93.

Knox, Keith T. 2023. 'Image Processing Methods That Reveal Erased Handwriting: Developments of the Last Two Decades'. In *New Light on Old Manuscripts: The Sinai Palimpsests and Other Advances in Palimpsest Studies*, edited by Claudia Rapp et al., 395–406. Österreichische Akademie der Wissenschaften Philosophisch-historische Klasse Denkschriften 547. Vienna: Austrian Academy of Sciences.

Lewis, Agnes Smith, ed. 1897. *A Palestinian Syriac Lectionary, Containing Lessons from The Pentateuch, Job, Proverbs, Prophets, Acts, and Epistles*. London: Cambridge University Press.

———. 1909. *Codex Climaci Rescriptus*. Horae Semiticae VIII. Cambridge: Cambridge University Press.

Lewis, Agnes Smith, and Margaret Dunlop Gibson, eds. 1899. *The Palestinian Syriac Lectionary of the Gospels, Re-Edited from Two Sinai MSS, and from P. De Lagarde's Edition of the 'Evangeliarium Hierosolymitanum'*. London: Kegan Paul, Trench, Trübner & Co. Ltd.

Malik, Peter. 2023a. 'Joshua Fragment from Codex Climaci Rescriptus: A New Edition Based on the Multispectral Images'. *Vetus Testamentum* 73 (4–5): 736–51.

———. 2023b. 'Psalms 135.13–136.7, 140.10–142.1 in Codex Climaci Rescriptus: A New Edition of the Greek Text Based on Multispectral Images'. *Zeitschrift für die alttestamentliche Wissenschaft* 135 (1): 16–40.

Mingana, A. 1939. *Catalogue of the Mingana Collection of Manuscripts*. Vol. 3, *Additional Christian Arabic and Syriac Manuscripts*. Woodbrooke Catalogues 3. Cambridge: Heffer and Sons, Ltd.

Moir, Ian. 1956. *Codex Climaci Rescriptus Graecus*. Texts and Studies: Contributions to Biblical and Patristic Literature 2. Cambridge: Cambridge University Press.

———. 1957. 'Two Septuagint Palimpsest Fragments'. *Journal of Theological Studies New Series* 8 (1): 1–11.

Morgenstern, Matthew. 2011. 'Christian Palestinian Aramaic'. In *The Semitic Languages: An International Handbook*, edited by

Stefan Weninger, 628–37. Handbooks of Linguistics and Communication Science 36. Berlin: De Gruyter.

Müller-Kessler, Christa. 1988. 'Die Überlieferungsstufen des christlich-palästinischen Aramäisch'. *Zeitschrift der Deutschen Morgenländischen Gesellschaft* 8: 55–60.

———. 1991. *Grammatik des christlich-palästinisch-Aramäischen.* Vol. 1, *Schriftlehre, Lautlehre, Formenlehre.* Texte und Studien zur Orientalistik 6. Hildesheim: Georg Olms Verlag.

———. 1999a. 'Die frühe christlich-palästinisch-aramäische Evangelienhandschrift CCR1 übersetzt durch einen ostaramäischen (syrischen) Schreiber?' *Journal for the Aramaic Bible* 1: 79–86.

———. 1999b. 'Review: Christian Palestinian Aramaic and Its Significance to the Western Aramaic Dialect Group'. *Journal of the American Oriental Society* 119 (4): 631–36.

———. 2014. 'Codex Sinaiticus Rescriptus (CSRG/O/P/S): A Collection of Christian Palestinian Manuscripts'. *Le Muséon* 127 (3-4): 263–309.

———. 2016. 'Christlich-palästinisch-aramäische Palimpseste im St. Katharinenkloster, Sinai mit dem Martyrium des Mamas von Kaisareia in Kappadokien (Arabic NF 66)'. *Oriens Christianus* 99: 76–84.

———. 2017. 'The Martyrdom of Arianos and the Four Protectores in an Unpublished Christian Palestinian Aramaic Palimpsest, St Catherine Monastery (Sinai, Arabic NF 66)'. *Collectanea Christiana Orientalia* 14: 115–25.

———. 2018. 'Three Early Witnesses of the "Dormition of Mary" in Christian Palestinian Aramaic from the Cairo Genizah (Taylor-Schechter Collection) and the New Finds in St Catherine's Monastery'. *Apocrypha* 29: 69–95.

———. 2019. 'An Overlooked Christian Palestinian Aramaic Witness of the "Dormition of Mary" in Codex Climaci Rescriptus (CCR IV)'. *Collectanea Christiana Orientalia* 16: 81–98.

———. 2019a. 'Proverbs 11:1b–15 as Transmitted in an Unpublished Christian Palestinian Aramaic Palimpsest from St Catherine's Monastery (Sinai, Greek NF MG 14)'. *Journal of Septuagint and Cognate Studies* 52: 157–65.

———. 2019b. 'The Unknown Martyrdom of Patriklos of Caesarea in Christian Palestinian Aramaic from St Catherine's Monastery (Sinai, Arabic NF 66)'. *Analecta Bollandiana* 137: 63–71.

———. 2020. 'A Palimpsest Fragment with Unattested Passages of Job 3:11c–4:3b in Christian Palestinian Aramaic under Sinai, Greek NF MG 14'. *Collectanea Christiana Orientalia* 17: 183–96.

———. 2021. 'On the Spellings of the Lexical Items *bʿš, bʿšwn', and mšbʿwn'*, and Other Peculiar Lexemes in Christian Palestinian Aramaic'. *Collectanea Christiana Orientalia* 18: 217–23.

———. 2023a. 'The Early Jerusalem Lectionary Tradition in Christian Palestinian Aramaic (5th–7th Century): Lections Containing Unattested Old and New Testament Pericopes in Unpublished Palimpsests (Sinai, Gr. NF MG 32; Georg. NF 19, 71)'. *Le Muséon* 136: 201–63.

———. 2023b. 'The Missing Quire of Codex Climaci Rescriptus Containing 1–2 Corinthians in Christian Palestinian Aramaic (Sin. Syr. NF M38N)'. In *New Light on Old Manuscripts: The Sinai Palimpsests and Other Advances in Palimpsest Studies*, edited by Claudia Rapp et al., 147–70. Österreichische Akademie der Wissenschaften. Vienna: Austrian Academy of Sciences.

Müller-Kessler, Christa, and Michael Sokoloff, eds. 1997. *A Corpus of Christian Palestinian Aramaic*. Vol. 1, *The Christian Palestinian Aramaic Old Testament and Apocrypha Version from the Early Period*. Groningen: Styx Publications.

———, eds. 1998a. *A Corpus of Christian Palestinian Aramaic*. Vol. 2A, *The Christian Palestinian Aramaic New Testament Version from the Early Period: Gospels*. Groningen: Styx Publications.

———, eds. 1998b. *A Corpus of Christian Palestinian Aramaic*. Vol. 2B, *The Christian Palestinian Aramaic New Testament Version from the Early Period: Acts of the Apostles and Epistles*. Groningen: Styx Publications.

Nienhuis, David R. 2007. *Not by Paul Alone: The Formation of the Catholic Epistle Collection and the Christian Canon*. Waco, Texas: Baylor University Press.

Parker, David C. 2008. *An Introduction to the New Testament Manuscripts and Their Texts*. Cambridge: Cambridge University Press.

Phillips, Kim. 2024. 'Codex Climaci Rescriptus I: Text, Codicology and Paratextual Features'. *Aramaic Studies* 22 (1): 12–73.

———. Forthcoming a. 'CCR VII Text and Codicology'. *Journal of Semitic Studies.*

———. Forthcoming b. 'The Anonymous Christian Palestinian Aramaic Homily in Codex Climaci Rescriptus IV: Edition and Linguistic Notes'.

Schulthess, Friedrich. 1910. 'Aramäisches II'. *Zeitschrift für Assyriologie und verwandte Gebiete* 24: 47–58.

———. 1924. *Grammatik des christlich-palästinischen Aramäisch.* Hildesheim: Georg Olms Verlag.

Sokoloff, Michael. 2002. *A Dictionary of Jewish Palestinian Aramaic of the Byzantine Period.* 2nd ed. Ramat-Gan: Bar Ilan University Press.

———. 2014. *A Dictionary of Christian Palestinian Aramaic.* Orientalia Lovaniensia Analecta 234. Leuven: Peeters.

Suciu, Alin. 2016. 'An Addition to the Christian-Palestinian Aramaic Literary Corpus: Logos XV of Abba Isaiah of Scetis'. *Journal of Semitic Studies* 61 (2): 449–61.

Von Soden, Hermann Freiherr. 1913. *Die Schriften des neuen Testaments: Text und Apparat.* Göttingen: Vanderhoeck und Ruprecht.

Wasserman, Tommy. 2006. *The Epistle of Jude: Its Text and Transmission.* Coniectanea Biblica New Testament Series 43. Stockholm: Almqvist & Wiksell International.

Williams, Peter J., Patrick James, Jamie Klair, Peter Malik, and Sarah Zaman. 2022. 'Newly Discovered Illustrated Texts Of Aratus And Eratosthenes Within Codex Climaci Rescriptus'. *The Classical Quarterly* 72 (2): 504–31.

INDICES

Biblical Index

Acts and Catholic Epistles

Pauline Epistles

1 Corinthians

1:6–12	F. 21r	58
1:12–17	F. 21v	59
3:17–23	F. 11v	60
4:1–6	F. 11r	61
4:6–10	F. 10v	62
4:10–15	F. 10r	63
13:4–11	F. 19r	64
13:11–14:4	F. 19v	65
14:4–7	F. 13v	66
14:8–14	F. 13r	67
14:24–30	F. 15r	68
14:30–37	F. 15v	69
14:37–15:3	F. 22r	70
15:3–10	F. 22v	71
15:24–31	F. 8v	72
15:31–37	F. 8r	73
15:38–42	F. 18r	74
15:42–49	F. 18v	75
16:16–24	F. 20r	76

2 Corinthians

1:1–3	F. 20v	77
1:23–2:4	F. 17r	78
2:4–11	F. 17v	79
4:18–5:6	F. 3r	80
5:6–12	F. 3v	81
6:3–10	F. 6r	82
6:10–16	F. 6v	83
6:16–7:3	F. 2r	84
7:3–8	F. 2v	85

Galatians

1:1–5	F. 123r	86
1:5–10	F. 123v	87
1:10–16	F. 130r	88
1:16–23	F. 130v	89
3:20–24	F. 39r	90
3:25–4:2	F. 39v	91
4:15–22	F. 125r	92
4:22–28	F. 125v	93
4:29–5:4	F. 128r	94
5:4–12	F. 128v	95
5:24–6:4	F. 46r	96
6:4–12	F. 46v	97

Ephesians

1:18–2:2	F. 63v	98
2:2–8	F. 63r	99
4:14–19	F. 56v	100
4:19–27	F. 56r	101
5:8–16	F. 59v	102
5:17–24	F. 59r	103

Philippians

2:12–19	F. 60v	104
2:19–26	F. 60r	105

Colossians

4:6–11	F. 62v	106
4:11–17	F. 62r	107
4:17–18	F. 57v	108

Index of Passages Appearing in the Textual and Linguistic Commentary

Acts and Catholic Epistles

Pauline Epistles

General Index

About the Team

Geoffrey Khan and Alessandra Tosi were the managing editors for this book.

Anne Burberry performed the copyediting of the book in Word. The fonts used in this volume are Charis SIL, Estrangelo Edessa, SBL Greek, and SBL Hebrew.

Cameron Craig created all of the editions — paperback, hardback, and PDF. Conversion was performed with open source software freely available on our GitHub page at https://github.com/OpenBookPublishers.

Jeevanjot Kaur Nagpal designed the cover of this book. The cover was produced in InDesign using Fontin and Calibri fonts.

www.ingramcontent.com/pod-product-compliance
Lightning Source LLC
Chambersburg PA
CBHW042043240426
43667CB00048B/2968
* 9 7 8 1 8 0 5 1 1 5 4 0 3 *